Preserving Emotion
in Student Writing

INTERDISCIPLINARY APPROACHES TO INSTRUCTION, PRACTICE, AND THEORY

Staci L. Shultz and CJ Kent
General Editors

Vol. 2

The Writing in the 21st Century series is part of the Peter Lang Education list.
Every volume is peer reviewed and meets
the highest quality standards for content and production.

PETER LANG
New York • Bern • Berlin
Brussels • Vienna • Oxford • Warsaw

Preserving Emotion in Student Writing

Innovation in Composition Pedagogy

Edited by Craig Wynne

PETER LANG
New York • Bern • Berlin
Brussels • Vienna • Oxford • Warsaw

Library of Congress Cataloging-in-Publication Control Number: 2020946162

Bibliographic information published by **Die Deutsche Nationalbibliothek**.
Die Deutsche Nationalbibliothek lists this publication in the "Deutsche
Nationalbibliografie"; detailed bibliographic data are available
on the Internet at http://dnb.d-nb.de/.

ISSN 2577-462X
ISBN 978-1-4331-8172-6 (hardcover)
ISBN 978-1-4331-8171-9 (paperback)
ISBN 978-1-4331-8190-0 (ebook pdf)
ISBN 978-1-4331-8191-7 (epub)
ISBN 978-1-4331-8192-4 (mobi)
DOI 10.3726/b17260

© 2021 Peter Lang Publishing, Inc., New York
29 Broadway, 18th floor, New York, NY 10006
www.peterlang.com

All rights reserved.
Reprint or reproduction, even partially, in all forms such as microfilm,
xerography, microfiche, microcard, and offset strictly prohibited.

Table of Contents

Acknowledgments	vii
1. Learning to Feel: Engaging Emotions, Narratives, Values, and Commitments in Composition JULIE CHRISTEN	5
2. Leveraging Student Emotional Motivations in Effective Classroom Writing: A Model-Based Approach SANDRA STANKO	17
3. "Dull Feelings of Just Getting By": Advanced Assistant Professor Experiences of Impasse and Mentorship K. SHANNON HOWARD	35
4. Emotion in Teaching and Administering Writing: An Ethics of Care for Writing Teachers REBECCA GERDES-MCCLAIN	45
5. Knowing Emotion: College Initiation and Self-Confrontation in the "Meta" Writing Classroom DIANA EPELBAUM	57
6. Integrative Learning as a Process for Linking Writing and Emotion JAMES P. BARBER & ETHAN YOUNGERMAN	85
7. Peaceful Pedagogy: Teaching Writing from a Place of Peace CRYSTAL SANDS	95
8. Affective Writing toward Feasible Futures: Helping Students Envision Triumph, Trauma, and Everything in Between JIM ZIMMERMAN & CATHRYN MOLLOY	105

9. *Authoring Well-being: Emotional Literacy as a Commonplace for First-Year Writing Pedagogy* — 117
   JESSICA SCHREYER, LAURA MANGINI, & SABATINO MANGINI

10. *Inverting Aristotle's Relationship between Invention and Pathos: 17 Students Write to the Freedom Writers* — 137
    JESSICA ROSE COREY

11. *Stirring Things Up: Rhetorical Dissonance in Writers' Revisions and Emotional Responses* — 147
    MATTHEW FLEDDERJOHANN

12. *First-Year Composition Students: Creating Their Own Stories* — 159
    JEANNE HUGHES

13. *We Awaken to Ourselves: Emotion, Reflective Writing, and the Study Abroad Experience* — 171
    TODD HARPER & MICHAYLA GREY

14. *Honoring Contemplative Practices in the Writing Classroom: A Personal and Pedagogical Exploration* — 187
    RACHEL N. SPEAR

15. *Dear Professor: Forging Student-Teacher Relationships through Course Letters* — 211
    ANN AMICUCCI

16. *Pet Pictures, Pop Culture, and GIF Game: (Re)Viewing Twitter as Multimodal Emotional Writing in First-Year Composition* — 229
    AMANDA M. MAY

17. *Performing Silence, Exhaustion, and Recovery: Articulating Faculty and Administrator Identity by Cultivating Mental Wellness* — 239
    SHERRY RANKINS-ROBERTSON & NICHOLAS BEHM

Contributors — 251

Acknowledgements

I am grateful for the hard work of all of the contributors to this collection, whose hard work made this collection possible. I wish to thank Staci Shultz, whom I consider a passionate scholar, dedicated teacher, and most importantly, a true friend. She proposed that I submit this collection, and through many conversations, we were able to shape the concept. I extend my deepest gratitude to Patricia Mulrane Clayton and Peter Lang Publishing, who patiently guided me through the process. I am grateful for Claire Giraudo's assistance with proofreading. Most of all, I am truly appreciative of the hundreds of students I've taught, tutored, guided, and counseled over the years; our interactions were the catalyst for this collection. I look forward to receiving inspiration from you in the years to come.

Introduction

I stumbled into the field of Rhetoric and Writing Studies (RWS) by happenstance. After spending two years trying to land a job teaching the classics of literature to high school students, I fell into a position as an Academic Support Center Assistant at Berkeley College, a small, proprietary school in White Plains, New York. One of my duties was to function as the writing tutor for a campus of approximately six hundred students. Here, I helped students with every facet of the writing process in a variety of genres. I mentored a great deal of writers who would get anxious at the very notion of having to put something down on paper for a professor. Oftentimes, I would read a series of awkwardly written sentences, and some version of the following dialogue exchange would occur:

ME: Tell me what it is you're trying to say.
(Student states their point in a very clear way.)
ME: Write down what you just told me.
(Student writes down what they had just said.)
ME: Which sentence do you like better, the one you wrote or the one you typed?
STUDENT: The one I just wrote.
ME: Why?
STUDENT: It just makes more sense.

Upon engaging in further dialogue with students in this type of situation, I would find students were nervous about composing for professors. For a student, writing an essay for a class is a high-pressure situation. When students write, they are being vulnerable. They are putting parts of themselves on paper for an audience to see. Moreover, that audience is assigning a grade, a letter that shows how worthy that vulnerability is. And for a student, that professor represents the ultimate authority on that work.

While serving in this capacity, a colleague, Michael Jacobs, turned me onto the work of expressivists such as Peter Elbow and Donald Murray, whose work I devoured. From there, I began to read journals in our field, such as *College English, College Composition and Communication*, and *Writing on the Edge*, and my interest in RWS was born.

A few years later, I found myself in a doctoral program at the University of Texas at El Paso (UTEP). Our seminars focused on topics such as Rhetorical History, Rhetoric and Technology, Critical Race Theory, and Composition Pedagogy, and we became exposed to scholars in a variety of expertise, such as James Berlin, Sharon Crowley, and Clay Spinuzzi. While such scholars are highly influential in our field, and their work has informed my teaching, the primary layer of my pedagogy continues to be emotionally engagement with writing, which was not discussed in any of my seminars. In a conversation I had with Kate Mangelsdorf, she even said, "Let's not throw out the baby with the bathwater," referring to expressivist scholarship.

In Helen Foster's Composition Studies course, I was able to apply my interest in writing anxiety to a project in which I would help graduate students develop strategies to overcome writer's block and writing anxiety. While my cohorts were taking electives in Communication and Rhetoric, I took a class in Theories of Counseling to develop knowledge.

After I finished my coursework, I designed such a project designed to help students working on Master's or doctoral projects across various disciplines. Our group would meet once a week for seven weeks, and students would be exposed to Donald Murray's idea of writing as process, definitions of writing anxiety and writer's block, and mindfulness meditation. Assignments consisted of designing a plan to help themselves write on a consistent basis, as well as committing to spending at least one hour every day working on their projects.

A major challenge was getting students to show up to these seminars on a regular basis. Oftentimes, commitments related to classes, work, and family took priority over this optional seminar, which students were not being compensated for attending. But, when students attended, they derived its benefits. One student told me it helped her confidence in her progress, and another indicated it removed her stigma of knowing she's not the only one who struggles with composing.

When we write, it is impossible not to go through some cycle of emotions. Writing to learn can help us to become emotionally engaged with what we're learning. Writing for the self can help us process emotions. And writing for social change can ignite our passions for our advocacy, as well as that of

Introduction 3

our audience. This collection of essays is meant to provide a revue of emotion as it relates to the composition classroom.

The first four chapters offer theories and ideas. In "Learning to Feel: Engaging Emotions, Narratives, Values, and Commitments in Composition," Julie Christen offers a theory of emotion as a complex process in how it facilitates our development of knowledge about the world. Sandra Stanko follows by proposing a five-step model that helps students establish explicit connections between their writing and the challenges they face in their personal lives. K. Shannon Howard follows by discussing the struggles students face with being stagnant in their writing and applies the ideas of "crip time" and "queer time" to such struggles; and Rebecca Gerdes-McClain posits an ethics of care as they relate to the emotional labor we endure in our work as teachers, scholars, and administrators. For the majority of the book, we see practical applications of these theories:

- Diana Epelbuam shares her pedagogical practices that enable students to develop their metacognitive skills as they relate to their emotions;
- James Barber & Ethan Youngerman argue that integrating emotion into academic writing spaces propels Integrative Learning, and they provide examples of student writing to support their argument;
- Crystal Sands provides instructors with practical, down-to-Earth strategies she uses to simply make her classroom a space where students can be themselves while learning;
- Jim Zimmerman and Cathryn Molloy examine pedagogy with a framework that has students writing to think about their futures in a "writing for health" approach;
- Jessica Schreyer, Laura Mangini, and Sabatino Mangini explain how their first-year writing classrooms function as a platform to help students develop emotional literacy through a series of low-stakes writing exercises, which contribute to true communities in their classrooms;
- Jessica Rose Corey follows by using her students' analyses of The Freedom Writers Diary to argue an idea of invention as an element of pathos;
- Matthew Fledderjohann discusses one Ph.D. student writer's encounter with rhetorical dissonance and the seemingly negative emotions it generated. He further discusses how negotiating those emotions helped him reshape the positioning of his values through revisions of a preliminary examination essay;
- Jeanne Hughes discusses how she applies many of these ideas to her classroom, with stellar results;

- Todd Harper, in conjunction with his student, Michayla Grey, shares how Michayla's experience studying in Todd's World Literature class abroad enabled her to become attuned to her emotional responses to the various texts with which she interacted.
- Rachel Spear discusses a composition course themed around mindfulness, during which she integrates meditation and writing process;
- Ann Amicucci shares a "pedagogy of course letters," during which she facilitated the student writing of reflective letters as pertained to their interaction with the course;
- Amanda May integrates technology into this process by describing how students in her freshman composition course used Twitter as a medium to write about their emotions.
- The last chapter switches the focus from student to teacher, as Sherry Rankins-Robertson and Nicholas Behm share the emotional realities of navigating through the academy.

While reading the proposals for this collection, I read many other great ideas that could not make it in here. But I am delighted to see that a number of scholars and instructors in our field are still giving credence to the idea that emotions are key in student writing. This collection is a tribute to this idea; as I read through these essays, I saw a few things I already practice in my pedagogy (for example, Rachel Spear's use of mindfulness meditation), and I thought of new ideas to incorporate in my classroom. I hope that these strategies can inspire others as they have me.

1. Learning to Feel: Engaging Emotions, Narratives, Values, and Commitments in Composition

JULIE CHRISTEN
University of Arizona

Twenty years ago, when my dad passed away from cancer, my mom gave me the best advice I've heard to date: "It's okay to cry." For both of us, this was just one small part of the grieving process, a process that has been recursive and epistemological. By epistemological, I mean that grief often serves as a means for trying to make sense of the experience of losing my dad and what it has meant to go on in our lives without him. Joan Didion writes about grief in *The Year of Magical Thinking* as something that "has no distance. Grief comes in waves, paroxysms, sudden apprehensions that weaken the knees and blind the eyes and obliterate the dailiness of life" (27). When I say grief is recursive, I mean something similar to that. It comes and goes, it ebbs and returns, requiring the griever to start over in some ways. Like writing, grief makes you return to your preconceived notions and interrogate them again and again before you can move forward.

I've spent much of my memorable life thinking about grief in some way, and most of my adult life thinking about writing. As a writer and writing teacher, I value the reflective practice that writing requires. In both of those roles and as a person more generally, I depend on this reflective practice in order to make sense of my experience, especially emotional experiences. When I first started teaching, I was struck by how unwilling my students were to engage with emotion in any way related to their writing. Their understanding of rhetoric is limited to logos, ethos, and pathos, with the latter being an appeal to be "used carefully in academic writing" or avoided altogether (Jensen 6). Contrary to my mom's wisdom, my students demonstrate Western culture's rejection of emotion. As one student stated in a conversation about determining credibility in research, we just "don't really trust sources that come from personal experience or appeal to emotions."

Because emotional awareness and interpreting my experiences by reflecting on my emotions have both played such a central role in my life, I'm especially put off when my students assert that we live in this bimodal world of facts and emotions. If that were the case, where do we sort values? Are values a fact, then, or simply an emotion? In this chapter, I center emotion as a key concept in a larger epistemological system about how we make up our minds about things and make sense of the world. In tracing the movements of this system, I highlight strategies for getting our students to think about themselves as fully human, as people who think with both emotion *and* facts as inextricable parts of our cognition. This all boils down to an analysis of how emotions shape our value judgments, expectations, motivations, and reflections.

This chapter traces the movements of this system by:

1. Considering how cultural proscriptions for emotion end up in composition classrooms and how even our own textbooks in First-Year Composition (FYC) fail us when it comes to emotion;
2. Considering how emotions shape the epistemic dimensions of our experiences, including our values, expectations, and value judgments;
3. Examining how these values and expectations influence and help us form our interests, investments, commitments, and motivations;
4. Engaging with these concepts through reflection on personal experience, which occurs in narrative. Ultimately, these strategies and behaviors are what help us make meaning.

Emotion Changes Our Behaviors and Perceptions

I define emotion as a specific, felt-response to a person or situation that makes us change something about our behavior or ways of understanding. I draw from Dale Jacobs and Laura Micciche's understanding of emotion from its root word *movere*: "a way to move." In simpler terms, it's a visceral feeling that leads us to do something differently. I consider emotion as an epistemic tool because it shapes our knowing and changes the way we interpret our experiences to construct new knowledge.

Considering specific emotions helps us achieve two things in our composition classrooms: (1) students learn to reflect on how their emotions shape the value judgments that they form opinions with and rely on in arguments;

and (2) students learn to recognize that their everyday emotional experiences are an integral part of how they think and not a distraction from how they are *supposed to* think.

Rhetorical studies has long recognized the value of emotional appeals, but this recognition has been overshadowed by our prevailing concern for helping students just be reasonable. Even our teaching resources in FYC reflect this concern. Most of our textbooks either do not productively discuss emotion as a rhetorical appeal, or they avoid the topic altogether. Gretchen Moon (2003) and Tim Jensen (2016) demonstrate how emotion has been mishandled in FYC in two reviews of popular FYC textbooks. Moon reviews 25 FYC textbooks published after 1998 and finds that textbook writers have "uncritically followed western culture's binary habits, which run deep and largely unchallenged" when it comes to emotion (39). Jensen's review of 25 textbooks published after 2010 points to specific gaps between rhetorical theory and what we actually teach first-year students: *we know* that emotion is valuable for composing practices but we treat emotion (oversimplified from pathos) as something to be avoided or "used carefully in academic writing" (6).

Jensen's notable exception is Mark G. Longaker and Jeffrey Walker's textbook *Rhetorical Analysis: A Brief Guide for Writers*, which includes a chapter on "Affect (Pathos Revisited)" that highlights the continuities between classical rhetoric and recent scholarship on emotion. Longaker and Walker consider emotion as a heuristic for making sense of experience, which plays in the following order: pathemata, affect, interpretation, emotion, and a change in behavior:

1. With *pathemata*[1], something happens to incite an emotional response (consider it an emotional exigence), which leads to an *affect*, a "bodily disposition" or response (210).
2. Our cognition kicks in to form an *interpretation* of what we're feeling, which becomes an *emotion*. For example, we might witness a near miss on campus during a heavy traffic time (pathemata). We gasp, feel our hearts race, our pupils dilate. These are non-cognitive, involuntary responses (affect) that precede cognitive responses.
3. We then *interpret* the situation: "That was a really close call," and feel an *emotion*: relief. In the final "stage," some part of our behavior changes. Maybe we pay closer attention to cars at intersections for a while, or put our phones away (or take them out to text a friend about what just happened).

This model for considering emotion is especially helpful for students because it allows for discussion on how our interpretations of various pathemata differ and it lets us consider *what underlying values* or expectations influence these interpretations. The key is, to get started we have to ask students to explicitly consider what they value most and then keep those values in mind as we navigate analyzing texts and creating arguments all semester.

For example, I once had a student tell the class about his uncle's pet deer. The deer had been injured, so the student's uncle took him in. When this student shared this story and a picture of the deer, most of the class reacted to how cute the story was—they smiled, said "Awww," and so on. But a few students, mostly male, smirked and shook their heads.

"Oh," I said to this handful of students, "You must hunt, then."

They nodded. They all experienced the same pathemata, but their affects were different because they had differing values for the story, which influenced their interpretations. It's a small thing, but these moments provide some concrete examples of how our emotions and values shape the way we interpret our experiences and make meaning. Specific examples like this one open up opportunities for discussing values, expectations, value judgments, and needs.

Emotion Shapes Values, Expectations, Value Judgments, and Needs

Jim W. Corder's work in "Argument as Emergence, Rhetoric as Love" creates further opportunities for bringing classical rhetoric and recent scholarship together with *narratives*. Corder considers the act of interpretation and meaning making as a narrative act. He writes, "Sometimes we can't find all that's needed to make the narrative we want of ourselves, though we still make our narrative. Sometimes we don't see enough . . . Sometimes we judge dogmatically, even ignorantly, holding only to standards that we have already accepted or established" (16). In other words, it's through the act of collecting our observations and experiences and forming narratives about them that we can make sense of things. Didion, too, draws on this line of reasoning when she writes, "We tell ourselves stories in order to live" (*White Album*). Corder's "standards that we have already accepted" are our values, expectations, value judgments, and needs. His point is that we're all narratives, and when we meet a "contending narrative" in another person, it's tough. It's especially tough when we care about that person, or when we're made to work closely with them. We have to listen to other perspectives and understand the values and emotions that undergird those perspectives if we want to get along.

In my spring FYC course, I ask my students to research the emotions and values that drive and influence discourse around public issues. Instead of choosing an aspect of an issue and arguing a "side," my students have to consider at least four viewpoints on their issue and investigate how certain values result in judgments about that topic. This semester, I had two students in one class give researched presentations on the border wall issue in Arizona. One student, who was from Nogales, which is half in Arizona and half in Mexico, went into the project blatantly opposing the wall. The other, who intended to enlist in the military after graduation, sat on the other end of the spectrum and supported the wall. The students presented on the same day, and I dreaded going to class that morning. I expected a fight. I was surprised to find, however, that the students were not only respectful of each other's research but that they were able to find common ground in their contending narratives. The student who initially supported the wall acknowledged the severity of mistreatment of immigrants and the negative environmental impacts a wall would create. The student from Nogales recognized the complexity of security along the border and, while he did not agree that a wall was a good solution, he came to understand where the other student was coming from. They recognized the difference in each others' values and where their narratives diverged.

Each of us thinks our own perspectives and opinions on various issues are reasonable; we believe that we make decisions that are rational, logical, and sensical, and most of us would never consider our opinions as something we form through emotion. By taking an inventory of their own values and then investigating how those values play out in public issues, students were able to at least understand how an opinion so opposite of their own could be formed.

Emotions, then, also play a central role in how we make value judgments. Social psychologist Jonathan Haidt describes this decision-making process using five "moral foundations," which have strong emotional resonances:

1. care/harm
2. fairness/cheating
3. loyalty/betrayal
4. authority/subversion
5. sanctity/degradation

Moral Foundations Theory considers these aspects of human nature as they correspond to our political leanings—for example, while both ends of the political spectrum care about *fairness*, the left considers fairness in terms of equality and the right considers it in terms of proportionality (138).

According to the work of Haidt and other social psychologists, our *moral emotions* also shape how we feel compelled to act in certain ways. With Hume's assessment that reason is "the slave of the passions," Haidt cites research that shows that when we are presented with pressing moral quandaries, the emotional centers of our brains are the first to respond, and then our cognitive centers kick in as we articulate justifications for how we feel about the issues involved. While Longaker and Walker's heuristic begins with affect (a non-cognitive response) and is *then* followed by a cognitive interpretation, Haidt's work considers visceral responses as part of a larger series of evolutionary adaptations that allow humans to "optimize responses" to various stimuli (148). For example, Haidt explains how *disgust* puts us at an evolutionary advantage that helps us avoid sickness (as in with rotting foods), and concludes that emotions like this are what help us form cooperative societies. In other words, we develop culturally approved emotions and responses to varying pathemata, and we use these frameworks to make up our minds about issues or make decisions about how to behave communally. These values are confirmed and passed down by the culture we live in and form "promises we make to one another" that dictate which behaviors we consider reasonable and which we reject (*Slouching Towards Bethlehem* 158).

Haidt makes the connection between culturally acceptable emotions and responses clear: "We feel pleasure, liking, and friendship when people show signs that they can be trusted to reciprocate. We feel anger, contempt, and even sometimes disgust when people try to cheat us or take advantage of us" (136). In the case of my students who researched the values and emotions shaping the debate on the border wall, their sticking points came from differences in Haidt's care/harm and loyalty/betrayal foundations. The student who supported the wall believed that building the wall was a matter of protecting Americans (care) and putting Americans first (loyalty to nation). The other student, in contrast, believed that we had a responsibility to welcome immigrants (care) and saw building the wall as a rejection of this responsibility (loyalty to humankind).

When I ask my students to think about the connections between emotion, expectations, values, and behaviors, I tell them to think about emotions as discrepancies between reality and expectations. If something happens that makes us feel frustrated or overwhelmed, we know there's something going wrong with how we *expected* something to go and how the world is actually working. For example, in most English departments we experience joy when a student asks a tough question in class because we *value* critical thinking and willingness to engage with the material. If we valued authoritarian, lecture-style learning, we might instead experience frustration that a student interrupted the flow of the class by asking a question.

These expectations—which are similar to Corder's "convictions"—shape our priorities, or what we find is worth spending our time and energy on. I often try to remind my engineering students, for example, that just because traditional "emotional arguments" do not *seem* present in the work of an engineer doesn't mean engineers are not guided and shaped by their emotions. "If you've ever talked to an engineer who has created something really cool or innovative," I say, "You'll hear all about how emotion drives their work. The passion, interest, and motivations are right there." Students demonstrate this example all the time when I ask them about previous writing experiences that stand out to them in their memory. It's always the same: writing experiences are memorable when students are excited about their topics. It's very common for me to get early reflective posts that say, "I was really excited about that paper because I got to choose the topic I was researching," for example.

Emotion and expectations are wrapped up with our investments and attachments, which also determine how much we are willing to engage with a task or person. Laura R. Micciche writes that emotion is "central to how we become invested in people, ideas, structures, and objects ... [it] generates *attachments* to others [and] to world views" (*Doing Emotion* 6). By considering emotion this way, we can start to think about how emotion enacts change—in our behaviors, our decision-making, and how we engage with the world. This is important for writers especially because it allows us to interrogate the lenses we use to consider issues. Micciche writes that even "how we think about what constitutes evidence and grounds for an argument—indeed, how we come to decide that an issue deserves to be 'argued'—is already shaped by our emotional investments in how things ought to be" (*Doing Emotion* 3). In other words, emotion shapes how we prioritize what's worth our time and intellectual engagement. This means asking our students (and ourselves) to think critically about how they can adapt their workflows in ways that *makes them* interested.

Emotion Influences and Helps Us Form Interests, Investments, Commitments, and Motivations

Shari J. Stenberg further expands on how the investments we form based on our emotions play a role in how we approach the world and build our narratives. She argues for a "pedagogy that values emotion as resource [and] considers how our emotional investments determine what we choose to see and not see, listen and not listen to, accept or reject" (60). This kind of pedagogical framework is only useful, though, if we can consider emotional investments in terms of our positionality, in how these investments "color the lenses through which we see the world" (61). The implications for this work are at least twofold:

1. Critically considering how our emotional values shape our investments and commitments allows us to identify gaps in our thinking and uncover opportunities for further growth as thinkers and writers. In other words, we find where we have more to learn.
2. Knowing how these values influence our investments allows us to reflect on how to make things that we don't inherently find interesting (like writing, work, relationships, etc.) worth our time and investment.

These are important moves in the epistemological system I trace because they give us opportunities to engage—to create meaningful connections, to solve challenging problems, to forge lasting relationships. It's not *all* about the writing; this is also *human* work.

If we frame emotion and writing in terms of values, attachments, and investments, we start to see how emotion is not only a rhetorical strategy or appeal, but a tool for engaging in ideas (as in writing), a means for reflection, and an experience that can be drawn from in order to form new interests and investments. Much of this work involves unpacking how our educations have shaped what we consider acceptable ways of thinking or approaching learning tasks. We do this by reflecting on previous writing experiences that tell us that personal experience is not a valid way of approaching arguments in writing or try to simplify emotion to pathetic appeals.

In one candid class discussion about Stenberg's chapter, my students brought up the fact that it's no wonder they do not know how to use personal experience in their academic writing, or how to use emotion effectively as epistemic tool. One student said, "One of the big emotions I kept coming back to [in Stenberg] was anger—on page 59. Anger as a need to defend one's investments in the values of the dominant culture. I think we're always told that anger is bad, so we never learn how to handle it or think about it." In a similar discussion a student connected to a line from the introduction of Micciche's *Doing Emotion*: "emotions have been schooled out of academic discourse" (5). He explained that "a lot of our writing in high school never focused on emotion; we just looked at the *tone* of the paper. We were never really taught to include emotion in our writing to make it better."

These previous experiences with writing reaffirm cultural stereotypes that personal experience is not evidence. Students tell me that their teachers "always told us not to use 'I' in our papers." They're supposed to be objective instead, and let their research pass through them, as though their personal experiences and values don't filter this research. These kinds of conversations allow students to "examine how our emotions have been schooled and how and why we respond emotionally to the world, [and] gain an opportunity for deeper reflection and insight" (Stenberg 43). That way, we can start thinking about emotion as not just an inevitable part of experience that requires taming or managing, but as an indication that further reflection might be needed in order to better understand our experiences and learn from them. I open up opportunities for this kind of reflection by engaging students with how their daily personal experiences influence their engagement with my class.

At the start of each class meeting, I ask my students to rate how they're doing on a scale of 1 through 5 (5 meaning great, 1 meaning terrible—probably a 1 wouldn't show up to class) and provide a quick reason. They're pretty good at this: "I'm a 2 because I almost got into a car accident on the way here and I'm still recovering from that a little," or "I'm a 5 because my parents are coming into town this weekend." I've gotten overwhelmingly positive feedback on this exercise because students feel like I better understand their needs and can cater the day's activities accordingly. In other words, I consider their emotions as an epistemic tool to adjust my teaching. Unfortunately, as soon as I ask them to do this in their academic writing, they're not sure what to do. Writing from personal experience or with emotion is reserved for fiction or for personal essays, not research and analysis. Even though most of the students in my spring courses have written a literacy narrative the previous fall, they can't quite seem to see how personal experience fits into academic writing.

I can't blame the overt avoidance of emotion in schooled writing on educators or academia specifically because these patterns just imitate cultural norms. As Stenberg points out, there are relevant social factors in play which "result in seemingly natural ways of categorizing emotion" and these social factors dictate whether we see emotion as appropriate to certain situations or not (49). In school, though, it's often safer to sweep emotions under the rug, rather than carefully analyze their rhetorical properties. "Just don't do it," seems to be the prevailing theme, even though we know that emotions are part and parcel of human experience and we know that emotions shape how we interpret these experiences.

Emotion is Necessary and Inherent to the Work of Writers (and to Ourselves)

Writing is inherently a meaning-making activity, which means we have to think about *all* the ways in which we know things in order to write effectively (*Naming What We Know*). We have to start asking ourselves why we find certain kinds of writing (or other activities or relationships) compelling, and we have to interrogate how our values and commitments filter these priorities. Ultimately, we have to ask ourselves which kinds of emotions drive our behaviors or influence our understandings. We have to engage in reflective practice, and we have to be able to weigh and mindfully consider how our emotions and values frame our approaches to writing (and all things, ultimately). In the composition classroom, this means asking students to continually bring their emotions and values into the conversation, instead of checking them at the door as they have been asked to do most of their educational careers.

In my rhetorical analysis assignment, I ask my students to consider how emotions influence their interpretations of the rhetorical situation in question. In response, more than one student has written something along the lines of, "My emotions did not influence my understanding of the situation or change the way I approached the writing because I could not relate it to my own life." When these students claim that emotions do not play a role in their writing experiences but they mention *frustration* at writing or being *bored* by their prompts, they disengage from their education because they don't view negative emotions as tools for changing their interpretations or behavior. It follows that when I ask students what their exigence is for writing—their problem or need to be solved by communication—the most common answer I hear is, "I was just writing it to get an A." This disengagement *prevents* reflective practice and allows students to go through their entire education without ever figuring out what's worth getting up in the morning for, or, as one of my mentors says, finding "where the jazz is." We *have to* ask our students to engage in this reflective practice in order to help them make meaning, both in the classroom and out.

Beyond education, Micciche considers this need for reflective work on emotion as an essential practice for situating ourselves in the world and engaging with it. She argues, "Without a framework for understanding emotion's legitimate role in the making of meaning and in the creation of value in our culture, we impoverish our own and our students' understanding of how we come to orient ourselves to one another and to the world around us" (*Doing Emotion* 1). It's through these critical engagements with our orientations that we become better thinkers, writers, and people who have to sometimes engage with contending narratives. We should help our students make themselves better, too.

Conclusion

I recently held a conference with a student who really grasped rhetorical elements and did nice critical work on audience, exigence, and constraints in his rhetorical analysis. He chose to write about a letter he had once written in order to make a complaint about a faculty member infringing on student privileges at his previous school. The notion of rhetoric as an activity that mediates action was very clear to him, but figuring out the role of emotion in this piece took some further thinking. "You mention some frustration and anxiety in your process of writing this letter," I said, "But I'm wondering how those emotions specifically impacted your decisions. What did you do about that frustration? How did it inform how you approached writing the letter?"

That got him thinking more, and this reflection ultimately ended in some further conversation about why thinking through rhetorical principles matters for a pre-business student who won't take any more writing courses after mine in his undergraduate career. "So this emotion and audience stuff is like, how I figure out what my financial advising clients need and care about then, right? I could use some of this to build better relationships with them?" He asked the right questions, and if we can keep getting ourselves (and our students) to think about how values and investments play a role in these interactions, we'll be that much closer to emotion as epistemic tool.

Note

1. According to Longaker and Walker, *pathemata* is essentially something that can be used to appeal to pathos; or anything that elicits an emotional response. Pathemata can be anything; it just depends on the values and expectations of the audience.

Works Cited

Corder, Jim W. "Argument as Emergence, Rhetoric as Love." *Writing about Writing: A College Reader*. 3rd ed., edited by Elizabeth Wardle and Doug Downs, Bedford St. Martin's, 2017, pp. 600–18.

Didion, Joan. *Slouching Towards Bethlehem*. Farrar, et al., 1961.

———. *The White Album*. Simon & Schuster, 1979, pp. 11–48.

———. *The Year of Magical Thinking*. Vintage, 2005.

Estrem, Heidi. "Writing is a Knowledge-Making Activity." *Naming What We Know: Threshold Concepts of Writing Studies*, edited by Linda Adler-Kassner and Elizabeth Wardle, Utah State UP, 2015, pp. 19–20.

Haidt, Jonathan. "The Moral Foundations of Politics." *The Righteous Mind: Why Good People are Divided by Politics and Religion*, Pantheon Books, 2012, pp. 128–54.

Jacobs, Dale, and Laura R. Micciche. *A Way to Move: Rhetorics of Emotion and Composition Studies*. Boynton/Cook Publishers, 2003.

Jensen, Tim. "Textbook Pathos: Tracing a Through-Line of Emotion in Composition Textbooks." *Composition Forum*, vol. 34, 2016. http://compositionforum.com/issue/34/. Accessed 9 Jan. 2018.

Longaker, Mark G., and Jeffrey Walker. "Affect (Pathos Revisited)." *Rhetorical Analysis: A Brief Guide for Writers*, Pearson, 2011.

Micciche, Laura R. *Doing Emotion: Rhetoric, Writing, Teaching*. Boynton/Cook Publishers, 2007.

Moon, Gretchen Flesher. "The Pathos of Pathos: The Treatment of Emotion in Contemporary Composition Textbooks." *A Way to Move: Rhetorics of Emotion and Composition Studies*, edited by Dale Jacobs and Laura R. Micciche, Portsmouth: Boynton/Cook, 2003, pp. 33–42.

Stenberg, Shari J. "Feminist Repurposing of Emotion: From Emotional Management to Emotion as Resource." *Repurposing Composition: Feminist Interventions for a Neoliberal Age*, Utah State UP, 2015.

2. Leveraging Student Emotional Motivations in Effective Classroom Writing: A Model-Based Approach

SANDRA STANKO

Why do you write? When students are posed this question, they most often respond with a typical "Because I have to" or "I want to get a good grade." These responses, however, can be said to more closely reflect answers to *what* the student hopes to be the end goal of the writing or *how* this goal might be achieved. Addressing the *why* of the writing process requires more individualist, intrinsic mining to identify the deeper motivations underlying the writing process. These motivations are often latent and emotionally based, below the surface of consciousness, but are, nevertheless, powerful contributors to potentially effective writing.

Drawing from learning theorists, including Murray, Dewey, Vygotsky, and Bruner, as well as the Self-Determination Theory (SDT) of motivation, this chapter will explore the intrinsic, emotional motivations underlying why students write and what they hope—even unconsciously—to gain from writing. The chapter will also make recommendations to stimulate this type of meaningful and effective writing within the classroom and will offer a specific tool, a Linked Value Balance Model, and a complementary worksheet to help students to meaningfully connect classroom writing with specific, identified emotional motivations for writing rooted in elements of personal value.

Why Do Students Really Write?

Focusing on the *why* of writing as opposed to the *what* reflects focusing on writing as a process rather than as a product. When writing is examined as a process, it becomes a conduit of discovery through language. It can even be argued that all forms of writing tap into the universal desire to share stories and experiences, where people want to exchange their narratives—stories, excuses, myths, reasons for doing and not doing—to organize experiences and memories and make sense of different aspects of their world (Bruner 4). Through narrative stories, people use "language or another symbolic system to imbue life events with a temporal and logical order, to demystify them and establish coherence across past, present, and as yet unrealized experience" (Ochs and Capps 2). Dewey described this coherence of one experience building upon another in creating new experiences as being "continuity" or "the experiential continuum" (*Experience and Education* 28). Similarly, Bruner described how narratives can be cumulative, what he calls "narrative accrual," saying that narratives "are eventually converted into more or less coherent autobiographies centered around a Self acting more or less purposefully in a social world" (18).

This type of organization and discovery through writing, said Murray, "is the process of using language to learn about our world, to evaluate what we learn about our world, to communicate what we learn about our world" (4). This process of discovery and sharing can yield a variety of related benefits, which can mirror a student's deeper potential emotional motivations for writing. Ryan and Deci found that these emotional motivations can involve the psychological needs of competence, autonomy, and relatedness, which reflect the essence of human thriving and can help to predict the wellness and vitality of an individual (*Self-Determination Theory* 5). To address these emotional needs, a student may consciously or unconsciously use writing for the personal benefits of healing, empowerment, self-development, problem-solving, and social connections.

Deliberately connecting the writing product with these personal, emotional benefits rooted in emotional motivation can yield a more fruitful and effective writing process, as well as product, for students. These emotional motivations and related emotional benefits from writing will be discussed in the following sections.

Writing for Competence and New Learning

Ryan and Deci described the emotional motivation of competence as being a person's need to feel masterful of topics and situations in their lives, evident in an inherent striving for knowledge and new growth (*Self-Determination Theory* 11). The degree to which a person experiences competence is reflected in their self-efficacy, which is the self-belief that one can identify, organize, initiate, and execute a course of action with a desired result (Bandura). A person is more likely to engage in behaviors where the promise of success is more likely (Ormrod 146). Because writing as process can result in new learning, it can build competence and support self-efficacy, yielding personal benefits such as healing, empowerment, and self- development. These benefits are possible essentially because this type of writing involves new learning through new perspectives and discoveries about a situation.

Dewey and New Learning

The process of discovery through language begins with personal experiences. Dewey asserted that learning originates from an individual's personal experiences, emphasizing the continuity of experience in which each experience affects the quality of future experiences. Dewey said, "The principle of continuity of experience means that every experience both takes up something from those which have gone before and modifies in some way the quality of those which come after" (35). Dewey believed that every experience is a moving force, which has value based upon what new experiences it is moving the person toward or into (14). In terms of self-efficacy, if a person has experienced success in a given activity in the past, he or she is more likely to expect similar success with the activity in the future; conversely, failure in a past activity may lead to an expectation of failure in the future (Ambrose et al. 78). Thus, the nature of an experience is determined by the individual and his or her interaction with the environment (both internal and external, past and expected future) at a given point in time (Dewey 43).

Writing for Healing

According to Dewey's theory, writing can result in new learning because of the continuity inherent in the process of writing about the experiences, one experience building upon another. The translation of experiences from abstract, prewriting concepts into more concrete, verbalized concepts in writing forces a kind of structure not only on the words but also on the experiences themselves. Elbow referred to this as the "germ event" in writing, where a person moves from abstract felt meaning into a piece of language (*Writing With Power* xviii). Tapping into Dewey's continuity of experience, Elbow recommended letting the writing process determine the outcome (*Writing With Power* 53), the writer using metacognition—thinking about thinking (Ormrod 364)—to generate new associations. As these new associations are made, the writer also makes new discoveries about the topic, experiences new learning, and gains new knowledge.

Writing for Empowerment

Just as writing can lead to new discoveries about both the syntax of the writing itself, as well as the writing topic, the new knowledge and perspectives that a person can gain through writing simultaneously provide the person with power (Foucault), which also gives the person a sense of control and ownership of the topic or situation. In this way, writing can lead to a sense of symbolic control over what may have appeared to be previously uncontrollable circumstances. Freire said that shifting this locus of control helps people to help themselves, "plac[ing] them in consciously critical confrontation with their problems,... mak[ing] them the agents of their own recuperation" (12). Empowered, the writer then becomes the agent for his or her own change, healing, empowerment, and self-development.

Writing for Self-Development

Writing has the ability to establish links among language, meaning making, and development of the self (Burnham 24–25). Writing can contribute to self-development because writing has been found to be a safe space for self-reflection, self-expression, and self-exploration.

In the process of writing for self-development, a person is expressing and developing his or her own voice. Just as each person has a unique speaking voice, with a unique "voice print," like a fingerprint, Elbow said that each person has a unique writing voice that mirrors the unique timber and range of his or her speaking voice (*Everyone Can Write* 194).

Similarly, Vygotsky said that a person's voice or written speech can be said to be a reflection of his or her inner speech, the internal dialectical dialogue he or she engages in when writing (*Thought and Language* 182). This inner voice can simultaneously shape and be shaped by social relationships and interconnectedness (Vygotsky, *Thought and Language*). Vygotsky described the concept of inner speech as having roots in experiences from a child's social development (*Thought and Language*). What begins as "external speech," essentially mimicked speech devoid of reasoning, evolves into "social speech" (speech for others) and "egocentric speech" (speech for one's self); egocentric speech then evolves into "inner speech" (Vygotsky, *Thought and Language* 228).

Inner speech specifically has a role in learning. While social speech is the "turning of thoughts into words, their materialization and objectification," inner speech is the reverse, as "overt speech sublimates into thoughts" (Vygotsky, *Thought and Language* 226). Through inner speech, learning occurs as words become "saturated with sense" (Vygotsky, *Thought and Language* 247), uniquely concentrated for the individual.

Writing for Autonomy and Evaluating the World

As was discussed previously, writing can be a way in which a person can build competence through new learning and the development of new perspectives about a situation. While competence focuses on the individual's perception of success in completing a given task, autonomy is an individual's ability to control or self-regulate one's actions (Ryan and Deci, *Self-Determination Theory* 10). This self-regulated learning can include learning strategies that involve setting goals, self-evaluation, self-reflection, and controlling one's motivation and emotions, among other activities (Ormrod 367–68). When a person experiences autonomy, he or she can experience pleasure in engaging in a task, willingly undertake challenges, and think meaningfully about problems, wanting to control what happens to themselves (Ormrod 451–52).

An aspect of autonomy is controlling one's decisions and actions through problem-solving. Writing for problem-solving is similar to writing for healing in that resolving the imbalance between the demands of a situation and a person's coping abilities through writing is essentially a problem-solving process.

Writing for Problem-Solving

Problem-solving through writing can involve seeing the writing process itself as being a "thinking problem" (Flower and Hayes, "Problem-Solving Strategies" 450). People have a set of problem schemas stored in their long-term memory, which includes knowledge about solving certain types of problems in specific ways (Ormrod 414). Writing as a process lets knowledge develop, so as the writer continues to write, he or she uses continual and more conscious guided guessing to recall what is known and to make new associations. Moreover, as the writer writes, he or she can alter goals as knowledge changes, adjusting where he or she wants to go in terms of writing based on the learning that is happening through the writing process (Flower and Hayes, "A Cognitive Process Theory" 290). Through this process, the memory schemas stored in long-term memory can change, creating new ways of presenting or framing an experience or problem, which can lead to new insights and solutions to problems (Flower and Hayes, "A Cognitive Process Theory").

Writing for Relatedness and Communicating with Others

Murray said writing as a process can enable people to communicate about their world and connect with other people. This psychological need for social connections can be described as relatedness (Ryan and Deci, *Self-Determination Theory* 11). Writers and researchers have used different images and metaphors to describe how writing can connect one person to another:

- Progoff used the metaphor of individual, personal wells all drawing from the same universal underground stream (34).
- McAndrew referred to people's "underlying webs of interconnectedness" (38).
- Elbow used the metaphor of a string to illustrate how one's writing is cast out "to connect yourself with other consciousnesses" (*Writing Without Teachers* 73).
- Woolf said that everyone is connected together by art, of which all humans are part: "Behind the cotton wool is hidden a pattern; that we—I mean all human beings—are connected with this; that the whole world is a work of art; that we are parts of the work of art" (17).
- Britton, referring to Gordon Pradle, said that people are engaged in "the conversation of mankind," which he said can also lead to "'the dialogic imagination'—the creative possibilities of cooperative talk" (182).

These interconnections made possible through writing can result in personal growth for both the writer and the reader.

Writing for Social Connections

The collaborative nature of writing enables writing's social connectedness. The writer experiences relatedness in being able to share personal narratives with others. At the same time, the readers benefit from sharing in the writer's story. "Other people's stories send us scrambling through our own story looking for correlations, similarities, or different possibilities," said Baldwin (125), insights which Progoff said can then be assimilated into the people's own lives (34). Through the process of engaging with another's narrative, the reader interacts with the narrative in a personal way, treating "the occasion of a narrative recital as a specialized speech act" (Bruner 17). Bruner described how the reader views the narrative through the lens of his or her own personal experiences and background knowledge, the writer's words being filtered through and interpreted by the reader's own internal voice and inner speech.

Nature of Motivation

This chapter thus far has focused on how writing can help to meet a person's psychological needs of competence, autonomy, and relatedness (Ryan and Deci, *Self-Determination Theory*) through yielding benefits related to healing, empowerment, self-development, problem-solving, and social connections. Whether or not a student is able to realize the end benefits of writing, however, is dependent upon one important factor: motivation.

In a nutshell, "motivation produces," said Ryan and Deci, and concerns the elements of energy, direction, persistence, and equifinality ("Self-Determination Theory" 69). Bruner also asserted that effective learning includes, among other elements, a desire or motivation to learn. In addition, Bruner spoke about the role of motivation in narrative writing, saying that "some measure of agency is always present in narrative and agency presupposes choice—some element of 'freedom'." (7).

Self-Determination Theory (SDT) categorizes motivation as being either intrinsic or extrinsic. SDT defines intrinsic motivation as being "the inherent tendency to seek out novelty and challenges, to extend and exercise one's capacities, to explore, and to learn" (Ryan and Deci, "Self-Determination Theory" 70). The roots for intrinsic behavior are within the person, and the rewards are internal as well, often in the form of personal satisfaction. Ryan and Deci characterized people who experience intrinsic over extrinsic motivation as having more interest, excitement, and confidence, which is manifested as enhanced performance, persistence, and creativity, as well as a heightened sense of vitality, self-esteem, and general well-being ("Self-Determination Theory" 69). These intrinsically motivated individuals may also experience "flow," which is characterized as being "a state of complete absorption, focus, and concentration in a challenging activity, to the point that a learner loses track of time and completely ignores other tasks" (Ormrod 442).

Conversely, extrinsic motivation focuses on behavior directed toward external outcomes. SDT differentiates between four types of extrinsic motivation, differentiated by the source of their roots and whether or not the roots are value-based: integrated regulation, identified regulation, introjected regulation, and external regulation (Ryan and Deci, "Self-Determination Theory" 72)

The second two forms of extrinsic motivation (introjected regulation and external regulation) can be said to be "controlling" forms because the root is external; these forms of extrinsic motivation have been associated with negative effects on psychological functioning, academic performance, and well-being (Garn et al. 264). In terms of self-efficacy, if a person attributes success to external or uncontrollable causes, the perception of future success diminishes (Ambrose et al. 78).

The first two forms of extrinsic motivation (integrated regulation and identified regulation) can be said to be "internalized" forms because the root is internal; like intrinsic motivation, these forms of extrinsic motivation have been associated with positive psychological functioning, as well as positive academic and well-being effects (Garn et al. 264). In terms of self-efficacy, the person with this type of motivation sees that success is attributable to internal and controllable causes, so future success is expected (Ambrose et al. 78) (see Table 2.1).

In this vein, a Linked Value Balance Model is proposed that is intended to activate and leverage the most effective types of student motivation to generate more personally meaningful—and academically effective—classroom writing. This model, along with the accompanying worksheet can be used in the classroom to increase student motivation for writing and to enhance learning.

Table 2.1 Effective Forms of Personal Motivation

	Root	Reward	Example	Potential Inner Speech
Intrinsic Motivation	Internal, value-based	Internal	A student wants to engage in an activity because it is enjoyable and personally satisfying.	"I want to write because I enjoy the process of writing."
Integrated Regulation Motivation	Internal, value-based	External	A student personally enjoys receiving good grades because of receiving external praise for those good grades.	"I strive to write well to receive praise for my good grades."
Identified Regulation Motivation	Internal, non-value-based	External	A person makes a commitment to getting good grades to pass a course.	"I want to write to get a good grade because I have learned that good grades will enable me to pass the course."

Linked Value Balance Model

The Linked Value Balance Model puts into action the benefits of writing for new learning and perspectives, increasing the potential for realizing personal growth benefits through writing. The Linked Value Balance Model is comprised of five steps: identify life challenges, identify emotional needs, identify elements of value, engage in freewriting, and develop personal writing goals.

At the end of this chapter, a resource titled "Developing Your Meaningful Writing Process Worksheet" based on the Linked Value Balance Model is provided, which can be used within the composition classroom to engage students in the writing process prior to beginning a writing assignment. The teacher can guide the student through the steps of the model, providing supplemental guidance as needed (see Appendix).

The five steps of the Linked Value Balance Model are described in more detail below, along with specific references to exercises in the worksheet that support each step of the model.

Step 1: Identify Life Challenges

As has been discussed, stories are the webs that interconnect individuals, and each person has several to tell. The first step of the Linked Value Balance Model asks students to identify the life challenges which comprise the current life stories that they want—and need—to tell, selecting the most pressing life challenge. This step is reflected in Exercise 1 of the worksheet. Life challenges typically can involve the following areas: work, family, health (physical, mental, or emotional), home environment, spirituality, and finances.

Step 2: Identify Emotional Needs

Going hand in glove with a life challenge is an underlying emotional aspect that needs to be addressed, which will likely involve meeting the general psychological needs of competence, relatedness, or autonomy (Ryan and Deci, *Self-Determination Theory*). These can also be the inherent personal benefits that can be realized through writing that have been discussed, including healing, empowerment, self-development, problem-solving, and social connectedness. The second step of the Linked Value Balance Model asks the students to identify these needs and then narrow them to the most important emotional need. This step is reflected in Exercise 2 of the worksheet, along with self-reflective questions to help the students to consider what emotional needs they may have.

Step 3: Identify Elements of Value
Just as every person has life challenges, every person has elements that he or she values the most. In the third step of the Linked Value Balance Model, students are asked to list their top elements of value, the things that are most important to them right now. From these, they should select their most important element of value. These activities are reflected in Exercise 3 of the worksheet, including examples of the elements of value. By focusing on the elements of value, the Linked Value Balance Model is tapping into those sources of motivation with an internal root (intrinsic, integrated regulation, and identified regulation), which are the most effective forms of motivation (Ryan and Deci, "Self-Determination Theory").

Step 4: Engage in Freewriting
In considering the areas of challenge and related needs, along with the elements of value, the students are asked to engage in freewriting in the fourth step of the Linked Value Balance Model, using these identified foci collectively as a springboard for new insights, what Elbow also refers to as loop writing (*Writing With Power* 61). Four brainstorming techniques are provided in Exercise 4 of the worksheet, which range from the most structured to the least structured: sentence stems, lists, clustering, and freewriting (Adams). The students should then circle the most meaningful words, phrases, or concepts which emerge from the freewriting exercises. These are the important connections that the students have made among the elements, which form the emotional basis, or scaffolds, upon which writing goals will be developed in the fifth step of the Linked Value Balance Model.

The student can use any or all of the brainstorming techniques. Using these techniques to make associations among needs and value elements is using Dewey's idea of continuity in layering previous knowledge onto new knowledge, which can ideally result in new associations and new learning. Because freewriting involves writing whatever comes to mind pertaining to the element of value and accepting the words that arrive (Elbow, *Writing With Power* xvi), the freewriting activity specifically can also tap into a student's inner speech (Vygotsky, *Thought and Language*) and enable these associates to emerge in his or her own unique voice (Elbow, *Writing With Power*).

At this point, the instructor can explain how the needs that the students identify (healing, empowerment, etc.) can be addressed through the process of writing. Using Vygotsky's theory of the zone of proximal development (ZPD), where the ZPD identifies those functions that are not yet fully developed but are instead in an "embryonic state" (*Mind in Society* 86), the instructor can explain how the connections among the elements become the scaffold which assists in the development of the person's personal writing.

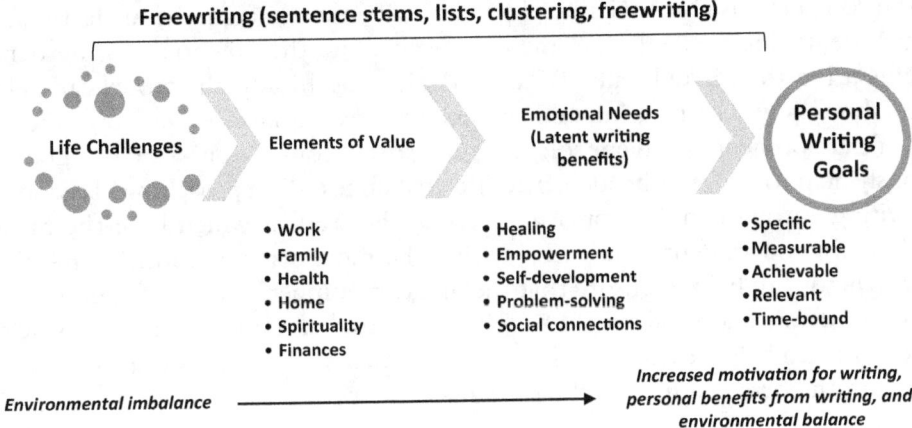

Figure 2.1 Linked Value Balance Model of Writing

As the individual works with these personally established connections, he or she also learns how that element is related to the writing process, potentially increasing the person's value of writing through this associative relationship.

Step 5: Develop Personal Writing Goals
What should have emerged from the exercises so far are raw associations among life challenges, elements of personal value, and emotional needs, the latter of which can be benefits of engaging in writing as a process. This step in the Linked Value Balance Model is where the student introduces structure to these concepts, writing one or two goals for the classroom writing process through Exercise 5 on the worksheet. These goals should take the form of SMART (Specific, Measurable, Achievable, Relevant, and Time-bound) goals. These goals can then be used collectively as a purposeful guide for the student, imbuing the required classroom writing with personal value.

The proposed Linked Value Balance Model can potentially result in an increased motivation for the writing process, as well as increased personal benefits from writing and an increased environmental/life balance, ultimately resulting in more meaningful and academically effective classroom writing (see Figure 2.1).

Conclusion

Students who enter the composition classroom are often carrying burdens related to work, family, health, home environment, spirituality, and finances, but they fail to see the connections between those and the writing activities of the course. This chapter has explained how connections can be made among a student's life challenges, elements of value, and the potential writing benefits using the Linked Value Balance Model. Specifically, the model can help to show how writing's inherent benefits related to healing, empowerment, self-development, problem-solving, and social connections can simultaneously help to address the identified life challenges. By approaching classroom writing through the personal interests of the student which have the most value for the student—and will provide the most personal motivation—the instructor can help to ensure that the greatest number of students can realize the academic and professional benefits of writing as a process, as well as help to maintain balance between the various elements of a composition classroom and in the personal lives of the students.

Appendix: Worksheet Complementing the Linked Value Balance Model

Developing Your Meaningful Writing Process Worksheet

Exercise 1: Identify Life Challenges

What life challenges are you facing right now? These challenges can typically fall into these broad categories: work, family, health (physical, mental, emotional), home environment, spirituality, and finances.

What are your current life challenges? List them below and circle the top challenge.

Exercise 2: Identify Emotional Needs

Your specific life challenges can generate emotional needs for you, which can generally fall into the categories of competence (feeling confident in what you do), autonomy (feeling that you are capable of doing what you want to do), and relatedness (feeling connections with others). These needs can cause you to feel associated needs for:

Healing
Do you feel that you need to recover from something physically, emotionally, or mentally?

Empowerment
Do you feel stripped of power in a specific situation? Do you feel overwhelmed by a situation, person, or other element?

Self-development
Are there areas in which you feel you need to grow? Do you feel lacking or inferior in a specific situation?

Problem-solving
Are you facing specific problems in your life right now? What problems do you feel that you need to solve?
Social connections
How do you feel about your relationships with others? How is this area lacking in your life?
What emotional needs are most demanding in your life right now? List them below and circle the top emotional need.

Exercise 3: Identify Elements of Value
Elements of value comprise what is most important to you, which can usually fall into the same broad categories as life challenges: work, family, health (physical, mental, emotional), home environment, spirituality, and finances.
What is most important to you right now? What do you value the most? List these below. Circle the most important element of value.

Exercise 4: Engage in Freewriting
What are your answers from the previous three questions? List them below.

> From Exercise 1: *What is your top life challenge?* _____
> From Exercise 2: *What is your top emotional need?* _____
> From Exercise 3: *What is your top element of value?* _____

For this exercise, you will reflect upon the results from the previous three exercises through engaging in freewriting. Freewriting is just writing without thinking or worrying about what you are writing, which is intended to tap into the creative, emotional right brain while quelling the analytic and critical tendencies of the left brain.

Consider all three of your responses in completing any or all of the freewriting exercises below, which range from the least to the most structured. What connections can you identify among your most important elements? Circle the most meaningful words, phrases, or concepts.

Sentence Stems

One of the easiest ways to generate new ideas is to complete a thought or concept with what comes first to mind. Incomplete sentences are provided for you to fill in the blanks.

In my life right now, I am facing _____.
This challenge makes me feel _____.
I value _____.
This valued element is related to my life challenge in _____.
My life challenge makes me feel like I need _____.
Writing about _____ makes me feel _____
_____.

I will believe _____ about myself following my writing.

Lists

The listing technique invites you to jot down words in a list form that come to mind as you consider your life challenges, emotional needs, and elements of value.

    1.
    2.
    3.
    4.
    5.

Clustering

Clustering is an associative way of generating ideas, where you write down one idea and draw a line to a new, related idea, forming an interconnected web of ideas among your life challenges, emotional needs, and elements of value.

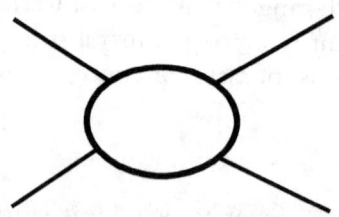

Freewriting

Freewriting is writing in long form anything that comes to mind as you consider your identified life challenges, emotional needs, and elements of value. Write without stopping and without thinking about what you are writing. You may also consider giving yourself a time limit for your writing, such as three, five, or even ten minutes.

Exercise 5: Develop Personal Writing Goals

Up to this point, you have been brainstorming elements related to your life challenges, elements of value, and emotional needs and have explored connections among these elements through freewriting:

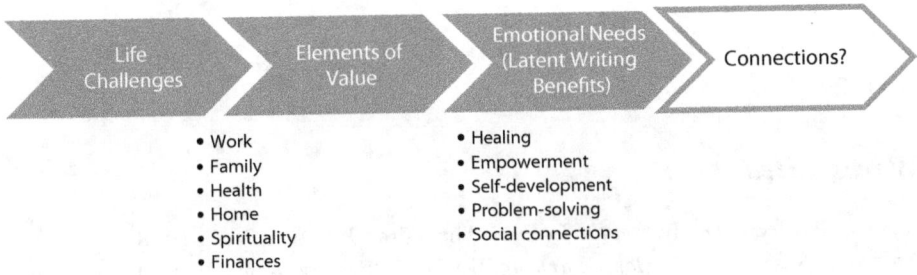

- Work
- Family
- Health
- Home
- Spirituality
- Finances

- Healing
- Empowerment
- Self-development
- Problem-solving
- Social connections

Taking into consideration that emotional needs can be met through the latent benefits of writing, this exercise guides you in creating personal writing goals which can help to direct and guide your writing. These goals are typically short-term goals that can help you to have personally meaningful and relevant, as well as effective, classroom writing. Thinking of these goals in terms of SMART (Specific, Measurable, Achievable, Relevant, Time-bound) goals can help to ensure that the goals are most effective. These questions can help you in constructing a SMART goal:

> **Specific:** What writing goal do you need to achieve? What life challenges, elements of personal value, and emotional needs are involved? What connections have you identified among these elements?
> **Measurable:** How will this goal be measured or quantified?
> **Achievable:** How is the goal able to be met?
> **Relevant:** How is the goal relevant to the situation?
> **Time-bound:** What is the target due date? When will this goal be met?

Using the information and insights you have discovered through the freewriting exercises, write one or two goals for your writing that are SMART goals. Below is a template to help you in structuring your SMART goals.

I will complete ____ by doing ____ [Specific writing goal] by the deadline of ____ [Time-bound aspect]. This activity relates to ____ [Specific life challenge] and ____ [Specific element of personal value] by addressing ____ [Specific emotional need] through ____ [Specific connection(s)]. This goal is relevant to my classroom work and personal life because ____ [Relevant aspect]. I will know that I have achieved this goal by ____ and ____ [Measurable, Achievable aspects].

Goal 1

Goal 2

Works Cited

Adams, Kathleen. *The Way of the Journal.* The Sidran Institute Press, 1998.

Ambrose, Susan, et al. *How Learning Works: 7 Research-Based Principles for Smart Teaching.* Jossey-Bass, 2010.

Baldwin, Christina. *Storycatcher: Making Sense of Our Lives through the Power and Practice of Story.* New World Library, 2005.

Bandura, Albert. *Self-Efficacy: The Exercise of Control.* Freeman, 1997.

Britton, James. "James Britton: An Impressionistic Sketch: A Response." *College Composition and Communication,* vol. 41, no. 2, 1990, pp. 181–86.

Bruner, Jerome. "The Narrative Construction of Reality." *Critical Inquiry,* vol. 18, no. 1, 1991, pp. 1–21.

Burnham, Christopher. "Expressive Pedagogy: Practice/Theory, Theory/Practice." *A Guide to Composition Pedagogies,* edited by Gary Tate et al., Oxford, Oxford UP, 2001, pp. 19–35.

Dewey, John. *Experience and Education.* Touchstone, 1938.

Elbow, Peter. *Everyone Can Write: Essays Toward a Hopeful Theory of Writing and Teaching Writing.* Oxford UP, 2000.

———. *Writing With Power.* 2nd ed. Oxford UP, 1998.

———. *Writing Without Teachers.* 2nd ed. Oxford UP, 1998.

Flower, Linda, and John Hayes. "A Cognitive Process Theory of Writing." *Cross-Talk in Composition Theory: A Reader.* 2nd ed., edited by Victor Villaneuva, National Council of Teachers of English, 2003, pp. 365–87.

———. "Problem-Solving Strategies and the Writing Process." *College English*, vol. 39, no. 4, 1977, pp. 449–61.

Foucault, Michel. *Power/Knowledge: Selected Interviews and Other Writings 1972–1977.* Pantheon Books, 1977.

Freire, Paulo. "Education as the Practice of Freedom." *Education for Critical Consciousness.* Edited and translated by Myra Bergman Ramos, Continuum, 1974, pp. 3–83.

Garn, Alex, et al. "Parental Influences on the Academic Motivation of Gifted Students: A Self-Determination Theory Perspective." *Gifted Child Quarterly*, vol. 54, no. 4, 2010, pp. 263–72.

McAndrew, Donald. "Chaos, Complexity, and Fuzziness: Science Looks at Teaching English." *The English Journal*, vol. 86, no. 7, 1997, pp. 37–43.

Murray, Donald. "Teach Writing as a Process Not Product." *Cross-Talk in Composition Theory: A Reader.* 2nd ed., edited by Victor Villanueva, National Council of Teachers of English, 2003, pp. 3–6.

Ochs, Elinor, and Lisa Capps. *Living Narrative: Creating Lives in Everyday Storytelling.* Harvard UP, 2001.

Ormrod, Jeanne Ellis. *Human Learning.* 7th ed. Pearson, 2016.

Progoff, Ira. *At a Journal Workshop: Writing to Access the Power of the Unconscious and Evoke Creative Ability.* Penguin Putnam, 1992.

Ryan, Richard, and Edward Deci. *Self-Determination Theory.* The Guilford Press, 2017.

———. "Self-Determination Theory and the Facilitation of Intrinsic Motivation, Social Development, and Well-Being." *American Psychologist*, vol. 55, no. 1, 2000, pp. 68–78.

Vygotsky, Lev. *Mind in Society: The Development of Higher Psychological Processes*, edited by Michael Cole et al., Harvard UP, 1978.

———. *Thought and Language.* Translated by Alex Kozulin, The MIT P, 1986.

Woolf, Virginia. *Moments of Being.* 2nd ed. Edited by Jeanne Schuleind, Harcourt Brace, 1985.

3. "Dull Feelings of Just Getting By": Advanced Assistant Professor Experiences of Impasse and Mentorship

K. Shannon Howard

Information science and communication scholar Steven Jackson explains that times of repair and maintenance in any act of innovation often go unnoticed or discarded. Having spent years of studying the work of mobile phone repair workers, Jackson developed a theory of the "broken world," which asserts that the idea of repair, or the condition during which "screens and buttons fail, firmware is corrupted, and the iPhone gets shipped back" deserves as much attention as the phase that typically characterizes production or creation of something new (226). Unfortunately, he says, such work is rarely visible in any meaningful or thrilling way. Although Jackson specifically critiques the obsession with innovation or innovators in technology and media, his thoughts may arguably now apply to the life of a professor teaching writing. The emphasis in universities now is one of innovation, deliverables and futurity. For example, professors may be asked to deliver a certain number of graduates who earn their Master's degrees in writing studies. Instructors of composition may be asked to submit just how many freshmen have withdrawn or failed first-year writing classes in order to study retention. Freshmen learn revising techniques in the first-year writing classroom in order to experience writing as recursive, yet the completion of assignments, despite decades of emphasis on processes rather than products, remains the typical goal.

In the material world, scholars and students alike still adhere to a linear model of time, and this model often limits how the process of writing takes place. Deliverables and futurity neglect the phases of production that may typify what writers, professors, and students regularly experience in terms of impasse. If, as Laura Micciche famously says, many central ideas in composition come from "emotioned ways of seeing our work," then feelings of stagnation, maintenance, and listlessness have a role to play in how we perceive ourselves. Not only do such feelings have a role to play, but time, as I will discuss later, is often "cripped" or "queered" in the writer's mind, thereby rendering traditional models of production unhelpful. Although both crip time and queer time possess different histories and contexts of usage, both call for new ways of experiencing the material world, ways that depart from the normative schedules or habits of those in power.

Debra Hawhee, in her work on the body and rhetoric, argues for a "transdisciplinary" approach to problem-solving, one in "favor of a broad, open, multilevel inquiry" that goes beyond cross-listing certain courses in a college catalog. I take such an approach in the forthcoming pages. Drawing from feminist, disability, and affect theories, Jackson's "broken world" concept, and the narrative of a recent popular culture text, this chapter argues that perceptions of impasse, more commonly and perhaps reductively known as writer's "block," need not be negative. Additionally, I suggest that composition as a field rely less on notions of futurity and more on what concepts of atemporality offer students and ourselves. As Hannah Rule argues, by engaging intimately with work by Susan Wyche, Jody Shipka and Paul Prior, and Brian McNely et al. (411–17), the theater, or scene, of writing production has received new focus over the past two decades although notable scholarship on this topic occurred prior to twenty-first century. Linda Brodkey, for one example, troubled the notion that the "scene of writing" has always been a "romantic" one, where the writer composes frequently and productively in a cloistered space, perhaps a garret (397). She stressed the importance of instructors dispelling such images in order to teach composition more effectively.

This infatuation with the writer's immediate space and the production happening within it has sometimes resulted in a naïve approach to materiality, one where the human controls the props on her stage of production and, as Brodkey critiques, isolates herself to access her genius. Because recent humanities scholarship has now embraced a material turn, or a focus on the nonhuman agents involved in rhetoric and daily life (Bennett, Barnett and Boyle, Grant, Rickert), nonhuman agents like coffee shops, ambient music, and even the arrangement of letters on a laptop have often come to signify more than just props in a scene. Still, what happens when the coffee served to us is weak or the music experiences a glitch? How does the *flawed* material world intersect with writing production, and what role do temporal constraints play in such a world? Ann Cvetkovich, extending Lauren Berlant's ideas, explains that a state of writer's block, or impasse "suggests that things will not move forward due to circumstance—not that they can't but that the world is not designed to make it happen." In turn, she also argues that today's society requires "better ways of talking about ordinary life, including the dull feelings of just getting by" (159). The comment about the world's design intersects with Jackson's concept of maintenance. It may be time to consider "the possibility that slowing down or not moving forward might not be a sign of failure and might instead be worth exploring" (Cvetkovich 21). This concept requires that we spend time understanding how time might operate differently in the world of impasse.

Affect theorists would remind us that intention is difficult to untangle from the "many bodily (and mental) processes [that] take place subliminally, below the threshold of awareness" (Leys 456). Human intentionality may take us to a certain point, but it fails to deliver us at certain pressing moments in our careers and mentoring work. Often perceptions of futurity intervene here. Many writers hold fast to the belief that the world itself does not support their production in a specific place and time; therefore, they must wait until the rain stops, a study cubicle becomes available, or a difficult home situation resolves itself. This is not to say that such beliefs are always false. Graduate students writing their master's theses repeatedly informed me that they will be able to work on their stalling projects "this summer" because of various reasons—summer, in a sense, ceased to exist as a season and became the ideal space and time to reverse unproductivity. However, once summer became the stage upon which productivity was set, the pressure to fulfill that goal would become too immense. The very things they imagined would be inspirational became hostile—the sun was too hot, the coffee too weak.

Graduate students also confront more serious problems in the form of personal challenges. I found myself frustrated at my lack of counseling skills at various times when a student experienced a tiring custody battle with a recalcitrant ex-husband. I was tempted at several points to remind this student, perhaps inappropriately, that there may not be an "optimal" time to finish a degree, that such battles in life (translation: such impasses) persist for years. Even though I told this student that completion of degrees did not matter in the face of such stress, I still reminded her that it might be better to drop her program or continue the project but not allow herself to get stuck "in the middle," paying for courses and graduation fees when she had no clear path to finishing. This advice stemmed from my own insecurities regarding numbers of graduates in my program and my own narrow vision of how academics measure time and effort. Donald Murray has argued that writers need to be "accepting" about the "doing nothing" phase of their work. Some delays, he argues, are "essential" to finding the right "information, insight, order, need, [and] voice" (720). Still, Murray's advice often goes unheeded by those of us bound up in administrative promises to graduate more students, or produce more output. A capitalist system requires that students be part of that output in order to make the degree a viable one.

Likewise, the desire for material comforts limits our openness to such phases of work and also tempts us into purchasing goods in exchange for better outcomes, such as more caffeine, a better lamp, or a more ergonomic chair. Bruce Horner, years ago, countered voices like Murray's by cautioning writing teachers that the work of writing instruction is always bound up in a materialist culture that seeks "commodification" and that some reactions to this state of things entail a naïve focus on process to the point of denying a product's use value (209). After all, graduate students will need to defend their thesis projects eventually. They require diplomas and credits and deadlines to move into their future careers.

Although Jackson stresses the importance of the fixer/maintainer/repairperson to contribute to the greater good, I would stress that the broken world he describes cannot be controlled or truly fixed, for, as he mentions, the world's nature is "to break." In the years preceding my tenure application, the position of department chair rotated three times, new provosts, chancellors, and deans replaced old ones, and the composition program underwent a major overhaul. Replacing and reinventing the proverbial wheels of governance reminds a faculty member just how uncertain daily work conditions may be. The same conditions that lend a spirit of precarity to faculty work also impinge on graduate student work. The graduate student faces her first group of freshmen writers when she signs up to be a teaching assistant, often in the second year of master's study. Brock Dethier, in his clear and brief advice to such new teachers, warns them that if they wish to pursue their own writing at the same time they teach, they will always feel as if they are "steal[ing]" time from their students and the course preparation in which they engage. He even concludes with a comment that new teachers should not "worry about trying to get the next chapter written this semester" on top of their other responsibilities (160–61). Christine Casanave explains that a "lack of tenacity" in finishing a graduate thesis may be due to an inability to articulate why the student has started a graduate program in the first place. In this sense she refers to the insights that the past, or an originary moment/starting line may provide. Several of my graduate students had both problems: a new set of freshmen to mentor in the present and reasons for pursuing graduate study they had failed to articulate at the starting point.

Linear structures of time, particularly ones featuring optimistic or optimal endings, often fail to provide comfort to the professor as well as the stalling graduate student. Family and friends often told me that as soon as I finished my tenure application and my book manuscript I could find release from stress. This is and was hardly the case. Being mired in these two projects was not contingent on the relief I would feel when they ended; rather, I felt the impending completion as just another hurdle. I feared the "what now?" moments of succeeding at both endeavors and being left directionless, no matter how carefully I orchestrated a new line up of research projects for my forthcoming years. The images or metaphors I associated with production were bound up in analogies where impasse was a gap or detour that hardly deserved acknowledgment. The train was always supposed to leave the station or the caterpillar was supposed to transform into the butterfly.

There were always fewer words on both global and local levels to describe the phase of metamorphosis connected to maintenance or repair and to the acceptance of a broken world. For instance, because my department had recently adopted a focus on transfer in the composition program, words like "future" and "bridging" peppered the meetings I attended, and consequently, I became immersed in a language of predictable deliverables, all while listless and uninspired by my own work and watching graduate students stall in theirs. Additionally, in filing state level reports to justify the need for a new Master's program, my predecessors promised that a certain number of students per year would graduate. This would offset the starting costs of investing in a new tenure-track hire (my own). Bound up in this plan was the fear of losing my job since it was created in part by this very report. As a result, I failed the student in the custody battle who needed my emotional support during a difficult time.

Redirecting my perception of impasse was made easier by an example from popular culture during the summer before completing my tenure application. Most people born in the 1970s and early 1980s are familiar with the 1984 film *The Karate Kid*. In this narrative, the underdog teen with a chip on his shoulder, Daniel LaRusso, manages to unseat the reigning teen karate champion Johnny Lawrence, a boy who has also begun bullying Daniel for flirting with his former girlfriend. During this film, Johnny embodies what Daniel is not: his family has money, he is a leader both in school and in his karate class, and he has a large cohort of friends. In contrast, Daniel's main friend is Mr. Miyagi, a maintenance man and karate expert who works in the run-down apartment complex where he and his mother live. The original movie ends with Johnny's comeuppance and his admiration for Daniel who, thanks to Mr. Miyagi's mentorship, wins the tournament with an iconic crane kick to Johnny's face. Despite the pain and embarrassment, Johnny hands Daniel the trophy and says "you're all right, LaRusso" in a moment of great sportsmanship.

However, the new streaming show *Cobra Kai* rewrites a section of that ending. In launching the new YouTube premium streaming episodes, the showrunners play back the final tournament footage where Daniel defeats Johnny. This is, in part, a sequel that reveals, piece by piece, the new adult lives the characters inhabit and how they were affected by the tournament. Although the outcome of the 1984 tournament is the same, the camera zooms in on what happens when Johnny receives Daniel's surprise kick to the face. The original film shows Johnny recovering after a moment. He stands, gives the trophy to Daniel, and makes amends. In this iteration, the camera's bird's eye view shows Johnny remaining face down, his body splayed like a corpse that has received a fatal gunshot wound. Because the showrunners focus on this moment, it enables them to construct a graphic match between that embarrassing fall and Johnny's body in 2017. In *Cobra Kai*'s first episode, Johnny sleeps on his bed alone in the same exact position, the table beside him littered with junk food and alcohol. In creating this match, the writers make clear that Johnny has been at some kind of impasse, that he has been, in fact, so changed by the loss that he refuses to get up. Decades have passed, and the visual the audience receives about Johnny is one where he has remained suspended in time, deflated and immobile, a person who peaked in high school and cannot recapture his golden days of youth and confidence. Even as Johnny the adult appears physically different from Johnny the teen: the man eats and drinks like a teenager, fixing spam with ketchup for breakfast and buying slices of pizza from the corner mart. He eschews social ties and gets fired from his odd job as a maintenance man for the San Fernando Valley upper class—one of the teen characters mocks him in the pilot with the proclamation of "You're the guy who cleaned my dad's septic tank!"

What happens next is the story of how he gets back on his feet. Johnny eventually opens his own karate studio, attempts to reconcile with his prodigal teenage son, and later comes face to face with Daniel LaRusso only to have one of his students defeat Daniel's sole student in a similar competition to the one the men fought years ago. What makes this rather pat ending work is the twist: Daniel's student loses, yes, but this student is actually Johnny's son Robby, a boy who sought revenge against his father by seeking out Johnny's former high school nemesis. In this sense, Daniel still walks off with the real prize, a relationship with Robby, while Johnny's students cheer and hold their trophy high.

What is so effective about this outcome is it stresses the way impasse persists despite positive changes in material circumstances. All of Johnny's efforts to improve himself, both physically and economically (he now exercises, cuts back on his drinking, and finds enough students to pay the rent on his dojo and support himself) has still kept him mired in a broken relationship that mirrors Jackson's "broken world." In watching and understanding Johnny's journey, I identified with him. Johnny had earned his trophy by the season's end, but he still felt discouraged. I had a book contract that year and ample material to "show off" my first five years as a professor, but I still felt let down by the system that pushed me to design marketing plans and social media content that would somehow increase my numbers in the graduate program. I felt success in my book project, but a month after I submitted the manuscript, a colleague wrote a Facebook post, denouncing publishers whose work did not include a commitment to open source materials and scolding scholars for allying themselves with such publishers. Likewise, linear time ceased to comfort me as promises of completion simply multiplied my anxieties. After my submission of tenure materials, I had to wait for months for the decision. It was like existing between two frames of reference: the assistant and the associate level of academic work. Graduate students must feel a similar tension between their roles as students and teachers in their second year of graduate work. We all confronted the strange, inexplicable nature of impasse and felt shame that the flow of material goods (in my case the book and the tenure application) did nothing to inspire us to move forward. Moreover, nothing in our surroundings like summer sunshine, pets, or strong coffee offered solace.

In this case, literacy scholar Bronwyn T. Williams (like Hawhee in her emphasis on transdisciplinarity), would recommend that composition seek out new fields and avenues of study in order to find answers to problems like the kind described above. Scholars in disability studies and queer theory have found innovative ways to bypass time's linear structure and explore how events move sideways, forward and backward in our experiences even when time passes according to the calendar. In this conception of time, it is also common to experience "time stopping" completely, as illness or queerness separates the bodily experience of one person from another's bodily experience. Such scholars refer to nonstandard views of time as "queer" or "crip" because of this structure. This designation may be helpful in exploring, in a less judgmental way, what blocks or stalls writers like ourselves and our students. Ellen Samuels explains how she connects crip time with the work of writing:

> If I were to write a best-seller, though, I think it would be about vampires . . . Because *crip time is vampire time*. It's the time of late nights and unconscious days, of life schedules lived out of sync with the waking, quotidian world. It means that sometimes the body confines us like a coffin, the boundary between life and death blurred with no end in sight.

Writer's block, or impasse, works similarly; the writer exists "out of sync" with the production of deliverables. Again, pop culture provides a visual that resonated with me in this period of my career. In *Cobra Kai*'s pilot episode, the camera zooms in on Johnny's body sprawled atop his covers, and this notion of late nights and unconscious days, all merging into decades of impasse, rings true. Indeed, that impasse begins with a punch that causes him to fall flat on his stomach in 1984. His choice to stay there queers time and keeps him figuratively "stuck" for decades. Alison Kafer draws on images of "falling" and "tripping" as key to the experience of losing control of place and time and failing to hide one's disability or queerness (36). Although Johnny's character experiences no visible disability or queer leanings, his inability to move past his fall disables him and, at least visually, connects him to Kafer's images. It still does when he, as an adult, finally wins a trophy for his dojo.

Still, Kafer suggests that crip time and queer time need not always keep us figuratively and metaphorically down. She explains, "Crip time is flex time not just expanded but exploded; it requires reimagining our notions of what can and should happen in time, or recognizing how expectations of 'how long things take' are based in very particular minds and bodies" (27). Lessons of cripping and queering time may help us mentor students in ways less confined to capitalist structures. A refusal to participate in what Jane Bennett calls the "hyperconsumptive" tendency of Americans to collect "ever-increasing numbers of products" (5) to comfort ourselves in times of impasse might also help. The desire to control writing's rooms and the events of impasse paradoxically hides what Bennett refers to as "the vitality of matter" around us (5). Constructions of queered and cripped time also fall into this category; for, as Christopher Lee explains in his study of jet lag as an object, scholars have often studied time in connection with a "range of moods, sentiments, and anxieties." More to the point, Lee argues that "time is not structured by past, present, and future alone. It is also organized and defined by emotive states and cultural habits of living" (21). This concept will become central to the writer and teacher who must also accept the world's nature to break and seek repair. Phases of repair and maintenance, existing both inside and outside of traditional frames of time, are necessary for both teachers and students to accept the impasses they confront.

More research is needed on how queer or crip versions of time might aid the field of composition, if only to offer emotional resonance for those feeling "out of sync." The internal struggles and maintenance tasks of writers often remain invisible or misunderstood, perhaps because they remind us too much of the broken world of which Jackson speaks. University administration and even composition administration's new focus on futurity keep us mired in material goods and services in the form of deliverables. With all of this bad news, it is no wonder most of us would rather focus on what we believe we can control. Still, in the midst of impasse, important reparative work may take place, and facilitating some of that work should be part of our work as leaders or mentors, even when the "dull feelings of just getting by" affect us most of all.

Works Cited

Bennett, Jane. *Vibrant Matter: A Political Ecology of Things*. Duke UP, 2009.
Boyle, Casey, and Scot Barnett, editors. *Rhetoric through Everyday Things*. University of Alabama, 2017.
Casanave, Christine. "What Advisors Need to Know about the Invisible 'Real-Life' Struggles of Doctoral Dissertation Writers." *Supporting Graduate Student Writers*, edited by Steve Simpson, et al. University of Michigan Press, 2016.
Cobra Kai. Directed and written by Jon Hurwitz, performances by William Zabka and Ralph Macchio, 2 May 2018, *YouTube Premium*, www.youtube.com/watch?v=_rB36UGoP4Y.
Dethier, Brock. *First Time Up: An Insider's Guide for New Composition Teachers*. Utah State UP, 2005.
Grant, David M. "Writing *Wakan*: The Lakota Pipe as Rhetorical Object." *College Composition and Communication*, vol. 69, no. 1, Sep. 2017, pp. 61–86.
Hawhee, Debra. *Moving Bodies: Kenneth Burke at the Edges of Language*. U of South Carolina P, 2009.
Horner, Bruce. *Terms of Work for Composition: A Materialist Critique*. State U of New York, 2000.
Jackson, Steven. "Rethinking Repair." *Media Technologies: Essays on Communication, Materiality, and Society*, edited by Tarleton Gillespie et al., MIT P, 2014, pp. 221–60.
Kafer, Alison. *Feminist, Queer, Crip*. Indiana UP, 2013.
Lee, Christopher J. *Jet Lag*. Bloomsbury, 2017.
Leys, Ruth. "The Turn to Affect: A Critique." *Critical Inquiry*, vol. 37, no. 3, Spring 2011, pp. 434–72.
Murray, Donald. "The Essential Delay: When Writer's Block Isn't." *The Norton Book of Composition Studies*, edited by Susan Miller, W.W. Norton, 2009, pp. 715–20.
Micciche, Laura. *Doing Emotion: Rhetoric, Writing, Teaching*. Boynton/Cook, 2007.
Rickert, Thomas. *Ambient Rhetoric: The Attunements of Rhetorical Being*. U of Pittsburgh P, 2013.
Rule, Hannah. "Writing's Rooms." *College Composition and Communication*, vol. 69, no. 3, Feb. 2018, pp. 402–32.

Samuels, Ellen. "Six Ways of Looking at Crip Time." *Disability Studies Quarterly*, vol. 37, no. 3, 2017, http://dsq-sds.org/article/view/5824/4684.

Williams, Bronwyn T. "Seeking New Worlds: The Study of Writing beyond Our Classrooms." *College Composition and Communication*, vol. 62, no. 1, 2010, pp. 127–46.

4. Emotion in Teaching and Administering Writing: An Ethics of Care for Writing Teachers

REBECCA GERDES-MCCLAIN

In this chapter, I argue both that emotion is a significant source of knowledge about the work we do which can be productively interrogated and that using emotion in this way can guide us as writing teachers and administrators to more ethical decisions. In particular, I suggest the ethics of care, a feminist moral philosophy, as the ideal moral theory for evaluating the ethical decisions inherent in our work. Too often the ethical decision-making we face as writing teachers and administrators is invisible or merely implicit in our research. Adopting an ethical framework—and, importantly, one that values and interrogates emotion—as a heuristic for guiding our actions from an ethical perspective not only provides a consistent framework for such decisions, it reaffirms and makes explicit our field's commitment to people.

The realization that emotion is undervalued both in academia generally and our field specifically is not new. Laura Micciche argues that "emotion [is] a valuable rhetorical resource" that is "central to how we become invested in people, ideas, structures, and objects" (7). She uses theories of emotion from Sara Ahmed's *The Cultural Politics of Emotion* to jumpstart her work revealing the ways emotion already underlies much Writing Studies pedagogy and scholarship (Micciche 8–9). Additionally, Writing Studies historian Jacqueline Jones Royster's avowal of her personal connections to—or emotional investment in—her historical subjects in *Traces of a Stream*, as well as her work with Gesa Kirsch in *Feminist Rhetorical Practices*, stresses the validity of emotion, intuition, and human relationships/relatedness as research tools. An ethics of care shares many of these values, particularly the idea that emotion is a valid form of knowledge devalued in patriarchal, logo-centric epistemologies.

An ethics of care emerged as feminist moral philosophers from Amanda Baier to Michael Slote to Virginia Held responded to and complicated psychologist Carol Gilligan's *In A Different Voice*. While previous theories of moral development argued women tended to remain stuck in "lower" forms of moral reasoning (in Kohlberg's famous hierarchy of moral development, for example, those who remained focused on how their actions affected or would be perceived by others were stuck in level 2 and failed to reach the "highest" moral reasoning associated with "an objectively fair or just resolution" found in level 3), Gilligan posited that girls were showing an alternative model for making moral decisions rather than a lower, less desirable level of moral reasoning (21–22). Ultimately, Gilligan saw girls' persistent concern with other people not as a juvenile obsession with societal approval, but as a moral reckoning for the ways self and other are always connected (*In a Different* 2). Feminist moral philosophers used her observations to jumpstart critiques of existing moral philosophy—often focused on abstract principles and the individual divorced from other human relationships—by "embracing emotion" as a tool to develop a moral theory designed for the complexity of unique, interrelated human contexts (Held, "Taking Care" 59). An ethics of care can provide new insights into why emotion in our work as writing teachers and administrators matters and what we can—and should—do with emotional reactions both to our work and to that work's effect on others. Is it ethical to put students in uncomfortable emotional situations? What is the moral value of preparing students to see writing as an emotional process? What kind of moral considerations should guide the advocacy of Writing Program Administrators (WPAs) for contingent laborers in their programs? While I will not develop detailed solutions to specific questions like these, I will demonstrate how an ethics of care contributes to understanding the emotion inherent in our work through a moral lens. Our work as writing teachers and administers is obviously and unavoidably emotional. What do we do about this reality? When and why does it matter if we feel good or bad about the work that we do? How can naming, confronting, and analyzing our emotions guide us to be more ethical writing teachers and administrators?

A Personal Accounting: Where Emotion Gets Me (and Where It Doesn't)

The value of personal experience as research tool comes not just from Writing Studies embrace of *Feminist Rhetorical Practices* but also from feminist interjections in other fields like psychology and moral philosophy. In Writing Studies, Royster and Kirsch argue that expressing the personal experience of one's place or emotions enriches research (Royster and Kirsch 94–95). In other words, what we bring to our research in the form of our experiences, ethical commitments, and embodied experience is just as important as traditional forms of scholarly knowledge-making. Similarly, Gilligan argues that responding to emotion within psychological and moral research—which requires naming and acknowledging that emotion—has moral "integrity and validity" (*In a Different* 3). In short, scholars in a variety of fields have demonstrated the scholarly value of owning and articulating personal situatedness. To this end, in the conclusion to their collection *Ethics of Care: Critical Advances in International Perspective*, Barnes et al. note the importance of narrative accounts to this work: "Fundamental to the processes of change [in how we acknowledge and respond to our personal positions and power in our research] is the embodiment of personal, professional and political insights. It is notable that a number of scholars working in this tradition incorporate personal narratives [. . . in] their arguments" (236). In this vein, I include the following narrative to highlight my own personal situatedness, emotional reactions, and embodied experiences and how these elements have shaped this research.

Recently, after participating in an interview with PhD Candidate Kate Highfill about the role of emotion in my work as a WPA, I received a follow-up email. The email read, in part, "If you have a minute, could you answer a follow-up question that has arisen as I go through the transcripts: What are things that you've done that you don't believe in? i.e. How have you had to compromise your ideals/ethics/morals in order to keep your job?" The question, while a logical extension of our conversation during the interview, felt like a bit of gut punch. I experienced the tell-tale physical signs of a deep emotional reaction: my stomach clenched; a tight feeling settled in the center of my chest; I could feel my shoulders tensing.

I replied:

> That's a tough question. [...] While I'm never the one actually making the decisions I think are unethical [...], I don't think that means I'm in the clear morally. It's easy to look at the crummy stuff happening everywhere and say (accurately!) that I simply didn't have the power to win this or that battle. But I don't think that absolves me. The more I think about it, that is a tactic that is purposefully used to "get things done" [...] No one, it feels like, has the power to do things better. And it feels like that is by design.
>
> There are so many small lines getting crossed all the time. For instance, when our course caps went up without additional compensation (so more labor, same pay); I didn't make that call but I am the one enforcing and explaining it to the people most affected by it. So my labor does several things that don't feel so great: I protect those making what I think are bad decisions (for students and

teachers) by serving as a kind of buffer obscuring some of the human costs of these decisions, I make decisions like this as tenable as possible by still continuing to support and expect excellent teaching no matter the labor situation, and even when I'm doing my best to advocate for faculty I'm always having to make strategic decisions to let some things go to argue for others. [...] All of these things are literally what my job exists to do. [...] I really don't know what to do with this, especially because I love my job. I'm still trying to decide if there is a way to do this work ethically in the current reality. I want to think there is and I'm thinking hard about it, but the little voice in my heart is pretty pessimistic about the whole thing. [...]

Ugh—Sorry! I think you got some messy emotional sorting-through that might be beyond what you wanted. I guess I'm in a place where I love my job, but the labor conditions surrounding that job (for other people in my program, people I have some authority over) make me wonder if doing this work is immoral. I want to say that sounds defeatist . . . (if everyone who can do what we do were to quit, would that get us anywhere better?) but I'm also feeling really gross about how much better compensated my work is than other people's. Everything in me says it's wrong. And what am I doing about it?

After I sent the email, I remember taking a deep breath. I got up and took a walk around campus; I felt less anxious, but more wound up. Though brimming with energy, it was the uncomfortable and charged energy I feel when faced with a problem I have no idea how to confront. Sitting down to plan professional development, revise committee documents, prep class, or think through my scholarship felt impossible and inauthentic at the moment. I wanted to do work that would *matter*, in terms of the moral quandary I had described, but I had no idea how that might look.

Though I had already submitted the proposal for this chapter before that exchange, it's a moment I keep coming back to when working on this project. That afternoon, I was able to articulate a handful of important things that have occupied me intellectually ever since, but I was only able to do that because I was paying attention to and consciously voicing an *emotional* reaction. In my quoted reply, I used some version of the word "feel" four times. By stopping to describe my *feelings* of guilt, frustration, and growing pessimism I began to consider the ethics of my employment in ways that I had not done, consciously, before. And the I reason I'm confident that these issues matter, while strengthened by my analysis of my experiences and my familiarity with scholarship on labor and WPA work, is because these issues *feel* important and uncomfortable. My feelings are why I'm writing this chapter.

And yet, in many real ways, there is little room for this kind of an insight in our discussions of teaching and administrating writing. Not only am I articulating emotions—those slippery, feminized, stand-ins for "irrational" conclusions in our cultural shorthand—I am linking them to moral propositions. The majority of researchers in the field no doubt believe the knowledge they generate contributes to something good in the world, but how often do we talk explicitly about morality? Part of this, I suspect, stems from the good we want to do: rather than forcing our moral understanding of the world in ways we've come to critique in the history of colonialism and other enterprises of domination, we lean on ideas about "objectivity" in order to avoid these pitfalls. Yet, by allowing moral judgments to lurk unstated in nearly every call to action we make, we seldom articulate the moral principles and reasoning that shape why we believe in our work and hope others will be influenced by it.

The above email exchange and my emotional response to it led me somewhere important. I worry my work is unethical—actually doing more harm than good in the world—because of current labor conditions that I feel largely powerless to change. Emotion got me here, but then what? If we take seriously the call of feminists to honor our emotional connections and motivations to our research, what does it mean when those emotions suggest that the work we are doing is either morally flawed or, more hopefully, could be more morally productive? Articulating my emotions helps identify tensions and problems that matter. But how can it help me solve them?

An Ethics of Care: Emotion and Connectedness in Morality

For a long time, I would have rejected the idea that moral philosophy was a tool for pointing us toward next steps as I was scarred by a negative experience. That experience began during my PhD coursework, when a literature professor reviewing one of my drafts remarked that I kept making claims about "ethically unconscionable" labor conditions without explaining the philosophical system I was using to make these claims. At first, the reply shocked me. I had assumed that the behaviors I was calling out—exploiting contingent laborers, demanding more work for the same, or less, compensation—were obviously "wrong." It felt like a waste of time to develop an extended literature review to support those claims. But the more I thought about it, the more I understood his point. If my moral reasoning was unarticulated, how could it help me wade through the messy applications of morality that happen constantly in life? My emotions might persuade me that something was "wrong" but, since I wanted to do something productive about that wrongness, I needed to be able to articulate how and why I was recommending some actions and not others. In short, as I began to think more seriously about my future as a WPA, I realized that making "ethical" decisions would be neither easy nor natural and that moral philosophy could be a tool for dealing with this. But, beyond a single undergraduate philosophy class over a decade ago, I had no explicit philosophical training. Worse still, my memories of that class were hazy at best. My solution was to start small, with a handful of popular books on philosophy written to general audiences.

I started with Peter Singer's *Practical Ethics*, which is also where things started to go south for me. At one point Singer, supporting abortion rights, analyzed abortion debates until he ended up questioning several premises underpinning different positions. Eventually, he unpacks these premises until he arrives at the conclusion: if "... the fetus does not have the same claim to life as a person, it appears that the newborn baby does not either" (Singer 151). He uses this to reason that newborn babies can be ethically killed in a variety of situations and, in evaluating these arguments, claims "in attempting to reach a considered ethical judgment about this matter, we should put aside feelings based on the small, helpless and—sometimes—cute appearance of human infants" (152). In addition to resenting the implication that having an emotional reaction to a claim like this means I'm swayed solely by "cuteness" (discounting the possibility that my emotion might be connected to more "mature" or "appropriate" evidence), the truth is I was viscerally disgusted with his claim. Yet, it wasn't my disagreement or disgust that bothered me most; I understand the value of the logical exercise and playing out conclusions to their ends. What bothered me was that, for him, the fact that I—and others—*felt* this position was wrong was simply irrelevant. The way emotion was surgically removed from his moral reasoning process, and was taken for granted as an obvious good, was far from helpful; instead, it was like a willful ignoring of what human beings, emotion, and life are actually like. I struggled to imagine how anything from such a philosophy could be useful or do the things I wanted a moral philosophy to do—to help me understand and account for the impacts of my actions, including emotionally, on the people around me. I tried reading a few other moral philosophy texts but came across the same basic problem. As far as I could see, philosophy was a kind of logic game in which human emotion and the complicated connections between people were "removed" to discover "universal" truths. The problem, for me, was that without attention to emotion, these "truths" seemed worthless. These were not principles I was interested in *using* to do things and the constant (sometime explicitly stated) suggestion that my response was clouded by my "irrational" emotion was frustrating. I admit that my reactions were partly emotional, but by using the fact I acknowledged my emotional response to discount and my label my response as "irrational" meant I was cut out of the conversation. My viewpoint was welcome, but only if I could strip away its emotional components. But those emotional components were—if not entirely my viewpoint—a vital part of it.

Suffice it to say I did not embed moral philosophy into my chapter revisions. Mentally I wrote off moral philosophy writ large as intellectual masturbation, convinced that—whether the problem were with me or with the theory—it wasn't something I cared to use.

Years later, working on an article on embodiment and labor, I came across theories of "care labor" that referenced "an ethics of care." Following the trail of citation I eventually discovered Virginia Held's article "Feminist Moral Inquiry and the Feminist Future." According to Held, "Moral theories [...] should give us guidance in confronting the problems of actual life in the highly imperfect societies in which we live. We need moral theories about what to do and what to accept here and now" (Held, "Feminist Moral" 153). Despite the alignment between Held's goals for moral philosophy and my own, I remained suspicious. After all, I imagine that Peter Singer and his ilk believe their moral theories have this kind of application, though I would disagree. But Held continues:

> Traditional moral theory is frequently built on what a person might be thought to hold from the point of view of a hypothetical ideal observer, or a hypothetical purely rational being. Morality is to reflect what Thomas Nagel calls "the view from nowhere." A hypothetical moral being is thought able to distance himself from the particular self interests and distorting passions of actual, embodied human beings, located in particular social and historical contexts. Feminists have often been critical of these attempts to ignore the reality of embodiment. As Susan Bordo puts it, the view from nowhere embodies the ideal being of everywhere, and the individual who is everywhere is necessarily disembodied (Held, "Feminist Moral" 159).

This critique, a much smarter and more sophisticated articulation of my dissatisfaction with moral philosophy, encouraged me to reconsider my earlier dismissal of the field and immerse myself in the scholarship and debate surrounding an ethics of care.

As mentioned earlier, an ethics of care was moral philosophy's response to Carol Gilligan's research on the different moral reasoning observed in boys and girls and her argument that these differences represented not inferior moral reasoning on the part of girls but a different ethical framework for discussion-making. Ultimately, the inescapable links between humans is the bedrock of the ideas about care she sees expressed by the girls she observed:

> As a framework for moral decisions, care is grounded in the assumption that self and other are interdependent, an assumption reflected in a view of action as responsive and, therefore, as arising in relationship rather than the view of action as emanating from within the self and, therefore, "self governed." Seen as

responsive, the self is by definition connected to others, responding to perceptions, interpreting events, and governed by the organizing tendencies of human interaction and human language. Within this framework, detachment, whether from self or from others, is morally problematic, since it breeds moral blindness or indifference—a failure to discern or respond to need (Gilligan, "Moral Orientation" 36).

The "detachment" championed by most Western moral philosophy was, understood in these terms, deeply flawed. It was Nel Noddings, an American moral philosopher, who first proposed an entire moral system around these ideas. For Noddings (and at least initially Gilligan), these findings suggested an inherent gendered division in moral reasoning that has since been critiqued as essentialist (Noddings 23). While the claim that this style of moral reasoning is unique to women has been complicated greatly (and today is rejected by most philosophers working on an ethics of care), the recognition that patriarchal ideas about men and women, as well as logic and emotion, can help to explain why this moral system has been associated so strongly with women. Additionally, the idea that "traditional," or justice, ethics and an ethics of care are mutually exclusive is also challenged, both by Michael Sloat and Virginia Held, though in different terms. Like all philosophical and theoretical models, an ethics of care is not uncontested or completely formalized.

However, while many important debates about the applications and definitions of an ethics of care exist, consensus has emerged around several principles. First, an ethics of care is committed to exploring how our relationships to people and situations impact our moral obligations. Held states emphatically that "It is the relatedness of human beings, built and rebuilt, that the ethics of care is being developed to try to understand, to evaluate, and to guide" ("Moral Feminist" 59). Second, an ethics of care is interested not only in the ideas and emotions associated with care but also with care as physical, embodied experience (Held, "Moral Feminist" 60). Bodies, physical sensation, and labor matter to an ethics of care. Third and finally, "In the epistemological process of trying to understand what morality would recommend and what it would be morally best for us to do and to be, the ethics of care values emotion rather than rejects it" (Held, *Ethics* 10). These three principals—close attention to the relationships between people, an awareness of the embodied experience of caring, and an openness to emotion as a valid site of knowing and knowledge-making—make an ethics of care valuable to Writing Studies. The work we do, both in the classroom and as administrators not only affects real people, engaging in that work has real emotional and physical consequences that matter as we consider what our labor ought, and ought not, to do.

Next Steps: Toward Action and a "Better" Future

Moral philosophy should help us do things, and do them well, in the world. An ethics of care is such an attractive moral framework to me, in part, because its responsivity makes it particularly useful in these terms. Held encapsulates care's dual role as a pragmatic tool we can use both to do things and as a morally complex concept we can use to understand the world by talking about care as "both a practice and a value" ("Moral Feminist" 69). Practice refers to actions we take while value refers to the moral mean-making we use to arrive at and evaluate those actions. In both cases, the goal of care is to "express the caring relations that bring persons together, and [to] do so in ways that are progressively more morally satisfactory" (Held, "Moral Feminist" 69). My professor in graduate school was right to suggest that in order to critique existing systems, some kind of a heuristic—something one can apply, adapt, and respond to—is useful. Without it, many are left where I was the day I responded to Kate about her question on whether I had done things I thought were morally wrong as a WPA: dissatisfied, angry, and ready for change but struggling to not only articulate those feelings but also to translate them into sustained and organized action.

But now that I've articulated care as an ethical framework for addressing this issue, what—if anything—has changed? What can I *do* that I couldn't do before? I think the answer is twofold. First, having established the suitability of an ethics of care for Writing Studies, we can begin to conceptualize what this would look like, in more concrete terms, for us as teachers, scholars, and administrators. This, in turn, will allows us, as a field, to advocate for practices that support "progressively more morally satisfactory" next steps on issues from labor exploitation to social justice to the gatekeeping function of the FYC course.

As a WPA currently struggling with the limits of my authority, an ethics of care has made me ask important questions. Who is my "care" supposed to be responsive to? While much of our scholarship assumes care for students as our reason for being, as an administrator, I feel both a moral responsibility to care for teachers in my program and pressure to direct my caring energy away from individual people and toward the institution as a whole. When asked to do specific things, like review retention data for FYC courses to suggest programmatic interventions, what happens when directing my care toward students and teachers puts me in tension with caring for the needs of the institution? Relatedly, I see struggles over what, exactly, is it that we (as individual teachers, a field, and within institutions) want Writing Studies and specially FYC to do in terms of caring labor. For example, there is a disconnect between the caring labor described by administration (requiring faculty to use early alert software, requesting pedagogies that intervene for at-risk students, and expecting teachers to give meaningful personalized feedback to each student) and the labor conditions they insist are necessary (larger classes, higher teaching loads, less paid professional development). I'm also reminded by an ethics of care that care is embodied, by which I mean that caring labor is physical labor that requires effort and expertise. Thus, to promote caring practices in my program, I need to take seriously the question of what kind of physical and intellectual conditions are required to support this effort. Being able to theorize these "caring" behaviors as *labor* that is not only important but to some degree specialized may also help to articulate their importance and value, especially if care for students is truly the goal of administration.

If nothing else, forcing these conversations should help the reveal the real priorities of both Writing Studies teachers and scholars and the administrations we labor within. Even if this leads me to conclude that my role as a WPA, as understood by my university, is *not* to care for students or teachers but to care for the administrative and fiscal needs of the university, this would be useful information. Bluntly put, the needs of university administrators (in terms of protecting university systems and resources over student and teacher needs) are not the things I value and if I cannot align my values with my institutional role, then I need to reassess my career path. In short, having clarity about our role in the system, good or bad, empowers us, as individuals and as a field, to make moral decisions.

Works Cited

Baier, Annette C. "The Need for More than Justice." *Justice and Care: Essential Readings in Feminist Ethics*, edited by Virginia Held, Westview Press, 1995, pp. 47–58.

Barnes, Marian, et al. "Conclusion: renewal and transformation—the importance of an ethics of care." *Ethics of Care: Critical Advances in International Perspective*, edited by Marian Barnes et al., Policy Press, 2015, pp. 233–44.

Gerdes-McClain, Rebecca. "Re: Transcript." Received by Kate Highfill, 28 Jan. 2019.

Gilligan, Carol. *In a Different Voice: Psychological Theory and Women's Development*. Harvard UP, 1982.

———. "Moral Orientation and Moral Development." *Justice and Care: Essential Readings in Feminist Ethics*, edited by Virginia Held, Westview Press, 1995, pp. 31–46.

Held, Virginia. *The Ethics of Care: Personal, Political, and Global*, Oxford, 2006.

———. "Feminist Moral Inquiry and the Feminist Future." *Justice and Care: Essential Readings in Feminist Ethics*, edited by Virginia Held, Westview Press, 1995, pp. 153–76.

———. "Taking Care: Care as Practice and Value." *Setting the Moral Compass: Essays by Women Philosophers*, edited by Cheshire Calhoun, Oxford Press, 2004, pp. 59–71.

Micciche, Laura R. *Doing Emotion: Rhetoric, Writing, Teaching*, Boyton/Cook Publishers, 2007.

Noddings, Nel. "Caring." *Justice and Care: Essential Readings in Feminist Ethics*, edited by Virginia Held, Westview Press, 1995, pp. 7–30.

Royster, Jacqueline Jones, and Gesa E. Kirsch. *Feminist Rhetorical Practices: New Horizons for Rhetoric, Composition, and Literacy Studies*. Southern Illinois UP, 2012.

Singer, Peter. *Practical Ethics*. 3rd ed. Cambridge UP, 2011.

Slote, Michael. *The Ethics of Care and Empathy*. Routledge, 2007.

5. Knowing Emotion: College Initiation and Self-Confrontation in the "Meta" Writing Classroom

Diana Epelbaum

Writing is self-confrontation. An extended, sometimes torturous, process of meeting and re-meeting oneself. I have witnessed my own students develop a range of elaborate strategies to avoid this self-confrontation. I have seen students riddled with writing anxiety crumple their papers over and over, erase or cross out feverishly, speak brilliantly and sit absolutely stumped before a blank paper, focus intently on spelling every word and placing every comma, forgetting to think. I have seen students with false confidence compose winding sentences with a flourish, adding words they didn't understand or misapplied, neglecting to make meaning. I have seen students write short, choppy sentences all beginning the same way and cycle through the same dead-end ideas over and over. Each of these writing habits signals an attempt to exercise control on the page prematurely. As experienced writers know, control does not always precede words. The illusion of control, however, easily stunts emotion.

I argue in this chapter that metacognitive practice attendant to emotion enables sustainable, transferrable student self-efficacy. This chapter pivots on praxis, correlating classroom strategies for teaching metacognition with teaching students to identify, access, and work through emotions that may hinder productivity and their individual writing processes. Through metacognitive awareness, students can learn to accept that staying with uncomfortable emotions may be necessary for task completion and self-efficacy for transfer, more broadly. Assuming that self-confrontation is an end in itself, as it is for many experienced writers, students may have to live in their emotions, push beyond them, or even befriend them, in order to look inward. I begin by reviewing relevant research on the ties between affect and metacognition, with emphasis on productive and unproductive emotions—or those that aid with, or obstruct, a writer's goals—and then suggest that what may render *all* emotions generative is metacognition. Writing instructors should conceptualize both the classroom and the professor as "texts" to be read, stopping frequently for metathinking, and focusing on reflection, rhetorical analysis, Writing About Writing (WAW), and teaching for transfer—all in the context of emotion and process. This paper outlines these and other individual strategies, interweaving students' affective process responses in reflections and course evaluations.

Emotion, Cognition, and Self-Efficacy, Entwined

"Writing anxiety," a more comprehensive, contextualized understanding of a writer's dispositional fear of writing than "writing apprehension," which links evaluation anticipation to hesitation, is the term I will use in this paper to account for the range of experiential variables influencing students' ability to put words on the page.[1] Experienced writers indeed know that writing anxiety—the most common "negative" writing emotion—can be intensely productive for both the person and the process. Writing anxiety for experienced writers, however, can be significantly different from student writing anxiety, which frequently stems from, among other factors, poor integrative understanding of individual process, unsuccessful management of shifting rhetorical contexts and purposes, and discomfort with the nuts and bolts skills of composing. In an education system that assigns unreasonable, overblown value on the "writing product" (and grading), and astonishingly little value on the variegated purposes and situations for writing, or on the wide variety of composing processes that may facilitate authentic writing, student writing anxiety that begins in learned systems of constraint intensifies in "real-world" writing's insistence on flexibility. As students move from restricted forms and product performance anxiety to process emphasis and exploratory research, they must make a cognitive leap that may be too large for uninitiated students without explicit instruction and metacognitive reorientation. Sally Chandler suggests that "students required to change the way they write . . . often encounter intense internal conflict" and demonstrate "fear that manifests as resistance," an emotion that "may derive from pressure to shift identity" (60). FYC instructors, then, are taxed not only with the teaching of writing, but also with the *unteaching* of writing, with the naming and redirecting of deeply engrained, negative writing emotions, including troublesome iterations of writing anxiety. It is through metacognition, I believe, that we can ease students' initiation, equipping them to better handle emotions like anxiety and fear.

As scholars, we too require initiation when we move into new fields; with students, openness about shared emotions like insecurity and uneasiness is a wonderful place to begin dissolving myths of "good" and "bad" writers that confuse our writing purposes, feed writing paralysis, and obstruct writing's emotional benefits, including self-confrontation. Normalizing and destigmatizing difficulty and allowing space for our own vulnerability, as well as our students', shifts the power dynamics in the classroom and creates room for building resilience through failure—ultimately, positively influencing self-efficacy. Many students in my metacognition-emotion oriented writing courses (developmental, standard, and advanced) in the past three years, demonstrated powerful shifts in approaches to failure. One offered a curious assessment of her growth in the course, displaying the profound understanding that transitions are discomfiting and require definitional repositioning: "I don't think I'm necessarily a better writer but a different writer."[2]

Writing skill, self-efficacy, facility with academic discourse, perception, and emotion are all bound up in highly complex, variable ways. More than thirty years ago, Alice Brand and Jack Powell explored emotion and the writing process, distinguishing between "negative passive" emotions like shame, boredom, confusion, and depression, and "negative active" emotions like anger, anxiety, frustration, and fear (282), suggesting through field research for the first time that not all negative writing orientations are necessarily unproductive. Brand and Powell researched a range of writerly emotions rather than foregrounding writing anxiety as the principal negative emotion, and relief as the principal positive (284). Later, in her design of, and assessment with, the Brand Emotions Scale for Writers (BESW), Brand did indeed find writing anxiety to be the most prominent negative emotion amongst all writers ("Writing and Feelings" 296), but continued to reject an approach that isolated these emotions or viewed all negative emotions as inhibitory. Brand and Powell felt that anxiety originates from different sources for skilled and unskilled writers; for example, students may have continued, as well, to feel anxiety *after* writing in expectation of evaluation (284). Higher levels of "negative active" emotions, like anxiety, were reported by students when composing self-sponsored pieces, rather than teacher-prompted writing in class, perhaps, as the authors hypothesized, because schooling trained them in passivity, conveying that it would be inappropriate to express (or even feel) "negative active" emotions like anger and frustration (283–84). Motivation could likewise account for this discrepancy, with students channeling emotions "actively," or productively, rather than passively, in self-sponsored work. Brand's study confirmed that emotion is at the heart of the writing impulse and process: students who wrote for themselves had more positive affective orientations, which impacted performance positively ("Writing and Feelings" 297).

Neither did other early researchers, even while conflating "apprehension" and "anxiety," believe that the umbrella term "anxiety" conveyed the nuances of the emotion, or its many sources, or its various manifestations within the composing process. When Daly and Miller created their Writing Apprehension Test (WAT) (1975), they surveyed apprehension as a generalized emotion, and found that students manifested writing anxiety by failing to submit assignments, for example, while writing-apprehensive adults "perceived their occupations as having significantly less written communication requirements than did those with low apprehension of writing" (Daly and Miller 244, 247). The WAT has seen continued use. Sacramento State includes the WAT on its website, dividing the results into three categories of apprehension: evaluation, stress, and product. Evaluation apprehensives fear grades; stress apprehensives experience writer's block; product apprehensives don't buy into the value of the writing task or of writing in general (Sacramento State). In particular, inauthentic writing for fabricated audiences, like the five-paragraph essay, does not inspire active emotions that motivate students to compose or revise. Tasks that feel both confusing and meaningless to student writers amplify performance anxiety, as one of my students expressed: "when I'm writing, I'm constantly thinking about what the teacher wants and how they would prefer my writing. This challenges me to almost *pretend to write* and give them what they want instead of how I see my writing" [emphasis mine]. As an alternative, asking students to carefully consider and consistently revise the stakes and exigencies of their work, articulating them for their intended audience, is metacognitive work that can serve to alleviate sources of anxiety (or perhaps, apprehension) like evaluation, stress, and product—and likely other sources, too.

Early researchers found that writing skill and writing emotion are interlinked. Linda Flower and John Hayes, for example, discovered that unskilled writers often reach satisfaction sooner than skilled writers (377–79), even as they haltingly start and stop, scan at greater rates, and edit rather than revise as they go, as Sondra Perl found (324). Satisfaction here is a complex emotion—positive, on the one hand, but "negative passive" if equated with complacency. In Brand and Powell's study, "negative passive" emotions like boredom and confusion were more prominent for self-identified unskilled writers than for self-identified skilled writers, pre- and post-writing (283–84), but importantly, these unproductive emotions were not immovable. Those rated unskilled by their instructors exhibited the greatest gains in positive emotions, like inspiration and relief, by writing (283). Writing itself, Brand

and Powell's study suggests, is the antidote to writing anxiety and to a range of other writing-focused negative emotions. Metacognitive practice, I argue, facilitates the administering of this antidote, and sometimes substitutes as the antidote itself.

Studies in self-efficacy support the idea that metacognitive practice is meaningful to both writing productivity and positive affective process response, and writing emotion is intimately connected both cognitively *and* socially in complex processes of mutual reciprocity. Brand notes that student writers' self-perceptions more intuitively and meaningfully correlate with feelings about academic writing than do their teachers' evaluations ("Writing and Feelings" 299). Peter Khost surveys habits of mind self-efficacy (outlined in the Council of Writing Program Administrators' *Framework for Success in Postsecondary Writing*) in students who completed metacognitive writing prompts about their academic writing, finding that metacognitive awareness improved habits of mind self-efficacy. In the study, self-efficacy beliefs determined emotional responses to tasks and courses: those who rated themselves more highly on self-efficacy beliefs for the habits of mind of curiosity, openness, creativity, and persistence were also more satisfied with their courses at the end of the term (282).[3]

With "satisfaction" and "relief" the governing positive emotions of the writing classroom, it is important to remember that more complex (and more productive) positive feelings like "inspired," "surprised," or "adventurous," hold potential to radically alter student self-efficacy. Rather than training students to write through their "negative active" emotions in order simply to relieve them, we should demonstrate and create the conditions in which they can access a range of positive emotions that move them towards the identity shift required to become what Nancy Sommers and Laura Saltz call "novice writers." Chandler argues for the lifting of student emotional barriers as a first priority in the writing classroom: "once students feel comfortable, instructors can help them reflect on connections between emotional positioning and writing in ways that can set up less traumatic transitions between discourses" (66). Emotional conditioning and metacognition need not be distinct, however; metacognition itself is central in facilitating productive emotions, even as we move students toward higher-order critical examination of the relationship between emotion and writing, and ultimately to greater understanding of their own writing processes. Beginning on the first day, continuous collective metacognitive discourse on process and emotion then, can open channels for emotional movement, jarring students out of cognitive misperceptions and emotional defenses that block engagement with, and retention of, "new discursive patterns" (Chandler 66). Greater self-efficacy can be expected to attend these cognitive and emotional breakthroughs, including ones that move students like my own toward purposeful scholarship: "My research inquiry is really frustrating me, not that this is bad, just frustrating. I think that this is good because I know that I am passionate about it."

Concomitant shifts in self-efficacy and initiation into college writing require withstanding and attending to the emotional toil of cognitive growth. Because cognitive labor is easier than emotional labor, students may delay or repress active, productive emotions that may stir them out of familiar forms. In Chandler's study, students tasked with writing critical analyses instead wrote "conversion narratives"—what Chandler sees as reversion to standard forms where "new cognitive terrain" became too challenging to manage emotionally. Emotional resolution is required in order to tamp down flaring negative emotions, or to secure them firmly in the past; conversely, anxiety and uncertainty may endure without "closure" (61–63). Metacognition around emotional effort and genres perceived to be centered in feelings and "vulnerability," as Chandler highlights, may help students merge their cognitive understanding—of what's required in an assignment, of the demands of college analytical writing—with the emotional labor required to execute those demands, helping them "step into the discursive patterns they cognitively embrace" (Chandler 65). It may draw attention to subconscious crutches like familiar forms, driving them to take greater risks in their writing.

Finally, scholars across the research spectrum agree that self-efficacy beliefs (task-specific and global) are indeed prognostic of performance[4] (Khost 278) and may be complicated by the social.[5] Because "emotions are discursive" (Chandler 53), self-efficacy may be fluid within the Composition classroom, where group misconceptions about academic writing may collectively magnify individual emotional defenses built up through years of schooling. If emotional experience can be socially constructed, then self-regulated learning, and hence, self-efficacy, may be rooted in the group as well as in the self.[6] Instructor evaluation, classroom dynamics, and local institutional contexts may constitute this social realm. Curricular focus in metacognition and emotion, then, creates the social conditions necessary for increased self-efficacy.

Classroom Models for Metacognition and Emotion Emphasis

In this section of the paper, I delineate classroom practices and activities centered in metacognition that inspire expansive emotional engagement, and in turn, catapult students into "new cognitive terrain," the adoption of "new discursive patterns" (Chandler 63, 65), and integrative personal systems of cognition and emotion. In two explicitly framed metacognition courses, "Writing about Writing" for advanced students, and "Writing about Writing" for a standard research seminar, and two semesters of developmental courses with metacognition-emotion emphasis, students self-reported gains in positive affect and reflected on scaling emotional walls that censored their voices. Appendices A and B provide an example of a central course assignment, rubric, and student product from an advanced first-year writing course. The following activities can be incorporated into any class that asks students to write, regardless of level, theme, discipline, or course objectives.

Ticker Metacommentary

Metacommentary, scripted or spontaneous, can be imagined as a news ticker, an ever-present prefacer of, and occasional merger with, course content. It serves to model the course ethos and reinforce key ideas, like "writing is hard"; something as simple as a "meta" byline in activity instructions or course assignments functions as acknowledgement of the importance of purposeful tasking. In class, a direct "why do you think I asked you to do that?" will often suffice to assuage a sometimes pervasive sense of "pointlessness" in task completion. Over time, students form the habit of thinking in terms of purpose,—"this semester I have become a more conscious writer and avid reader. My reading weaknesses are that I read without purpose"—critical for self-efficacy transfer.

Further, centering metacommentary frequently in emotion trains students to cognitively check in with inhibitory or unproductive emotions, generates productive positive emotions like enthusiasm and motivation, and inspires self-efficacy. Student responses to these courses reflect an openness to emotional inquiry—"Enter, Writ 201. What is this class? Why do I leave excited to read and write? The analysis and introspectiveness of the writing process in the class has saved me"—and through emotion, even track meta-awareness as its own course outcome—"At the beginning of the term, I was excited and intrigued by the idea of meta writing, in the middle I wasn't so sure, but by the end I was shocked by just how meta I got." In these reflections, the very language of the course has seeped into conscious articulations of metacognition's emotional benefits.

Writing as Thinking

Writing as thinking activities include visual brainstorming techniques like "dialogic journaling," "idea threading," diagramming, and "mind mapping" (Hyman and Schulman 105–21). *Bard Institute for Writing and Thinking*'s immersive writing model asks participants to freewrite *into* or *out of* a text through a series of multimodal "writing provocations" that make visible the act of both entrance and departure into textual space. "Pause, reflect, write, share" teaches students the habit of detaching momentarily from their writing, pausing to frame a new inquiry, jot down a response, identify the emotional or cognitive source of an emotional stall, or record a brief next step. Whether for a draft, text, or class discussion, each takes no more than a few moments and repositions the writer/thinker for reentry into the material. In all writing as thinking methods, the importance of the "emotional check-in" is paramount: "did that technique *feel* more or less generative to you?" "With which technique did you feel the least bodily resistance?" "Which technique did you enjoy the most?"

Extended Metaphors

Metaphors help us both conceptualize and relate, making them an excellent tool in the metacognition-emotion classroom. We all naturally use metaphor to make ourselves understood, and student writers are no exception: "I felt like writing, was like painting a picture and that all I needed to make a painting beautiful was the right colors. However ... painting without a solid concept is just coloring on a canvas," "I know that I need to work on my effort ethics," "In drafting my inquiry, I tried my best to jam it with possible angles and directions—like possible escape hatches to use if one idea dries up or the entire paper starts to go south." My courses lean heavily on metamoment metaphors, some that arise spontaneously, and others prepared. Active reading, I tell my students, is like scuba diving, wherein the deep reader can experience sea life—or changes in temperature (it gets colder), or color (it gets darker the deeper you go)—in ways those at the surface cannot (Levine).

Extended metaphors facilitate all kinds of writing application work. For example, you might prompt students to "create and extend a metaphor that captures the state of your first draft and then create and extend a metaphor for your vision of your 'final' draft. What emotions are associated with both metaphors? What concrete steps do you need to take to get from where you are to where you want to be?" Or, "create and extend a metaphor for concision/paragraph unity/use of evidence/your voice." For example, students arrived at these creative metaphors for concision: cutting dead ends on hair, clarifying butter, straining orange juice to the pulp, choosing the fastest and most direct route for driving. This activity can be completed in any mode (visual/linguistic/aural/gestural/spatial) for added effect, and then applied through a discrete revision task. In another activity, students listed "Meta Takeaways" for an extended metaphor exercise that asked them to plot literature review source conversations as a Twitter feed. In one, a new metaphor of a solar system—sources rotating around the core research inquiry—emerged [Appendix C]. Since metaphors are personal and carry emotional weight, their conscious use in the composition process may boost both task-specific and global self-efficacy.

Multimodal Strategies

Visual Strategies

Early in the term, I have students visually map their writing process for a product they commonly write (whether academic, creative, or personal), superimposing emotions, represented as they please, onto the map [Appendix D]. This visual map can be repeated at different points in the term with different processes (like research), or with different aims: instead of mapping emotion, students might map revision onto their process (where and when do you revise?). Students could create a WAW comic or meme as a way to visually express a more difficult concept or a recurring emotional challenge. Annotation maps visually represent textual annotations to demonstrate comprehension, deepen annotation practice, or track emotional engagement with material, and can be generated for any "text," visual and oral among them [Appendix E].[7]

Color-coding in isolated craft or style lessons for the purposes of rhetorical analysis might have students highlight all their signal phrases (one color for effective, one color for ineffective), or deconstruct a paragraph (one color for evidence, one for analysis). Color visualization makes evident necessary revisions by drawing attention to imbalances, ineffective ratios, or poorly-executed chunks of writing. Other variations on segmentation and piecing might ask students, per Michael Harvey's *The Nuts and Bolts of College Writing*, to write out the thesis and all topic sentences as one paragraph, looking for essay-level coherence, flow, and logic (72–74), or per Gwen Hyman and Martha Schulman's "Says/Does" activity in *Thinking on the Page*, to "make an inventory in the margins" of what each paragraph is saying, and what it's doing (172–78). In the Question/Answer Method, a student paragraph model serves for a collective development workshop. Students ask the paragraph clarifying, context, and extension questions, and question numbers are inserted into the paragraph where the writer's "answers" will appear. As students develop the paragraph's core ideas, they also naturally begin to excise repetition and verbosity, which leads to meta-discussion about how development and concision can be concurrent outcomes in revision, and why writers form habits like writing around, rather than into, ideas. Each of these visual exercises illustrates the vital function of the parts to the whole, compelling examination of the emotional uses of "faking it" in confused or deadwood-filled drafts. In rhetorical analysis of successful drafts, we explore the interplay of emotions and craft: what emotions is the writer harnessing or appealing to, and why?

Oral Strategies

In one oral activity with dual cognitive and affective resonances, students perform scholarly conversations in a student-authored Literature Review by reading aloud source voices. The conversation can be read cold or parsed first. Whether the student writer has properly distinguished among, and signaled transitions between, voices becomes immediately clear as assigned source readers attempt to find where they "come in"; where the writer invokes two or more sources with the same claim or idea, the actors read those sentences chorally. It is easy to hear when sources are truly "in conversation" and when they are standing side by side, speaking past each other. For the student writer, there is often a strong emotional response to hearing the harmony or disjointedness of this conversation; this emotional feedback is just as critical as the peer review, and is then built into revision.

Conclusion: *The Mind-Body Connection*

In one particularly moving part of *The Body Keeps the Score*, a tome on forty years of advancements in trauma therapy, Bessel Van Der Kolk describes a therapy modality created by Richard Schwartz called Internal Family Systems Therapy (IFS), which requires a kind of identity fragmentation. In this therapy, patients must consciously separate out their multiple selves—their adult self and their inner child, for example, or the self before "the accident" and the one after—in order to first objectively see, and then compassionately approach, the earlier self (279–97). Our brains have enormous power to activate different selves, to step outside of our bodies and into our minds, and back again. I've come to see the WAW classroom as a kind of therapeutic space, where years of mixed writing experiences—classroom-based and self-sponsored, academic and creative—can be both deconstructed and felt, and then collectively, supportively explored through metacognition-emotion emphasis. It's a space where students can safely hold up to the light their many writing selves, and speak to them. There may be an inner doubter, a confident conqueror, a scared overachiever. Students can learn to rewrite the script for internal dialogues between these selves, using meta realizations as catalysts to shift real feelings that may be impediments to empowered self-efficacy. Responding to the emotional needs of split selves is encapsulated in one student's reflection:

> I think the idea I've come across *while* writing my paper (to make *myself* happy with the quality of the work I'm doing) will be valuable moving forward both academically and working on healing myself mentally. As much as I've grown, my self-critic has only come with me—maybe quieter—but it's still there. Learning to shift the way I criticize my work will help my perfectionism become more productive rather than a symptom of my anxieties.

Here too, as Brand and Powell found, writing itself became powerful medicine for this student's writing anxiety, out of which emerged an emotional purpose for composing: happiness.

When first-year students begin their journey into the "new cognitive terrain" of college writing (Chandler 63), they do so at the doorstep of emotion—except they rarely *know* how complexly bound their writing and emotions truly are.[8] In courses centered in metacognition and emotion, students cross the threshold of that door, often experiencing profound disorientation in so doing. Self-confrontation follows, becoming a value to pursue beyond the course. Pondering the emotional stakes of college initiation, this student, at the conclusion of our course, had come to see writing as a window to the self: "the meta has exaserbated [sic] my mental limits. What is writing? Who is writing? Who am I?"

Appendix A: Multimodal Essay Assignment

Task

For your first essay, you will consider the intersection of language and identity—as you have personally experienced that intersection—in greater depth. Please see our list of questions on the back of this handout for help with narrowing your focus.

Purpose, Audience, Evidence

Your essay may be reflective, narrative, or argumentative (this is your **purpose**). If you choose reflection, you might center your essay around a realization, or moments in your life that exhibit that realization. If you choose narrative, you might tell the story of how that intersection has factored into your identity. If you choose persuasion, you might use your life experiences as evidence in support of a central claim. These are merely examples, and your essay can have any emphasis with any of these purposes. While your life experiences are your **evidence**, you may also choose to pull evidence from the course texts. Your classmates are your **audience**.

Mode

You will choose an essay **mode** that best aligns with your intended **purpose** and **audience**. *Multimodality* means that you are *composing* (and of course, *thinking*) through (a) nonstandard mode(s). In other words, you are not *writing* an essay using the standard *linguistic* mode but rather composing a *visual, aural, gestural, or spatial* "essay," although you may of course combine modes. Here is a handy pie chart:

See the Digital Rhetoric Collaborative's page for a definition of these modalities: http://webservices.itcs.umich.edu/mediawiki/DigitalRhetoricCollaborative/index.php/Modes

Overview: Linguistic: words; Visual: images; Aural: sounds; Spatial: physical spaces; Gestural: movements

Length

There is no set length to this creative essay, as long as it explores language and identity deeply. Keep in mind, however, that this is an "essay," though not a typical one—which means that it is substantive in the way an essay is (and not like an exercise, a sketch, or a paragraph, for example).

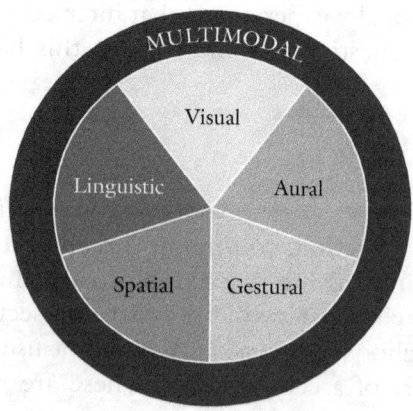

Figure 5.1

Timeline

- Proposal, 1–2 pages, at individual conferences, F 9/28
- Draft 1, in-class work, F 10/5
- **Final Draft, F 10/12**

Grading Criteria

See attached rubric.

Unit Learning Outcomes

- Read and respond to college level texts
- Develop and refine ideas in dialogue with class readings; enter an ongoing scholarly debate
- Design and produce a creative essay that clearly and logically reflects, narrates, or argues something about your personal stakes in the scholarly debate about language and identity
- Demonstrate an understanding of rhetorical concepts like purpose, audience, and mode
- Select a mode for your product aligned with your topic, purpose, and audience
- Improve your essay through a multi-draft revision process

The Assignment, in Your Own Words

Questions for our Task (student-generated questions):

> What is your identity and how does your home environment factor into/shape that?
> What is the line between language and dialect? How does this line move?
> How does how you speak shape people's perception of your identity?
> Does your identity shape the way you use language or do languages shape your identity?
> How can you reshape the way you speak to reaffirm your and others' identities?
> What is the relationship between codeswitching, codemeshing, and identity?
> How do certain sectors of American society reinforce or uphold linguistic prejudice?

What does language have to do with racism?
How do different dialects develop?
Is there a relationship between dialect and personality?
How do prejudices affect your relationship to your identity/the self?
How does your main language or dialect affect how you're taught? How you're taught SAE?
How can your dialects affect the kind of discourse communities/groups you join?
How can we validate a multitude of voices?
How do people switch voices? How do people develop a "voice"?
How has language influenced me as a person?
How has the construct of language influenced my personal language(s)?
How has language confined me to a certain community? Or opened me up to certain communities?
How have other people's words affected me as a person?
How have my languages given me power? Or taken away my power?
How does my language affect my art?
Can language be another form of cultural appropriation?
Authenticity/ medium of languages in storytelling (effectiveness)
How can learning a different language affect how you think?
Have I changed the rhetoric of_____ or has it changed me?
How I did learn the different languages/dialects/discourses I'm conversant in?
How did I learn to speak?
How do languages and knowledges inform each other? What do people who use different languages know that others don't?
How do my languages impact my self-concept? My insecurities?

Ideas for the Multimodal Essay (student-generated ideas):

Short film
Performance piece
Work of art (movement)
Comic/Graphic Memoir (panels)
Prezi/PPT (visual—series of images)
Song/Ballad
Expressive Dance
TED Talk/spoken word
Sonnet Hybrid

(Multi-) Modal Essay Rubric

EXPLORATION OF TOPIC: Does the multimodal essay establish a central idea? Engage a central question? Explore and develop the central idea deeply?

EXCELLENT (A)	GOOD (B)	COMPETENT (C)	INSUFFICIENT (D)
Essay has an appropriately focused topic and develops that topic clearly and explores that topic deeply.	Essay has a focused topic and mostly develops that topic clearly and explores that topic in some depth.	Essay has a somewhat focused topic and/or does not fully develop or explore the topic.	Essay lacks focus or does not develop or explore the topic with any depth.

ORGANIZATION: Is the development of ideas throughout the essay successful?

EXCELLENT (A)	GOOD (B)	COMPETENT (C)	INSUFFICIENT (D)
Essay is clearly and logically organized with an engaging introduction, a logically sequenced body with appropriate transitions, and a clear and convincing conclusion.	Essay makes a clear attempt at organization with a beginning, middle, and end, and an attempt to use transitions.	Essay has some inconsistencies in organization and/or lacks a sustained focus throughout with an inconsistent use of transitions.	Essay shows a lack of organization, which makes it difficult to follow the creator's ideas; there may be no clear beginning, middle, or end.

PURPOSE: Does the essay have a clear purpose? Does it clearly reflect, narrate, or argue?

EXCELLENT (A)	GOOD (B)	COMPETENT (C)	INSUFFICIENT (D)
Student demonstrates a clear understanding of the essay's purpose.	Student demonstrates a partial understanding of the essay's purpose.	Student demonstrates a vague sense of the essay's purpose; the audience is required to make assumptions.	The essay's purpose is unclear; the audience is left confused.

EVIDENCE: Does the essay use "evidence" in the form of personal experiences or text-based ideas successfully?

EXPLORATION OF TOPIC: Does the multimodal essay establish a central idea? Engage a central question? Explore and develop the central idea deeply?

EXCELLENT (A)	GOOD (B)	COMPETENT (C)	INSUFFICIENT (D)
Student carefully chooses strong, effective evidence to explore the central topic; chosen evidence aligns clearly with essay's purpose.	Student uses mostly strong, effective evidence to explore the central topic; chosen evidence mostly aligns with essay's purpose.	Student chooses evidence that may not support a deep exploration of the central topic; chosen evidence may not align with the essay's purpose.	The chosen evidence does not support an exploration of the central topic; the evidence may be confusing, inappropriate, off-topic, or misaligned with the essay's purpose.

MODALITIES: Does essay use the most appropriate modalit(ies) given its topic, purpose, and audience?

EXCELLENT (A)	GOOD (B)	COMPETENT (C)	INSUFFICIENT (D)
Student uses modality/modalities that most effectively convey the topic and purpose of the essay. It is perfectly clear why student chose video over photography, or performance over text, for example.	Student uses modality/modalities that convey the topic and purpose of the essay. It is somewhat clear why student chose video over photography, or performance over text, for example.	Student uses modality/modalities that may be unsuitable for the topic, audience, or purpose of the essay. It is unclear why student chose these modes.	Student uses modality/modalities that are inappropriate or illogical for the topic, audience, and purpose of the essay.

ORIGINALITY/CREATIVITY: Is the essay original and creative?

EXCELLENT (A)	GOOD (B)	COMPETENT (C)	INSUFFICIENT (D)
The essay illuminates the topic in a new way.	The essay engages the audience, and begins to illuminate the topic in a new way.	The essay suggests that there may be a new way to see the topic, but does not effectively convey this perspective.	The essay does not challenge the audience to see the topic in a new way.

OVERALL EFFECTIVENESS: Was the essay successful, overall?

EXCELLENT (A)	GOOD (B)	COMPETENT (C)	INSUFFICIENT (D)
The audience's attention is maintained, and the purpose of the essay is achieved.	The audience is mostly interested, and the purpose of the essay is achieved.	Audience interest is not sustained, and the purpose of the essay is only partially achieved.	Does not capture audience's interest, and the purpose of the essay is not achieved.

Knowing Emotion: College Initiation and Self-Confrontation | 73

Appendix B: Student Multimodal Essay Supplement

This student performed a monologue for the class about learning to find his voice as an actor. Accompanying the monologue were a series of images he called "Words and Emotions." A few are included below, with the student's permission. Credit: Craig Jameson:

Figure 5.2 Loneliness

Figure 5.3 Love of Self

Figure 5.4 Pain

Figure 5.5 Insecurity

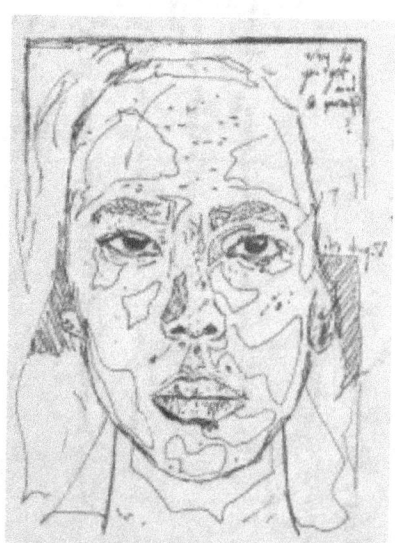

Figure 5.6 Truth

Knowing Emotion: College Initiation and Self-Confrontation 75

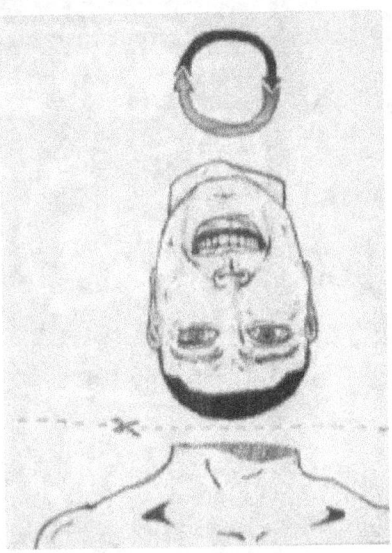

Figure 5.7 Joy

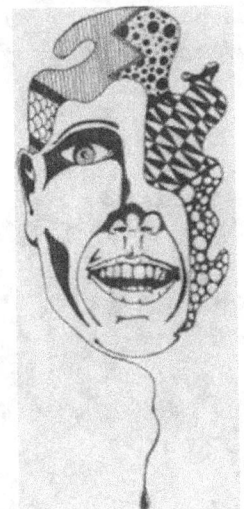

Figure 5.8 Depression

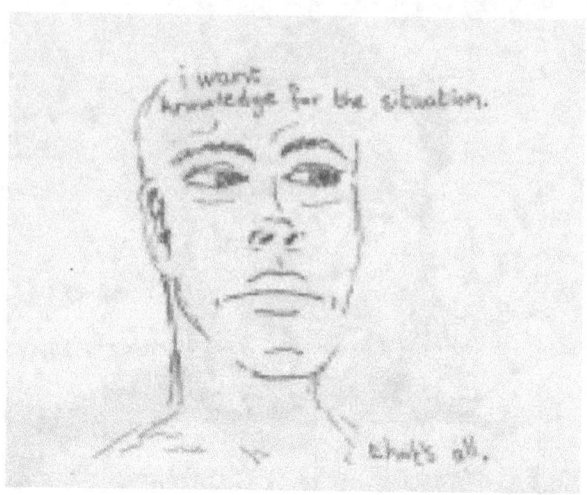

Figure 5.9 Confusion

Appendix C: Extended Metaphor Board Notes

Assignment: After our class model, plot one of your literature source conversation groups as a Twitter Conversation. Who is speaking to whom? What is the response?

Board Notes:

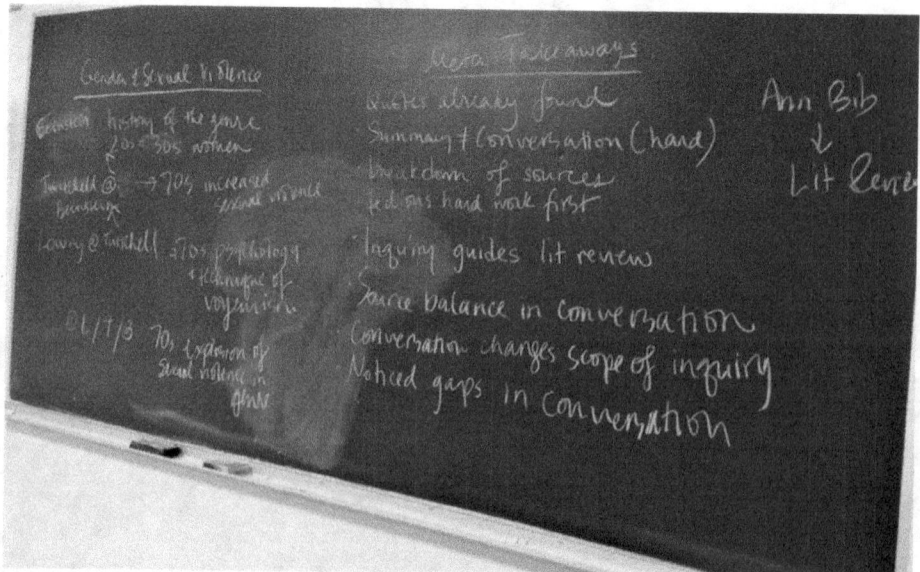

Figure 5.10

Knowing Emotion: College Initiation and Self-Confrontation 77

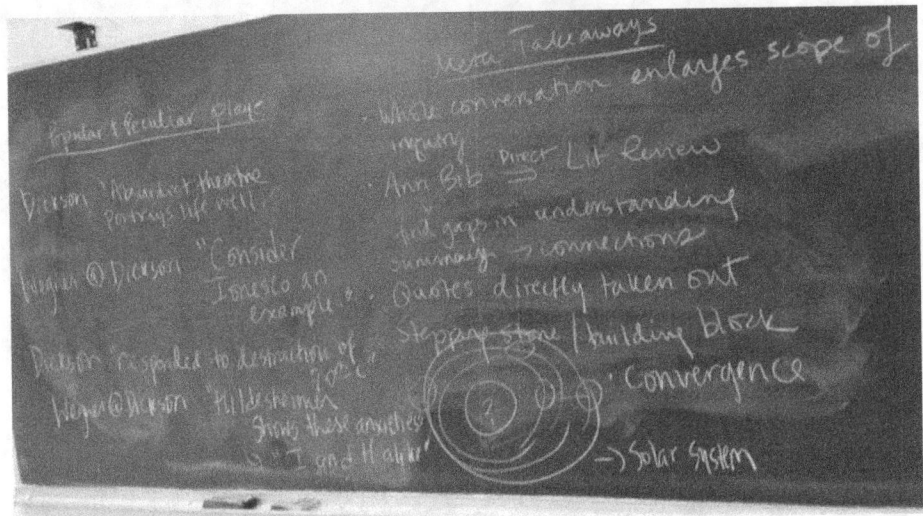

Figure 5.11

Appendix D: Emotion and Writing Process Maps

Assignment: (1) Choose a lengthier writing product that you commonly generate (academic essay, short story, poem, creative project, etc.), (2) On blank paper, with colored pencils/markers, draw a visual representation—or if you prefer, a map—of your writing process for that product, including the steps. Your visual must somehow represent emotions you typically feel when engaging with that process.

Student examples:

Figure 5.12

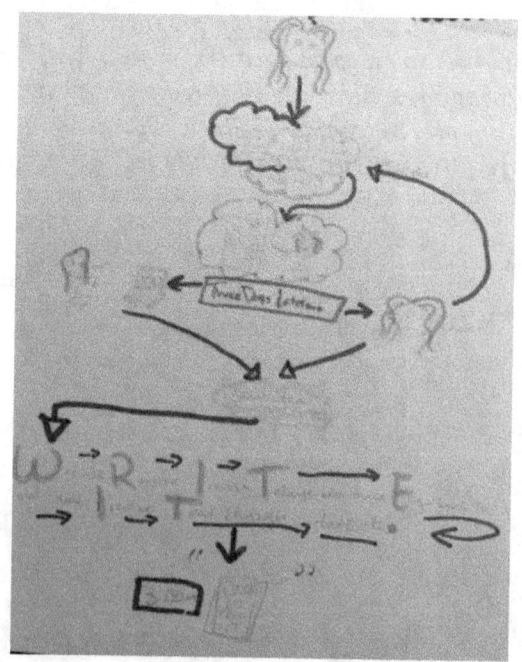

Figure 5.13

Knowing Emotion: College Initiation and Self-Confrontation

Figure 5.14

Figure 5.15

Appendix E: Annotation Maps

Developmental students annotated the Introduction to Thinking on the Page: A College Student's Guide to Effective Writing, *Gwen Hyman and Martha Schulman.*

Knowing Emotion: College Initiation and Self-Confrontation 81

Figure 5.16

Figure 5.17

Notes

1. Lynn Bloom narrows contextual factors that feed writing anxiety to intellectual (writing knowledge, skill), artistic (risk attitudes), temperamental (self-efficacy), biological (physiological factors during writing), emotional (attitude), social (social support), and academic (academic environment) (Wynne 11–12). Daly, Faigley, and Witte, as well as Clark, also differentiate "writing anxiety" from "writing apprehension" by suggesting that "anxiety" manifests in a wider range of writing comportments (Wynne 8–11). For a detailed literature review of the conflation of these terms in scholarship, and of their proposed distinction, see Wynne, 6–12.
2. Yet another student response highlights this shift. A developmental student began to see difficulty as a sign of progress when she commented that "throughout the semester I've noticed that I struggled a little more than last semester with getting my ideas down for the first two papers, but I also noticed that my process of writing has gotten better."
3. In a writing program survey that our institution, Marymount Manhattan College, administered to all first-years in Spring 2018 at the conclusion of the two-semester stretch sequence (with 237 responses, at a 65.7% response rate), 13–17% of students rated three of the four metacognitive skills we asked about, including rhetorical analysis, rhetorical awareness, and writing as thinking, "no improvement" after writing coursework. Those who felt misplaced, believing their skills to be higher than the level of their first-semester course, were more likely to report "no improvement" in these categories (62–65% of that group). Self-reporting misplaced students as a broader category (the course level was either too high or too low), were significantly less satisfied with their writing courses (29.3% "extremely/very satisfied") in comparison to those who felt the level was "just right" (63.9% "extremely/very satisfied"). This data suggests a correlation between strong metacognitive habits and self-efficacy; those who already felt versed in these habits or who did not believe themselves to have gained in metacognition, believed they were misplaced at higher rates than their counterparts, and were ultimately left with the lingering *emotion* of discomfort, or improper initial placement, even at the conclusion of the academic year. These same students reported lower rates of overall satisfaction with their writing courses.
4. Lower self-efficacy, accompanied by awareness of this perception of deficit, in cases of ESL students has been found to motivate students to seek additional help, which in turn then intervened in this predictive model, improving writing performance (Khost 278).
5. Alfred Bandura's four "sources" of self-efficacy beliefs, in descending order of strength—"mastery experience," or having completed the task before, "vicarious experience," having watched others perform the task, "verbal/social persuasion," external encouragement of ability, and "emotional or physiological state," or a feeling in the moment about one's ability—do not equate self-efficacy with more global perceptions of the self, as these "fail[ ] to establish the requisite standard of task-specificity" (Khost 276). Anastasia Efklides, however, finds that "self-regulated learning," driven by self-efficacy, functions at the intersection of "person" characteristics like general metacognitive knowledge and "task" processing characteristics like comprehension, and therefore is not solely task-specific.
6. See Dale Jacobs and Laura Micciche, *A Way to Move: Rhetorics of Emotion in Composition*.

7. See comic artist Nick Sousanis's extraordinary visual thinking work with students, including annotation maps and visual syllabi.
8. This revelation usually comes early, as here, where students chose reflective exercises from Elizabeth Wardle and Doug Downs's *Writing about Writing: A College Reader* introduction to "threshold concepts," responding affectively, almost without fail. Together, we tagged an astonishing range of emotional words and phrases: "circle paper," "honeymoon phase," "obsessed," "inspiration," "struggled," "nervous," "boring," "afraid of run-on sentences," "aggravated," "flexibility," "make someone feel," "comfort," "cure," "fatalistic," "absolutely terrifying," "uninteresting," "toxic," "anxious," "struggle," "uncomfortable," "really surprised," "understanding," "passionate," "ignored," "why?," "love faded," "never praised," "envied writers," "I suck at reading poetry," "nothing wrong with my story," "stress set in," "beliefs that drove me," "stifling writer's voice," "music to my ears," "more personal and more thoughtful," "couldn't even create meaning for myself," "how I feel about myself as a writer," "lose the self," "second personality," "resonate more deeply within myself," "they couldn't connect to it," "angered me," "made me upset," "so stumped," "epiphany," "so stressed out," "traumatized me," "surprisingly grateful."

Works Cited

Bandura, Albert. "Self-Efficacy: Toward a Unifying Theory of Behavioral Change." *Psychological Review*, 1977. *ProQuest*, http://ezproxy.gc.cuny.edu/login?url=https://searchproquest.com.ezproxy.gc.cuny.edu/docview/63957362?accountid=7287. Accessed 16 Jan. 2019.

Bard Institute for Writing and Thinking. http://writingandthinking.org/. Accessed 5 Jan. 2019.

Bloom, Lynn. "Anxious Writers in Context: Graduate School and Beyond." *When a Writer Can't Write*, edited by Mike Rose, Guilford Press, 1985, pp. 119–33.

Brand, Alice G., and Jack L. Powell. "Emotions and the Writing Process: A Description of Apprentice Writers." *Journal of Educational Research*, vol. 79, no. 5, 01 Jan. 1986, pp. 280–85. EBSCO *host*, search.ebscohost.com/login.aspx?direct=true&db=eric&AN=EJ336858&site=ehost-live. Accessed 8 Jan. 2019.

Brand, Alice G. "Writing and Feelings: Checking Our Vital Signs." *Rhetoric Review*, vol. 8, no. 2, 1990, pp. 290–308. *JSTOR*, www.jstor.org/stable/465600. Accessed 16 Jan. 2019.

Chandler, Sally. "Fear, Teaching Composition, and Students' Discursive Choices: Re-Thinking Connections between Emotions and College Student Writing." *Composition Studies*, vol. 35, no. 2, 01 Jan. 2007, pp. 53–70. *EBSCOhost*, search.ebscohost.com/login.aspx?direct=true&db=eric&AN=EJ818660&site=ehost-live. Accessed 16 Jan. 2019.

Clark, Diane. *Toward a Theory of Writing Anxiety*, Diss., Arizona State University, 2005.

Council of Writing Program Administrators, et al. "Framework for Success in Postsecondary Writing." Jan. 2011, http://wpacouncil.org/files/framework-forsuccess-postsecondarywriting.pdf. Accessed 5 Sept. 2018.

Daly, John A., and Michael D. Miller. "The Empirical Development of an Instrument to Measure Writing Apprehension." *Research in the Teaching of English*, Jan. 1975. *EBSCOhost*, search.ebscohost.com/login.aspx?direct=true&db=eric&AN=EJ137933&site=ehost-live. Accessed 8 Jan. 2019.

Efklides, Anastasia. "Interactions of Metacognition with Motivation and Affect in Self Regulated Learning: The MASRL Model." *Educational Psychologist*, vol. 46, no. 1, 2011, pp. 6–25. *EBSCOhost*, search.ebscohost.com/login.aspx?direct=true&db=eric&AN=EJ912525&site=ehost-live. Accessed 24 Dec. 2018.

Faigley, Lester, et al. "The Role of Writing Apprehension in Writing Performance and Competence." *Journal of Education Research*, vol. 75, no. 1, Sept. 1981, pp. 16–21. *JSTOR*, www.jstor.org/stable/27539858. Accessed 9 Jan. 2019.

Flower, Linda, and John R. Hayes. "A Cognitive Process Theory of Writing." *College Composition and Communication*, vol. 32, no. 4, 1981, pp. 365–87. *JSTOR*, www.jstor.org/stable/356600. Accessed 16 Jan. 2019.

Harvey, Michael. *The Nuts and Bolts of College Writing*. 2nd ed. Hackett, 2013.

Hyman, Gwen, and Martha Schulman. *Thinking on the Page: A College Student's Guide to Effective Writing*. Writer's Digest Books, 2015.

Jacobs, Dale, and Laura Micciche. *A Way to Move: Rhetorics of Emotion in Composition*. Heinemann, 2003.

Khost, Peter H. "Researching Habits-of-Mind Self-Efficacy in First-Year College Writers." *Contemporary Perspectives on Cognition and Writing*, edited by Patricia Portanova et al., 2017, pp. 271–89. https://wac.colostate.edu/books/cognition/chapter14.pdf. Accessed 24 Dec. 2018.

Levine, Lisa. Personal Communication, 2004.

Perl, Sondra. "The Composing Processes of Unskilled College Writers." *Research in the Teaching of English*, vol. 13, no. 4, 1979, pp. 317–36. *JSTOR*, www.jstor.org/stable/40170774. Accessed 16 Jan. 2019.

Sacramento State. "The Daly-Miller Test: How to Calculate and Read Your Score." https://www.csus.edu/indiv/s/stonerm/daly_miller_scoring.htm. Accessed 2 Jan. 2019.

Sommers, Nancy, and Laura Saltz. "The Novice as Expert: Writing the Freshman Year." *College Composition and Communication*, vol. 56, no. 1, 2004, pp. 124–49. *JSTOR*, www.jstor.org/stable/4140684. Accessed 9 Jan. 2019.

Sousanis, Nick. *Spin Weave & Cut*. http://spinweaveandcut.com/education-home/. Accessed 22 Feb. 2019.

Van Der Kolk, Bessel. *The Body Keeps the Score*. Penguin Books, 2015.

Wardle, Elizabeth, and Doug Downs. *Writing About Writing: A College Reader*, 3rd ed. Bedford/St. Martin's, 2017.

Wynne, Craig. *Toward a Theory of Productivity Problems in Graduate Student Writing*. Diss., University of Texas at El Paso, 2014. https://cwynne.weebly.com/uploads/6/0/4/6/6046729/craig_wynne_-_dissertation.pdf. Accessed 18 Apr. 2019.

6. Integrative Learning as a Process for Linking Writing and Emotion

JAMES P. BARBER & ETHAN YOUNGERMAN

Laisa Garcia was stumped. The prompt in her FYC class asked her to explore a connection between an art object and a public issue. So far, so good. Except that there were so many art objects. And so many public issues. The freedom to select her own topic was curdling into an obstacle. Her sophisticated NYU classmates, she imagined, had no difficulty with this assignment, but as a first-generation Mexican-American from a small Texas border town, she didn't know where to begin. Until, that is, she remembered a principle of the class: use emotion to help forge intellectual connections. So Laisa began writing about how upsetting it is to live so close to Mexico, and yet have such difficulty empathizing with the experiences of immigrants; she wrote about how she was scared to watch the Oscar-winning film *Roma*, scared that she wouldn't be moved by the lives of the Mexican characters. These conflicting emotions led her, eventually, to the work of Jason de León, whose anthropological art exhibitions are made out of backpacks he finds discarded by migrants along the Mexico/US border. Using her own emotional ambivalence, Laisa constructed an argument about art's ability to introduce us to empathy, a trait she argued is sorely lacking in the political discourse around immigration. In an end of year reflection, Laisa noted that "From now on, I will write solely about the things I care about so that I may care about the things I write (my biggest takeaway from this class, by the way)."

There is often a false dichotomy delineated between "personal" and "academic" writing (Bartholomae 62; Elbow 72). But while RWS has pushed for bringing emotion back into the college classroom (Jensen; Moon 33), research in the field of higher education offers new theoretical insights. In this chapter, we argue that integrative learning research reveals that emotion can be a guiding force of student writing, not just to describe emotions, but as a way to make meaningful connections between life experiences and other sources of evidence. Likewise, a purposeful effort to bring emotion into the academic writing space fosters integrative learning.

Integrative learning, in short, is a highly coveted cognitive outcome (AAC&U; National Academies of Sciences, Engineering, and Math) which explicitly privileges (and practices) the bridging of contexts, the linking of disparate evidence and fields, and the mixing of settings and methods. Within the framework of integrative learning, the linking of academic writing and emotion is, in fact, expected.

Our own empirical research has used the grounded theory method to code and typologize two sets of data: extensive student interviews and award-winning student academic essays. Drawing on this research and a wider literature review, we offer principles and practices to use integrative learning to bring emotion into the composition classroom, in-class writing prompts, larger writing assignments, and even the process of selecting academic projects. Some of these practices are small (for example, the 280 characters of a Twitter post assignment), while others are as large as encouraging students to create a Researcher's Stance (see Appendix A). The goal is to offer a variety of entry points to the work of integrative learning.

Integrative Learning Explained

Integration of learning is an essential outcome of a college education. No matter where students go next in their careers, they will be at an advantage if they can quickly make connections across contexts. Barber analyzed nearly two hundred interviews with undergraduate students to examine how students integrate learning, and developed the following definition from his research:

> Integration of learning is the demonstrated ability to connect, apply, and/or synthesize information coherently from disparate contexts and perspectives, and make use of these new insights in multiple contexts. This includes the ability to connect the domain of ideas and philosophies to the everyday experience, from one field of study or discipline to another, from the past to the present, between campus and community life, from one part to the whole, from the abstract to the concrete, among multiple identity roles—and vice versa (593).

Through his grounded theory analysis, Barber (*Integration of Learning: Meaning Making* and "Integration of Learning: A Grounded Theory") identified three main approaches that college students used to integrate learning across contexts: connection, application, and synthesis. Connection was the least complex approach, and often was a fleeting recognition that two ideas or skills were related. Application, by contrast, was a more concrete approach, in which students used knowledge or skills acquired in one situation in another context. Finally, synthesis was the most complex approach to integration of learning, in which students brought two or more ideas or skills together to form a new way of seeing the world. Synthesis is a creative process of combining knowledge to advance understanding and generate new insights.

Youngerman (*Integrative Learning* and "Integrative Learning") examined 32 award-winning essays to explore how college students integrated learning in the writing process. Among other things, his research revealed students making integrative connections between written texts and the emotional ethos they developed within their discipline; for example, when one student was introduced to a real-world problem through a course reading, she applied the emotional training from her Social Work program to propose a safe and empowering response (*Integrative Learning* 72). Through his analysis, Youngerman created a typology of what students integrated in their writing, which serves as a guide for how students can introduce emotion into their writing. He found that students integrate learning in moments ranging from the contained (as when a student makes a connection between one source and another source) to the complex (establishing, say, a multifaceted contextualizing debate); in each of these situations, personal experience and emotional understanding emerged as one of the sources students integrated. Furthermore, Youngerman's work supported the notion of three approaches to integration of learning that Barber identified, and he found students connecting, applying, and synthesizing in their writing. As Youngerman enumerates:

> These integrations may happen by connection, in which sources are: positioned as equivalent; contrasted contextually, argumentatively, or hierarchically; connected via an intermediary or bridge; or connected in service of the formation of a problem. These integrations may happen by application, in which one author's language is brought to another author, or in which the realm of ideas or art objects are tested in or exported to the everyday world. These integrations may happen as a result of synthesis, through the process of: generating an idea; forming a judgment; following an implication; or gathering (*Integrative Learning* 148).

Next, we discuss how to implement integrative learning and emotion into writing assignments and activities in an academic setting.

A Crucial Caveat

Before we explore the implications of integrative learning for composition and emotion, we must consider the role of trust. In order for students to bring genuine emotion into their academic work and then share those feelings in writing, trust must be established between educator and student. Educators hold the power to create an environment where students can feel both vulnerable and safe enough to share emotion through writing with their audience(s), which may be the professor, their classmates, or a larger public. An intentional invitation to students to bring emotion into their writing—and their class experience—is crucial. Beyond that, how this trusting rapport is built will differ depending on the context and individuals involved. After all, for some students, the process of bringing emotion into an academic setting through writing will be a new idea: some students have been taught to check their emotions and life experience at the door when they enter the formal space of a classroom. For others, negative experiences bringing emotion into their writing may foster negative transfer, a reluctance to try again. Still others have had good mentors who supported them in expressing emotion through writing previously, but may be unsure how their current instructors feel about such a practice. In any event, it is vital to open the door for students to bring their prior experiences, their home lives, their full identities into the academic space through their writing. We as educators must encourage students to do so; this type of enthusiastic invitation will promote integration of learning across contexts.

The process of trust-building, both with and among students, takes time. Writing activities, prompts, and assignments should be scaffolded in such a way that the initial interactions are low-risk for students. These early writing prompts can invite students to share aspects of themselves as they are comfortable, without requiring substantive self-disclosure or emotion. Later in the semester as students become more familiar with the course content, the instructor, and their peers, assignments that expect greater emotion can be more effective.

Integrative Learning Applied

Implications for Shorter Writing Assignments. College students compose text with emotion every day, although not always in the form of writing for academic purposes. Writing in diaries, blogs, tweets, texts, and social media captions are short bursts of writing in digital spaces that happen frequently throughout the day. Many of these more casual genres and modes are excellent entry points to integrative learning, even if they are limited to 280 characters at a time through a tweet, may not adhere to grammatical rules, and may include emoji interwoven with text. Because these modes do express emotion in a written form, they are a foundation from which to build;

educators can help students apply what they already know from informal writing to bridge that knowledge into a different context—writing in an academic space. For example, Kassens detailed the uses of the microblogging social media platform Twitter for promoting writing, reflection, and community in Economics classrooms (101). And it bears repeating: the application of this familiar writing method into a new academic setting is not only a "backdoor" process for helping students express themselves; application of methods is, itself, an (integrative) learning outcome.

Implications for Project Design. Integrative learning research also has implications for how instructors design project selection work for their students. Michele Eodice, Anne Ellen Geller and Neal Lerner discovered, in their *Meaningful Writing Project*, that students find writing projects meaningful when they feel the "power of personal connection" (4). Instructors hoping to create meaningful writing projects for their students, then, should be looking for ways to allow students to bring emotion into the writing process. This could even be the essence of the selection process: students could be encouraged to write problem statements/research questions about the class text they feel most emotionally conflicted about. Letizia has framed the process of student thesis writing in the language of self-authorship: as students progress from initial thinking to complexity, they move, Letizia argues, from a place of fact-based claim-making to a more complicated intellectual space where they "own" their thinking (220). In this way, by bringing integrative learning into the initial writing process, instructors can be encouraging students to invest their writing with emotion and meaning, while also creating a scaffolded processes for increasing complexity. See Appendix A for a sample Researcher's Stance writing project.

Implications for Larger Writing Prompts. Perhaps most crucially, instructors can foster integrative learning in their larger writing prompts in a way that builds on the power of using emotion in academic writing. Students can be prompted to make a connection between their personal experience and a course reading. Or they can be led down a path of inquiry that demands that they synthesize multiple conflicting sources and theories, including their own lived emotional experience. By requiring this kind of meaning making, instructors can leverage the power of emotion in academic writing to foster integrative learning, and can leverage the complexity of integrative learning to encourage emotion in academic writing. See Appendix B for further suggestions. Regardless of how instructors incorporate integrative learning into their courses, we encourage framing this work with explicit instructions for students to bring emotion freely into their academic writing. For example, lead into one of the writing prompts in the appendices while noting that: "Writing can be a tool for expressing emotion and making sense of complicated ideas. In this course, I encourage you to bring your prior knowledge and life experiences into your writing. As you respond to the following prompt, think about your experiences broadly."

Implications for Curricular Structures. Integrative learning is often fostered through writing-based curricular structures like ePortfolios, capstone projects, and other writing/reflecting that takes place over longer periods of time than just a course or semester. Thinking across multiple moments in an undergraduate careers is, in and of itself, valuable and challenging integrative work. And in terms of content, the chances of a student thinking across disparate contexts are increased by encouraging the use of evidence, methods, and written assignments from multiple courses and semesters. But the incorporating of emotion into such projects can follow some of the same paths we've mentioned above. If students are curating an ePortfolio, they may be encouraged to select pieces of writing that still have emotional resonance for them; they may even be prompted to write a kind of researcher's stance "introduction" or "about me" section of their ePortfolio that explicitly explores why the pieces they chose are still meaningful to them.

Integrative Learning Principles for Writing

Returning to the three approaches to integration of learning that we introduced early in this essay (connection, application, and synthesis), we offer several principles in Table 6.1 that can be implemented across multiple courses or activities.

The practices we describe in Table 6.1 have been successfully implemented in undergraduate and graduate courses that we teach at our respective universities. The feedback has been positive both in terms of formal student evaluations, as well as informal comments from students. Including a variety of writing assignments and in-class activities that encourage different integrative approaches (i.e., connection, application, and synthesis) has allowed for students with varied experience to leverage integration. Those students with less exposure to integrating writing and emotion can find a foothold in connection and application, while those students who are more skilled with integration continue to grow using synthesis and combinations of the three approaches to complement one another.

And the benefits of valuing emotion are apparent in student written demonstrations of integrative learning. Here, an NYU student (Giorgio) integrates his own emotional experiences with Alice Walker's "Beauty, When the Other Dancer is the Self." He notes that

Table 6.1. Principles to foster integration of learning through writing and emotion.

Approach	Definition/ Characteristics	Principles
Connection	Realization of similarity (often fleeting); recognition that two ideas are related in some way.	Reflection prompts can help students make connections across disparate contexts and timelines (e.g., "Write for 10 minutes about an emotion that has surfaced for you in this class, and relate it to a time you felt that way in the past").
		Short assignments can be leveraged to introduce the skill of connection-making and seed the possibility of that connection-making being emotion-driven (e.g., "Compose a tweet about how you're feeling today, but add a mention of a writer we've read in class whose theories might help explain why you're feeling that way").
Application	Practical; uses knowledge, skills/ methods, or ideas learned in one context in another.	Students need support realizing that "nonacademic" strategies and identities can be relevant to coursework (e.g., "Describe a strategy you have used for problem solving. This could be from any identity you hold— as a family member, as a participant in a faith community, as a member in a student club or team, even in a romantic relationship. Now, explain how applying that strategy to one of the issues/problems we've identified in our course does and does not work.")
		Innovation often comes from old skills brought into new contexts.
Synthesis	Creative; brings together multiple parts to form a new whole.	Emotional learning can be an act of synthesis (e.g., "Write about a time that you brought two important people in your life together for the first time. What emotions did you feel as you introduced them?")
		Synthesis does not happen without scaffolding and challenge.
		Fostering the ability to create a new whole comes, in part, from challenging students' sense of form. Creative writing projects may enact such a challenge.

"[Walker] suggests to us what is perhaps the way to happiness: loving the scars that make us who we are. Unfortunately, this is much easier said than done. As Walker's story shows us, psychological wounds need time – sometimes years, even decades – to heal. [...] But if we are strong – or maybe just lucky – we will eventually heal, acquiring a deeper understanding of ourselves. At least, so it was for me." (qtd. in Youngerman, *Integrative* 74).

Even before the climactic final claim, it's clear that a connection – a "realization of similarity"—fuels this analysis of Walker's essay. The student integrates emotional experiences with an assigned text; "personal" and "academic" writing not only aren't separate, they empower one another.

We do not offer such evidence to suggest that the process of integrating learning is confined to a single course. The desired outcomes sometimes are not realized until months or years later. As writing teachers, we realize that we are not teaching a skill for a particular class or semester, but rather honing an essential communication skill that will benefit students personally and professionally for a lifetime.

Synthesis (aka Conclusion)

Compositionists have argued for the value of writing as a skill across the curriculum and, indeed, into the wider world beyond college. Integrative learning is, similarly, a learning outcome with reach well beyond the classroom—being able to synthesize information and experiences is a valuable career skill. Having strategies for appropriately and productively bringing emotion to bear on other pursuits is a valuable life skill. In this way, integrative learning is not just practically aligned with writing courses, but is also aligned with the larger transfer mindset of rhetoric and composition forces like the Teaching for Transfer movement (Yancey et al. 7). Using emotion in writing through integrative learning is a way of helping students bring their experiences from outside the classroom into their academic lives, and a way of helping students bring what they are learning inside the classroom into their lives more broadly during college, as well as into the future beyond graduation.

Appendix A

Researcher's Stance Assignment: in many Social Science traditions, a section called Researcher's Stance is an expectation of the article/study genre. In it, the researcher explores the experiences, worldviews, outlooks, and identities which have shaped how they've constructed the current research project.

They may enumerate personal experiences which, upon reflection, they can now see as having led them to their current project. The ethos here is not to foreground bias/limitations so much as it is to offer a moment of reflective synthesis. The writer takes the space to explore their positionality and how that is connected to their methods, site selections, research questions, and even epistemological assumptions. You have already written a paper proposal (congratulations on turning it in!). Now try, in 3–5 pages, to bring together the various parts of your life, your education, and yourself; write a Researcher's Stance. Among other things, this is a challenging organizational task: how do you order the various parts of who you are to help someone else understand why you care about what you care about? Finally, take stock of your proposal: does this work make you want to change anything about the proposal—explain!

Appendix B

Experience Assignment: select one of our class readings that resonates with you. Now think about an experience you've had in the last 3 months that can NOT be fully explained by that reading. In 2–3 pages, try to explore that incomplete connection. What part of your experience IS clarified by our reading? What part of what you experienced can't be captured or explained by this text? Perhaps this connection even reveals something to you about the text, about the successes and limitations of its explanatory power.

Works Cited

Association of American Colleges & Universities (AAC&U). "A Statement on Integrative Learning." 2004. Retrieved from http://wacenter.evergreen.edu/sites/wacenter.evergreen.edu/files/statementintlearning.pdf.

Barber, James. *Integration of Learning: Meaning Making for Undergraduates through Connection, Application, and Synthesis.* 2009. PhD diss., University of Michigan, *ProQuest Dissertations and Theses.*

———. "Integration of Learning: A Grounded Theory Analysis of College Students' Learning." *American Educational Research Journal*, vol. 49, no. 3, 2012, pp. 590–617.

Bartholomae, David. "Writing with Teachers: A Conversation with Peter Elbow." *College Composition and Communication*, vol. 46, no. 1, 1995, pp. 62–71.

Elbow, Peter. "Being a Writer vs. Being an Academic: A Conflict in Goals." *College Composition and Communication*, vol. 46, no. 1, 1995, pp. 72–83.

Eodice, Michelle, et al. *The Meaningful Writing Project: Learning, Teaching and Writing in Higher Education*. Utah State UP, 2017.

Garcia, Laisa. "Re: Mercer Street." Received by Ethan Youngerman, 28 May 2019.

Jensen, Tim. "Textbook Pathos: Tracing a Through-Line of Emotion in Composition Textbooks." *Composition Forum*, vol. 34, 2016, files.eric.ed.gov/fulltext/EJ1113431.pdf.

Kassens, Alice. "Tweeting Your Way to Improved #Writing, #Reflection, and #Community." *Journal of Economic Education*, vol. 45, no. 2, 2014, pp. 101–09.

Letizia, Anjelo. "Student Writing for Self-Authorship and Democracy: Engaging Students Critically." *Journal of College Student Development*, vol. 57, no. 2, 2016, pp. 219–23.

Moon, Gretchen. "The Pathos of Pathos: The treatment of Emotion in Contemporary Composition Textbooks." *A Way to Move: Rhetorics of Emotion and Composition Studies*, edited by D. Jacobs, Boynton/Cook, 2003, pp. 33–42.

National Academies of Sciences, Engineering, and Math. *The Integration of the Humanities and Arts with Sciences, Engineering, and Medicine in Higher Education: Branches from the Same Tree*. The National Academies Press, 2018.

Yancey, Kathleen, et al. *Writing across Contexts: Transfer, Composition, and Sites of Writing*. Utah State UP, 2014.

Youngerman, Ethan. *Integrative Learning in Award-Winning Student Writing: A Grounded Theory Analysis*. 2017. EdD diss., New York University, *ProQuest Dissertations and Theses*.

———. "Integrative Learning in Award-Winning Student Writing: A Grounded Theory Analysis." *AERA Open*, vol. 4, no. 3, 2018, pp. 1–13.

7. Peaceful Pedagogy: Teaching Writing from a Place of Peace

CRYSTAL SANDS

I come to education from a place of trauma. Growing up in an abusive home, I struggled with some of the classic symptoms of childhood trauma, such as anxiety and low self-esteem. As a first-generation college student, my trauma nearly kept me from succeeding in college. During my first year of college, I was floundering. I was a smart student, but my grades were all over the place, mostly related to issues with my writing. I could do well on tests but struggled every time I had to write an essay for a class. During my first semester, when I received my graded essays with "bad" grades on them, I was too ashamed to ask for help. I was worried that I did not belong in college, and if I drew attention to myself, someone might find out that I did not belong and require that I leave. My anxiety was so severe during my first semester of college that I was pretty sure I would not be back the next semester. But my advisor put me into another round of classes the spring semester, and I did not know what else to do with myself. I was working two part-time, minimum-wage jobs that did not seem at all appealing to me in the long term. *So I'll keep going for one more round*, I told myself.

Thankfully, that semester, I had a graduate teaching assistant for the second half of my Freshman Composition sequence who literally saved me. She could see I was scared, and a few weeks into the course, she stopped me after class and forced me to talk with her. She explained that my writing was mostly good but that I just had to work on some things. As she described the things I needed to work on, such as basic essay structure and sentence boundaries, they seemed doable to me. She kept emphasizing what I had done well, and a few weeks later, I was brave enough to ask her a question about my essay before I turned it in. I did not know what MLA format was. I did not even understand what word she was saying when she said "MLA." It sounded like "emelay" to me. She took the handbook from her bag and showed me where a sample MLA essay was. She spoke to me with such kindness, not like I was stupid, as I was sure I was. In that one semester, my confidence in my writing grew significantly, and though I would continue to struggle with confidence throughout my time in college, the kindness my teacher showed me is likely what made it possible for me to continue in college. Her kindness was pivotal for me, and a first-generation college student, the daughter of a convenience store clerk, and the product of an abusive childhood succeeded.

What are our students' stories today? How many of them come to our writing classes from places of trauma? According to a study on childhood trauma published in 2018, researchers studying children in rural communities found that childhood trauma is "surprisingly normative"; 60% of the children studied had experienced at least one trauma by age 16 and over 30% of the children had experienced multiple traumas (Borenstein). I was recently speaking with a former Dean about the state of teaching today, and he commented on how difficult it can be to teach such a traumatized generation. We spoke about the struggles with anxiety and depression we see our younger students facing. According to a 2019 study published in *Abnormal Psychology*, rates of depression for teens between the ages of 14 and 17 increased by more than 60% between the years of 2009 and 2017. Additionally, in 2017, one in eight Americans between the ages of 12 and 25 experienced "a major depressive episode" (qtd. in Heid).

With our students dealing with everything from climate change to school shootings all while living a good portion of their lives online via social media, it is no wonder we are seeing so many students struggling with anxiety and depression. And what of our nontraditional students? In addition to teaching in traditional classrooms with younger students, I also teach a high number of older adults, adults who are working full-time jobs, raising children, dealing with sick and aging parents, and doing everything they can to survive in a difficult economy. My students tell me stories of homelessness, cancer without health insurance, abuse, and every kind of financial crisis one can imagine. As their teacher, I feel that approaching these students with a kind of peace, kindness, and understanding is critical to their learning and growth as writers—and humans. How can we build their confidence in their writing and help them grow? After all, most of us are not trained as counseling professionals, yet we have much to overcome and much work to do in the writing classroom to help prepare our students for academic writing and writing in their potential careers? In my over twenty years of experience teaching writing, I have found there are ways we can help our students grow as writers while be highly cognizant of potential struggles with anxiety and lack of confidence, many of which may be related to issues of trauma of various kinds. As a teacher, I have found that I cannot allow myself to deeply process all of the tragic stories I hear, but I can create a learning environment that supports my students from a place of peace and kindness. And, in this peace and kindness, I have seen my students grow as writers.

When I first began teaching writing, my first job was teaching high school students. I did not last long in the public school system; after one year in the classroom, I decided to go back to school to complete my PhD. One of the first things my principal told me was that I was "too soft" as a teacher and that I needed to "be tougher" on my students. After a few months of trying to be someone I was not, the "tough" teacher, I was miserable—and so were my students. I decided, if I was going to make it through the year, I would need to be myself as a teacher. I started being a better listener to my students. I made sure I explained the reasons behind each lesson. I learned about the problems in their lives through the writing, and I could see that there was a reason they were "acting out" in class. I could also see that, as the "tough teacher," I was just like everyone else to them—someone who gave them no respect and someone they had to fight against. When I changed, so did my students' approach to me, and, therefore, their learning.

That was exactly twenty years ago. Today, after a career in traditional academia, where I worked my way into mid-level administration, I am back to doing what I love—teaching. I teach online almost exclusively, and I work with mostly first-generation college students who are working, supporting families, and trying, despite all that life seems to be willing to throw at them, complete their educations. In my teaching in the last few years, I have developed what I call a "pedagogy of peace," where I focus on adding peacefulness and support to the writing process instruction in my classes. I believe students. I support students. I give them second chances. And, I argue, most importantly, I build their confidence.

There are multiple benefits to the peaceful approach to writing instruction I have developed. Not only does my approach help with student issues of confidence and writing anxiety, my approach also helps me. There are almost no conflicts in my classes. I am able to remain positive and supportive for my students without the stress and anxiety that results from negative feelings between students and teachers. And there are others who see the benefits of a positive and peaceful approach to instruction. My colleagues in educational psychology have been saying for years that stress in a learning environment can negatively impact learning, but I think current national and world events have more faculty considering a more peaceful approach to their classrooms, whether they are online or traditional classrooms.

Some Literature

I read Mina Shaughnessy's *Errors and Expectations* in graduate school and knew I had found my path. In this groundbreaking book, Shaughnessy does more than explain student errors; she makes important connections between confidence and mistakes. Shaughnessy's call for compassion and flexibility in the classroom spoke to me as a teacher in training, but today, I read more teachers speaking to the importance of compassion in our classrooms.

In his 2018 piece for *The Chronicle of Higher Education*, Professor Gary Laderman explains why he likes to be the "easy" teacher for students and that being easy can equate with strong learning in the classroom, contrary to what some professors may believe. In his essay, he explains the reasons he aims for kindness in his classroom, and he argues that his students still learn a lot in his courses. Laderman writes:

> Something else most all share: They are on drugs, either prescribed or not—and I'm including the legal drugs (alcohol, cigarettes, vapes, and so on). They are also in the midst of serious existential struggles—around identity, family, self-worth, purpose, direction, and so on ... So part of my plan is to try to show love and empathy rather than contempt and derision, as some of my colleagues do. Hell, students already have enough stress and uncertainty in their lives ...

The "love and empathy" Laderman describes does not have to come at the expense of the teacher's well-being or learning in the classroom, and while Laderman does not teach writing, I would argue that his approach is even more critical in a skill-based course like writing. The stress associated with growing as a writer is stress enough for most of our students.

In his book, *Small Teaching: Everyday Lessons from the Science of Learning*, James Lang provides lessons for teachers on ways in which we can take advantage of what science teaches us about learning to build activities into our classrooms that work well for modern student learning. In his chapter "Motivating," Lang describes many of the strategies I have come to use in my own online and traditional classrooms and provides the research to support these approaches to learning. Lang cites research from Sarah Cavanagh, the director for the Laboratory for Cognitive and Affective Science at Assumption College, who explains the importance of emotions to learning because emotions play an important role in every single thing we, as humans do. Creating positive emotions, such as curiosity, excitement, and happiness, have a positive impact on student learning. In creating motivation, Lang also points to strategies, such as telling stories, sharing enthusiasm, and showing compassion, all critical elements to the peaceful pedagogy I have developed over the years and that will be described in more detail in my "Strategies" section below.

Strategies for Creating a Peaceful Learning Environment

My overall goal for my writing classes is to create a warm, positive learning environment, one that feels safe for my students, whether we are online or in a traditional classroom. Writing is hard. Some who teach writing may be naturally strong writers, but most of us deeply understand the difficult nature of writing. There is a heavy cognitive load involved in reading, summarizing, synthesizing, developing arguments, writing clearly and succinctly but also thoroughly developing ideas. To add to this, most of our students come to our classes without the writer's vocabulary needed to improve as writers. They may not know what a thesis is or, like me, have never heard of MLA. The stress of learning a new skill can be significant, and for most our students, academic writing is a new skill.

When I consider this stress in addition to the stress of our culture, I have no doubt that my students need as much emotional support as I can give them. And this is not easy. I am a highly empathetic person, and it is far too easy for me to feel so deeply for my students that I become depressed myself. One semester, I had a student with cancer, and her health insurance was refusing to pay for certain parts of her treatment. As she screamed at me over the phone about the research paper requirements, I knew her screaming had nothing to do with the research paper requirements, and I had to steel myself. I also had to remind myself that there is only so much I can do, but I also remind myself every day that there are *some* things I can do. So I do them. I present the following classroom management strategies.

Warm Tones in Communication

In a traditional classroom, we can create a positive, peaceful learning environment through the tone voice we use, the stories we tell, and the way we present ourselves as teachers. We can do these same things in online environments as well. When I first began teaching online in 2004, I was working at a traditional college, and my department chair was skeptical about online learning. But I had taken a couple of online courses as I was finishing up my doctoral coursework, and I was in love with online learning. I went through extensive training before I was allowed to teach my first online class, and after my first formal review from my department chair, I was allowed to teach online classes every term. My supervisor noted that she was impressed with the way I was able to establish a "warm" online presence, something that she was not sure was possible. Today, many in online education understand this is possible and know strategies for it. I just have a powerful emphasis on this warmth in my online classes.

I create this warmth in both the text I write and the videos I make. In my announcements, I bring kindness to my tone by focusing on what advice I can give students to help them do well. I also begin and end all of my discussion posts and email or course question responses with kindness. I thank students for their questions or responses and sign my message with a smile or with "warmest" or something that lets them know I see the communication in a positive way. In my videos, I try to be "real." I let them see a little bit of me, of my vulnerability. I talk about my own struggles and tell stories about my own experiences with the content, which I explore further below, but I do try to show a little bit of my authentic self. In one set of videos, one of my cats kept appearing in the background. At the end of the term, one of my students wrote me and told me that his daughter loved to watch my weekly videos with him because she was always watching and waiting to see my cat named Marley.

Sharing Stories

As a writing teacher, I think I always have a powerful quote from Donald Murray from my graduate studies about having to make sure our students *want* to write for us. In essence, they have to like us at least a little, and early on in my teaching career, I could see that I was going to have to do some sharing about myself, which is not easy for someone who is more introverted like myself. Thankfully, I found a strategy that worked well for me and also helped build confidence in my students. I was a struggling writer in college, so I could tell my stories. By sharing my stories with my students, I am helping to create a positive learning environment and letting my students know it is okay to struggle. I emphasize that, without struggle, there can be no learning, that it is all a process, and this works well.

Understanding Their Struggles

One of the hardest things for me is when I see some of my colleagues on social media making fun of their students for their struggles. I know we all need to vent about our students and our teaching loads at times. Writing teachers have difficult jobs, but I have seen some mean spiritedness at times from colleagues and think this is risky. I worry that these feelings may somehow come through in our teaching, so we have to be careful. It seems that every term, I have at least a few students that love to complain. They seem ready to complain about everything from the directions to the research requirements to the course management system. I have found, if not handled well in both online and traditional classrooms, the complaining can be contagious, and it does not take long before negative energy can overtake a classroom environment. I think teachers have to make sure we are not adding to any negative energy and ensure we are meeting negative with positive.

My peaceful strategies of kindness have helped reduce negativity issues in my classes, which makes my life and work so much better. From the first mention of a complaint, I immediately respond with kindness, understanding, resources if necessary, and offers of help and support. I have seen that "killing complaints with kindness" works quite well. Of course, there will sometimes be a student who continues with negative energy, despite my best efforts, but those instances have become increasingly rare in my classes, and I credit the positive energy that the negative emotions are met with for this improvement.

Giving Them the Benefit of the Doubt

We have all heard the stories about how many grandmothers can die in a semester, but I have taken an approach opposite of many of my colleagues. Instead of believing no one or trying to discern who may or may not be telling the truth, my approach is to *believe everyone*. In my study of human nature in the years I have been teaching, I can sometimes tell if a student is not being honest in a story, but how can I ever be for sure? So, I take the approach that I will not take the chance. I hear stories about miscarriages, death, violence, money struggles, broken computers, stolen computers, sick children, lost textbooks, and I simply believe them all. I have come to understand this: It does not really matter if my students are telling me the truth, at least in a way. What matters is that I have to try to find a way to help them move forward from whatever they are struggling with. Maybe their grandmother really died. Maybe they are just terrified to start writing the paper. Either way, I try to find a plan to help my students move forward.

I am as lenient as I can be within university requirements. I accept late work until the last day possible within deadlines I have set or the university has set. I allow for revisions, even in tight classes, though I have to give deadlines for those as well. And I always emphasize that I will help as much as I possibly can within reason, and I tell my students exactly what "within reason" means based on deadlines in the course. I can see that believing my students helps my students, and I have found that a very high percentage of them want to do better for themselves and for me after an experience like this. Writing is tough, and I need them to work for me in order to grow. It is for themselves as well, of course, but I need them to want to work for me as well.

Confidence-Building

One of the last and best classroom strategies I can offer is to find a way to build student confidence. This is especially true for any student dealing with any kind of trauma in their lives, but I have found that almost everyone can benefit from more confidence in their writing. In my written feedback, I always find at least one positive thing to say about their work, and I never give them more than three things at a time to work on for improvement. Learning is a process, and good writing takes time. If I try to "fix" everything for my students every time they write, they will become overwhelmed, and the negative energy created with that kind of feedback just is not worth it to me.

Peaceful Pedagogical Strategies

Of course, a peaceful pedagogy is more than classroom management strategies. In my work as a curriculum designer for my own classes as well as standardized classes at online universities, I find ways to bring peacefulness to the curriculum of the course.

Writing Process

A *flexible* approach to writing process is one of the most peaceful and effective strategies I use in my classes. The understanding that writing is a process in general and that we are *all* working on improving ourselves as writers helps my students with confidence. Any pressure I can take off of my students to feel like they have to be perfect reduces anxiety and helps facilitate growth. Writing process strategies have been proven to be effective and work well. In their 2007 meta-analysis, Graham and Perin cite the benefits of strategies, such as peer review, prewriting, and a writing process approach in general. And when taught within a peaceful approach to writing, these strategies can also help reduce some of the stresses of writing.

Writing about Writing

Based on the work of Elizabeth Wardle and Doug Downs, I use an approach to writing about writing that focuses on kindness. There is kindness in the WAW approach itself, as struggling to learn to write without the vocabulary of a writer or being able to think like a writer adds confusion to the instructional process. I add to this by using essays from writers who speak to their processes and struggles. Thinking back to my own experiences as a beginning writer, I needed help with a writer's vocabulary before I could even begin to think like a writer, much less find the courage to write. Writing about writing instruction with an emphasis on kindness helps re-emphasize the fact that we are all just writers trying to be better than we were before.

Grammar Instruction

I teach a very limited amount of grammar and usage in my classes. I connect this with the importance of vocabulary. I know my students are seeing things like "comma splice" or "passive voice" marked on their papers; if I can tell them what those things mean and what they can do about them, I see this as a profound act of kindness. Within this approach, I also rely heavily on the work of linguist Anne Curzan, who emphasizes the relativity of correctness and teaches students that there is a wide variety of ways of being "correct." Finding ways to empower students when it comes to grammar and usage helps build confidence and prepares them for their writing lives outside of our classrooms. Faculty in other disciplines often focus heavily on grammar and usage errors. Helping students build a writer's vocabulary, as per the work of Rei Noguchi, all while helping them understand the relativity of correctness can help reduce writing anxiety.

Providing Models

I always provide models for my students for difficult assignments and unique genres. I explain the risks of models to my students. I emphasize that the models I provide are just one way to approach the assignment. Thinking back to my own anxiety as a writer, having no idea at all what was expected of me was far more detrimental to my growth as a writer than leaning on a model too much.

Informal and Formal Results

While formal research on a peaceful pedagogy would be ideal, my experience tells me what there are some profound benefits to what I do. I have seen growth in my students' writing abilities and their confidence. Mostly, I have seen positive attitudes about education in general. I see hope in them, and hope is something critical to success and completion in higher education. We do not have to compromise academic rigor in order to adopt a peaceful, kind approach to instruction. I push my students as writers; it's just that I am working to build confidence and eliminate as much anxiety as I can while I push.

Students write me thank-you letters at the end of the term, or I will hear from a student years later with a thank-you note. In course reflection essays, I see in my students' writing that they are getting what I hope for them to get from my classes. I have older students writing about how scared they were to write and how they feel more comfortable writing in academia. I often witness the growth in their skills while this confidence grows. I have younger students writing about how much they thought they would hate the class but end up being thankful for it.

In an annual review at Walden University where I am a part-time faculty member, my supervisor made me sit and listen while she read positive reviews from my students. After the first couple, I started to speak, and she said, "No, just listen. There's more." And I began to quietly cry as she read message after message about how positively my students felt about their writing and their learning and how they gave some credit for that to me. I am the kind of person who needs to feel like I am making a difference in the world. Through a peaceful pedagogy, I feel like I am. When students have absolutely no frame of reference, no vocabulary, no experience at all with a genre, asking them to write something for a grade can produce anxiety levels so high that learning and growth become almost impossible.

Works Cited

Borenstein, Jeffrey. "Childhood Trauma Exposure Is All Too Common." *Psychology Today*, 14 Jan. 2019, https://www.psychologytoday.com/us/blog/brain-and-behavior/201901/childhood-trauma-exposure-is-all-too-common. Accessed 20 May 2019.

Graham, Steve, and Delores Perin. "A Meta-analysis of Writing Instruction for Adolescent Students." *Journal of Educational Psychology*, vol. 99, no. 3, 2007.

Heid, Markham. "Depression and Suicide Rates Are Rising Sharply in Young Americans, New Report Says. This May Be One Reason Why." *Time* 14 Mar. 2019, http://time.com/5550803/depression-suicide-rates-youth/. Accessed 20 May 2019.

Laderman, Gary. "Why I'm Easy: On Giving Lots of A's." *The Chronicle of Higher Education* 6 Aug. 2018, https://www.chronicle.com/article/Why-I-m-Easy-On-Giving-Lots/244144. Accessed 20 May 2019.

Lang, James. *Small Teaching: Everyday Lessons from the Science of Learning*. Josey-Bass, 2016.

Shaughnessy, Mina. *Errors and Expectations: A Guide for the Teacher of Basic Writing*. Oxford, 1979.

8. Affective Writing toward Feasible Futures: Helping Students Envision Triumph, Trauma, and Everything in Between

JIM ZIMMERMAN & CATHRYN MOLLOY

Writing instructors are famous for their concern for students' welfare and infamous for their contentious theoretical disputes about how best to teach writing. Complicating these realities, emotional and mental health problems are increasingly at the forefront of instructors' and administrators' concerns. For decades, some writing instructors have used a "writing as healing" approach wherein writers attempt to "get down on paper" the things that are bothering them, thus liberating their inner lives from these burdens and simultaneously making compelling connections between their private hurts and the sociopolitical realties that make them possible (Anderson and MacCurdy, DeSalvo, Herman, Payne). However, such approaches are rightly criticized because they enter hazardous therapeutic territory (Carello and Butler, Goggin and Goggin, Micciche, Worsham). Writing instructors lack the training and the long-term relationships necessary to invite and respond helpfully to students' emotional disclosures (Molloy and Zimmerman, unpublished paper).

Acknowledging that writing as healing methods can be problematic, this chapter pursues what we are calling a "writing for health" approach to productively engaging student writers' emotional lives. At its core, a "writing for health" pedagogical framework involves using future-oriented prompts that encourage students to explore the affective dimensions of what they think they want out of life. Assignments are cumulative in ways that reward writers for imagining and researching future experiences in a realistic manner, taking probabilities into account. Aspirational notions can be combined with observable trends and facts to help writers envision multiple possible futures that will be more specific and feasible, rather than vague and fantastic. We argue that instructors using a "writing for health" approach can facilitate rich exploration by creating feedback loops with students that will help them appreciate the vagaries of adult existence: the possibility of great success, disappointing failure, and everything in between.

Tapping into writers' abilities to compose probable futures with many contingencies in mind—both good and bad—is intended to promote metacognition and emotional growth. Rather than focusing on what went wrong in the past and risk fetishizing the emotional freight of those experiences, "writing for health" empowers students to build strong emotional connections to their future selves in order to suggest present action that might serve their future interests. In the process, we argue, the commitment to significant personal concerns will result in group cohesion, as well as better individual thinking, research, editing, and writing.

Writing that promotes health is based on two principles: first, it values informal, ungraded expressive writings that are anonymous and uninhibited, written for no audience at all, not even the self. Second, healthful writing is a cumulative, gradually more academic, scholarly, and professional project that culminates in carefully-designed, graded research-based assignments. These are intended to stimulate students in a non-threatening way toward the areas of human activity that they might find most interesting or rewarding five or ten years into the future. This research-based approach encourages students to customize the major assignments in order to meet their own needs. In the end, we emphasize the rigor of the research and the quality of the writing.

In imagining and piloting this approach, we combine the work of Daniel Gilbert (2006) with that of Pennebaker and Smyth (2016) to provide a theoretical framework. We specifically rely on their emphasis on future-oriented, emotional (or affective) work, which is supported by empirical studies that indicate the benefits of logical exploration of a student's future possibilities. The literature reveals an opportunity for students to, first, write expressively about the future—including possible difficulties as well as hopes and dreams—and follow such exercises with disciplined assignments aimed at learning more about themselves and the probabilistic futures they will inhabit. The ultimate goal is to use recursive writing practices to develop pragmatic pictures of what their prospective personal and professional successes could look like.

Although we avoid past-oriented "writing as healing" assignments, we address the inevitability that every writer's future will include daunting challenges. We indicate the ways students can benefit from envisioning and even embracing probable troubles as well as exciting successes. Pennebaker and

Smyth observed that "asking people to explore important issues in life and focusing on the potential benefits of these experiences can be helpful" (69). "Important issues" can include wonderful experiences and terrible ones, deliberate decisions and impulsive choices, as well as carefully formulated plans that work out and ones that don't.

Below, we sketch out a rationale for our position and offer some model prompts for use in a wide variety of writing courses. These assignments are aimed at greater student emotional self-efficacy through future-oriented, research-based therapeutic writing. Students can explore aspirations for any kind of future success, including money-making, creative work, and dedication to social change via nonprofit work. After this safe, non-threatening exploratory framework is explained, we share examples of expressive writing exercises and companion readings about emotional intelligence. Our emphasis is writer-centered prose, and we address issues relevant to writing anxiety. We first offer emotions-driven writing prompts designed to elicit anonymous, private writing that is, out of necessity, not graded. Research supports the idea that these ungraded exercises have the capacity to enhance the learning and writing students do in the more traditional, graded writing assignments that follow.

The Framework

To begin with, let's make it explicit that our approach works best when a writing course is viewed as a community of collaborative learners: novice writers and instructors come together to share candid, realistic visions of possible life experience, to look forward both hopefully and fearfully to the future. As writing instructors nourish these communities, they must value the solidarity that Richard Rorty promoted (1989) and the high standards appropriate to professional work. We believe any accidental promotion of competition in the writing classroom must be avoided, as well as any cruelty. Additionally, we suggest that instructors must espouse Jacques Ranciere's concept of "equal human intelligence" (1991) and refrain from the erroneous belief that they are more intelligent than their students. Likewise, instructors should make it clear that everyone present must commit to the idea of the future as a set of opportunities worth rigorous exploration. In this way, the future becomes Ranciere's "third thing" that everyone in the classroom can share throughout the course, with no one having the capacity to dominate or explicate as the group learns together.

When the writing classroom is non-threatening locus of learning where each writer is invited to project themselves into possible futures, collaboration is natural. Through shared research, informal presentations, and writing, students can feel safe as they engage in open, curious, and generous feedback and peer review. The result is a collaborative climate that engenders curiosity about social and technological probabilities as well everyone's individual possibilities. Students are more likely to establish meaningful, professional bonds via their shared purpose and motivation: to find out what they can through researching and writing about themselves in a forward-looking orientation. The common emotional content is that of forward-looking human experience, including the whole range of positive and negative emotions.

The subject matter or content portion of such a course is the enormous variety and richness of possible futures, and the metaphoric methodology is not healing or counseling, but coaching. Thus, by adopting a goal of equal intellectual and emotional health, the group of writers can systematically search possible futures as a means of invention that will not only give them practice as committed writers, but will also offer motivation to want to discover and share their findings. Quite the opposite of wallowing in disempowering narratives of personal defeat and pain, this focus on embracing and strategizing probable futures encourages agency and responsibility.

Through teaching agency in this way, we hope to increase and expand the disciplined practices and positive emotions that lead to competence and confidence. Curiosity and optimism, coupled with skepticism and commitment, can lead to students discovering lives they want to lead, even as they become aware of the probable trials and tribulations associated with the years ahead.

Affective writing explicitly addresses the full range of emotions, but rather than excavating the triumphs and traumas of a student's past, we turn their attention to the unknown future—an uncertain territory that nevertheless is associated with possibilities and probabilities worth formal study. To promise a future free from trauma is not realistic, but to explore the adult terrain with curiosity in a safe environment is to offer understanding not only of the students' lives ahead, but of others in families and communities living through those characteristic triumphs and traumas of adult life in private and public settings.

Writing pedagogy, despite all of the experimental developments of the past few decades, still promotes too much passivity in students. In that passivity, negative emotions are often fostered. We've witnessed a kind of creeping depression at the onset of adulthood encapsulated in the terror with which many of our students react to this question: "What are you going to do after college?" It evokes visible distress; the feeling of powerlessness is tangible. We need to recognize that it is a subtle, yet powerful and damaging form of cruelty to subject young people to questions they have no ability to answer.

"What will you do in five or ten years?" is an interesting question with vague, threatening, or even traumatic possible answers. Encouraging student writers to explore such questions thoughtfully, with the benefit of rigorous research and engaged feedback, can lead them to find meaningful and useful answers even as they develop new skills in research, writing, and editing.

Future-Oriented Affective Activities and Assignments

"The future" is a vague concept. It can mean next month or fifty years hence. Thinking about the future generates a spectrum of emotional reactions, and a general uneasiness is most often associated with the future. Ideas about career, geography, and family are blurry or even disturbing visions that most young adults have in common, and the problem of paying off college debt is terrifying to many. On the positive side, in any given group of students, some may be dreaming of a wedding, others look forward to studying abroad, or maybe someone savors their prospective commission as an officer in the military. On the negative side, one student may dread the certainty that he will be living back at home after graduation, while another is equally certain she will be finding it difficult to get accepted to law school. Those with a gravely-ill parent will be focused on life experience in a completely different way from those whose loved ones are experiencing no health problems. "The future" can mean next week to one person, a year from now to another, and 2030 to a third.

One way to begin the process of acclimating writers to the future is to ask the simple question, "How do you feel when someone asks you what are you going to do after college?" This question can prompt a brief session of expressive writing that is neither graded nor shared, but the topic can still be used as the basis of a discussion. (See Appendix for all of the writing prompts exercises, and assignments mentioned.)

Once it is clear that several students default to "I don't know" as the response to what they're going to do after college, and assuming some negative emotions are obvious when that question rears its ugly head, an instructor can offer a scenario like this:

> Suppose you are speaking with an older person who asks you the dreadful question, "What are you doing when you graduate?" Notice that "I don't know" is a conversation-killer. Is there anything you can say that has the potential to give something back and possibly prolong the exchange until it reaches more interesting or even useful territory?

In pairs or small groups, students can collaboratively compose responses that go beyond "I don't know." As students at the Naval Academy are taught, saying "I don't know" is not acceptable, and instead, should be "I'll find out." Without the military rigor, we are suggesting the same thing. Together, students coach each other to develop answers that will keep a conversation going. Such responses can feature interests, experiences, hopes, and of course the proverbial dreams (or fantasies). Each student should complete this exercise with several versions of their possible future. Whether it is called an "elevator speech" or a "cocktail party" gambit, it is a ready-made offering that provides an opportunity to have an interesting conversation, perhaps even to make a valuable connection.

When several students are willing to share their composed responses to the group, the instructor can inquire about the different kinds of emotion associated with having a ready answer that gives the interlocutor something to go on. The competence in composing an answer to a frightening, yet probable question can lead to greater confidence. Subsequently, such general responses about interests and hopes can be further developed by an assignment that asks students to research three possible experiences they could imagine having in the next five or ten years. The assignment might require that at least one of the experiences be connected to a specific location, organization, or profession as an impetus to further research (see Appendix).

These informal introductory exercises and assignments, appropriate to the beginning of a first-year writing course (but also surprisingly useful with graduating seniors) create the climate within which later writing assignments can flourish. Additionally, there is an opportunity to have students write about how the current course can contribute to their future well-being. This segment can be a formal assignment that requires curricular research. It's also possible to add the question, "What kind of work-related reading and writing do you expect to be doing in your post-college life?" Students might, for example, create an infographic to chart how they'll use their time in school toward the myriad experiences they hope to have later.

By far the richest and most rewarding future-oriented writing assignment we recommend is the feasibility study. Although this may be ambitious for a first-semester freshman writing course, it fits very well in our first core course, "Introduction to Studies in Writing, Rhetoric and Technical Communication," where we see results that are characterized by intellectual and emotional satisfaction, as well as possible roadmaps that students may actually use.

The feasibility study is a three-stage process, with oral presentations, informal peer feedback, and graded feedback at each of the following stages: proposal, progress report, and deliverable. By immediately developing a classroom culture that features sharing and collaboration regarding the worries and opportunities of post-college life, instructors can feel confident that students will be willing to try out ideas in the classroom. One non-threatening method is to arrange chairs in the front of the room for an informal panel discussion in which students volunteer their vague ideas about what they would want to explore. After getting feedback from the group, the students can write up a rough draft of a proposal and submit it as a quiz. Following that (with instructor feedback), students can be assigned to write a formal proposal. That can be graded and the feedback associated with it can lead to the next step: progress. Progress can also be reported in a panel format, or if the students have something they want to present individually, it can be slightly more formal. In the end, the feasibility study takes the form of a report that documents what it would take to accomplish the student's desired goal.

This sequence affords students an opportunity to explore the practicalities of a future real-world project, such as starting a business, becoming a freelance travel writer, creating an app, founding a magazine, or directing a nonprofit organization. The idea is that students are able to discover the skills and resources needed to become what they aspire to be, while at the same time getting a taste of what the experience is like for older people who are actually doing the things the students imagine they would enjoy. Importantly, the feasibility study forces them to consider and research challenges, limitations, and possibilities for failing as much as it invites them to revel in the emotional riches of imagining wildly succeeding at something that is quite ambitious.

In a recent, memorable feasibility study, a student prepared a dynamic, multimodal project in Adobe Spark in which she began with affective content to explain the impetus for the design of a music app she calls "Musiconnect." She explained: "Loving myself and the life I was blessed to live has always been my biggest challenge in life. Once I found myself hungry for help in fighting the demons clouding my head, I decided to turn to music" (DeVincent n.p.). This is the entirety of her self-disclosure of emotional turbulence in her past. The rest of the report follows a feasibility study, replete with research, tentative in its claims to newness, and thorough in its examinations of limitations, competition, and material sustainability. Moving from self to community, she explained:

> MusiConnect is made for absolutely anyone. However, when creating the app, the main target audience was teens and college students. According to Jenae Cohn's study on smartphone use by undergrad college students in the article

"Devilish Smartphones' and the 'Stone-Cold' Internet: Implications of the Technology Addiction Trope in College Student Digital Literacy Narratives," "teens commonly refer to their social media use as 'addictive'" (Cohn). Because younger people spend so much time on their phones, and more specifically on social media, MusiConnect is a great option for young people to experience social media, as well as a music streaming app. (DeVincent n.p.).

Our major requires a community-based learning course, an internship, and a capstone course that facilitates the production of a professional portfolio for graduating students. The community-based learning courses afford students the opportunity to volunteer twenty hours of work in a setting they're interested in, whether it's "business and industry," "the community," "nonprofits," or "the health sciences." The experiences students have in work settings allow them to envision possible futures in these realms, even as they write, edit, and do social media for their host entities, and our capstone course offers them opportunity to make these emotional connections.

We are aware that, in Cintron's phrase, "the overproduction of mass desire" is a hazard for young people. The idea that everyone can obtain everything they wish for, to simplify Cintron's concept, is detrimental to what Daniel Pink calls "mastery" and what Tomas Chamorro-Premuzik calls "competence." The hard work of achieving something based on autonomously chosen purpose will never be undertaken by young adults who have no realistic ideas about the experiences of adulthood.

Ultimately, any future-oriented exercise or assignment, graded or ungraded, is emotionally valuable if it is constructed to emphasize the possibility of affective forecasting through imagination and actual research. In fact, "feelings," when closely observed and well-defined as a form of research become things students might feel better prepared to mediate. As we note above, expressive writing can be informative to the writer, even if it is discarded. The practice of writing expressively promotes the related practice of paying attention to one's moods. Getting to know oneself through the multiple possible futures afforded by affective forecasting is likely to reap dividends in the present in the form of intellectual and academic writing, as well as emotionally-focused work.

The Future on Paper and in Digital Formats

Forecasting emotional experience from the platform of research-based writing allows everyone in the writing classroom to engage with something with which no one has superior expertise. Everyone is an equal novice, which promotes sympathetic and generous collaboration. Whether it's curiosity about a future course in the curriculum or research on the future of various kinds of professional, personal, and community opportunities, each writer needs the help of imagination, writing, research, and other people.

What happened in the past is different in degree and kind from that which will happen in the future. The idea of counter-induction is relevant here because too often human beings expect things to go on as they always have, when in fact they have never gone on in the same way. This is especially the case for college students, whose past as young adults is so brief compared to what we hope will be their future. We want to find ways to show our students that the past was filled with givens, constraints and affordances independent of agency; the future depends on agency. What emotions we want, we can seek. What emotions we look for in our research and writing are the ones we can theorize and practice and increase the probability of experiencing more often than not. That said, we openly acknowledge that what gets done in a future-oriented writing assignment does not determine the distant future. The result might even be just as much or more about the present and the immediate future, about emotional understanding of adulthood and its many possible experiences, good and bad, joyful and fearful. The feasibility of embracing the future is increased by the practical approaches to seeing its many facets, and how everyone shares the mysterious unknowns awaiting them.

Appendix: Prompts, Exercises, and Assignments

1. Non-graded prompt, for the student's eyes only: Quickly list the feelings that come to mind when an older person asks you, "What are you doing after college?"
   After you have listed several, pick the one that feels strongest and write about it.
2. Non-graded prompt: Thinking about the same general question (e.g., "What are you going to do after you graduate?"), list as many interests, wishes and hopes as you can think of. Freely fantasize!
3. Exercise based on #2: With a partner, interview each other and mention the interests, wishes, hopes, and fantasies you are comfortable revealing. Then help each other compose a useful response to the question, "What do you want to do with your life?" Imagine an older person asking it—a person with connections, who would possibly help you if you gave them an inkling of your imaginary futures.

4. First graded assignment: using the answer you have composed in the exercise (#3), develop some possible future activities (internships, jobs, a career, hobbies, volunteer work, entrepreneurial ideas, or whatever else naturally follows from the general statement of interests, hopes, and wishes for your future. (250 words)
5. Exercise and freewrite: List all of the things about your various possible futures that you are looking forward to, based on the first graded assignment. After you have eight or ten or a dozen, rank them. Then write a paragraph or two about each of your top three.
6. Graded assignment: Select your top-ranked idea and imagine what it looks like in one, five, and ten years after graduation. Then do some research! (500 words)
7. Select your three top-ranked futures and imagine what they look like in five years after graduation. Then do the research. (500 words)
8. Decide on one possible future course of action (job, career, further education) as well as a particular calendar year in your future, and research it extensively. (1,500 words) This could take the form of a feasibility study (how to do it, what it would require, how probable the positive outcome is), a research paper, or a multimodal, digital project (blog, website, or some other form of digital presentation).

Works Cited

Anderson, Charles M., and Marian M. MacCurdy. *Writing and Healing: Toward an Informed Practice.* Urbana, IL, National Council of Teachers of English, 2000.

Carello, Janice, and Lisa D. Butler. "Potentially Perilous Pedagogies: Teaching Trauma is Not the Same as Trauma-Informed Teaching." *Journal of Trauma & Dissociation*, vol. 15, no. 2, 2014, pp. 153–68.

Chamorro-Premuzic, Tomas. *Confidence: How Much You Really Need and How to Get It.* New York, Plume, 2013.

Cintron, Ralph. "Democracy and Its Limitations." *The Public Work of Rhetoric: Citizen-Scholars and Civic Engagement*, edited by John M. Ackerman and David J. Coogan, U of South Carolina P, 2009.

Desalvo, Louise. *Writing as a Way of Healing: How Telling our Stories Transforms our Lives.* Boston, MA, Beacon P, 2000.

DeVincent, Diana. "Musiconnect," 2018. https://spark.adobe.com/page/dskML2LiCDs1t/.

Gilbert, Daniel. *Stumbling on Happiness.* New York, Knopf, 2006.

Goggin, Peter, and Maureen Goggin. "Presence in Absence: Discourses and Teaching (in, on, and about) Trauma." *Trauma and the Teaching of Writing*, edited by Shane Borrowman, U of New York P, 2005, pp. 29–51.

Herman, Judith. *Trauma and Recovery: The Aftermath of Violence—from Domestic Abuse to Political Terror*. New York, NY, Basic Books, 1992.

Micciche, Laura R. "Writing through Trauma: The Emotional Dimensions of Teaching Writing." *Composition Studies* vol. 29, no. 1, 2001, pp. 131–41.

Molloy, C., and Zimmerman J. ""I've Gotten a Lot of Sympathy and That's Not What I'm Looking For": Epistemic and Ontological Violence in Writing as Healing Pedagogies." *Violence in the Work of Composition*, edited by Scott Gage and Kristie Fleckenstein, unpublished paper.

Payne, Michelle. "A Strange Unaccountable Something: Historicizing Sexual Abuse Essays." *Writing and Healing: Toward an Informed Practice*, edited by Charles Anderson and Marian McCurdy, National Council of Teachers of English, 2000, 115–57.

Pennebaker, James W., and Smyth, Joshua M. *Opening Up by Writing It Down: How Expressive Writing Improves Health and Eases Emotional Pain*. 3rd ed. New York, Guilford Press, 2016.

Pink, Daniel. Drive: *The Surprising Truth about What Motivates Us*. New York, Riverhead 2009.

Ranciere, Jacques. *The Ignorant Schoolmaster: Five Lessons in Intellectual Emancipation*. Translated by Kristin Ross. Stanford UP, 1991.

Rorty, Richard. *Contingency, Irony, and Solidarity*. Cambridge UP, 1989.

Worsham, Lynn. 2006. "Composing (Identity) in a Post Traumatic Age." *Identity Papers*, edited by Bronwyn T. Williams, UP of Colorado, 2006, pp. 170–81.

9. Authoring Well-being: Emotional Literacy as a Commonplace for First-Year Writing Pedagogy

JESSICA SCHREYER, LAURA MANGINI, & SABATINO MANGINI

> Emotion matters to teachers because the classroom is alive with bodies, hearts, and selves, and because learning is joyous, exciting, frightening, risky, passionate, boring, disappointing, and enraging. Emotion matters are inscribed in the teaching situation, a point too often forgotten (Micciche, Doing Emotion 105).

Navigating the rocky terrain of college requires a certain skill set; is there any other location in which you are expected to branch out, connect, immerse, and yet be your own independent person all at the same time? There is no emotional GPS for college, and students often feel isolated, stressed, uncertain, and anxious. This can impact their academic achievement, social development, and general sense of well-being. First-year students, in particular, can struggle with acknowledging and understanding their emotions, and may lack the emotional literacy and support system they need to sustain a purposeful transition from the homes, people, discourses, and classrooms they've known to the strange land of college. As composition professors, we identified the exigency of working with students within the classroom to navigate this transition. This chapter is a narrative exploration of our attempts to integrate emotional literacy into a first-year writing pedagogy.

Exigence of Emotional Literacy

Spendlove defines emotional literacy as "our ability through thinking to recognize, manage, comprehend, and suitably communicate our emotions and to understand how they shape our actions and relationships and influence our thinking"; further, "emotions are profoundly cultural and social, and they are bound up with thought, rather than existing in opposition to it" (4);

they are "not additive or somehow separate from other forms of communication" (Micciche, "Staying"). Gauging our students' emotional intelligence is a powerful measure of their well-being, believed to "promote positive social functioning by helping individuals to detect others' emotion states, adopt others' perspectives, enhance communication, and regulate behavior" (Brackett et al. 96). These are well-developed concepts, but emotional literacy is not generally considered a driving force behind current writing pedagogies, often viewed as "a lesser strategy of argument, one that is distinct from and inferior to reason or logic ... emotions have long been categorized as anti-intellectual, as standing in opposition to reason or thought" (Winans 150). Viewing emotion as inferior limits our students' well-being in consequential ways.

The 2018 National College Health Assessment from the American College Health Association shared some troubling statistics: 31% of students indicated that within the two weeks prior to the study? they "felt overwhelming anxiety," 17.2% "felt so depressed that it was difficult to function," and within the last twelve months, 12.7% "seriously considered suicide" (14). Anxiety and depression were listed as the top concerns for students visiting campus counseling centers between 2013 and 2018, according to the Center for Collegiate Mental Health (CCMH) 2018 Annual Report. Although there was a 30% rise in students seeking appointments at counseling centers (between 2009–10 and 2014–15), enrollment grew by only 5% (Winerman 88). While the percentage of students who use counseling centers has grown, the stigma still leaves students feeling alone and reluctant to visit the centers. A University of Richmond student admits: "When you're going through [issues with bipolar disorder] and you're looking around on campus, it doesn't seem like anyone else is going through what you're going through. It was probably the loneliest experience" (qtd. in Reilly). Further, Wolf found that students' thoughts of suicide and self-harm are more prevalent in school environments with higher stigmas against mental health problems. The necessity of dialogue that is stripped of stigma is paramount, and helping students learn emotional intelligence and regulation is important for their success in college, their vocations, and their personal relationships. It is also crucial for students' well-being for college professors and the college community as a whole to acknowledge an "interrelationship between emotion and thought" and to "recognize that emotions are not simply private, individual experiences, but instead are embodied phenomena that are profoundly social and cultural in nature" (Winans 150). Our shared classroom emphasis on emotional literacy allows students to find a commonplace of non-stigmatized emotion in a safe space of camaraderie and composition.

Pedagogical Framework for Emotional Literacy

Classrooms can be a welcoming place to help students learn about and discuss emotions. Professors cannot take the place of trained professional therapists, but we can serve as models of people who work on developing our own emotional literacy. We celebrate writing of the self which embodies emotion; Magnet et al. point out "techniques of the self are often seen as 'aesthetic' or decadent individualized practices divorced from meaningful collective political action ... Arts of the self become practices of micropolitics when they enter into the life of a community or to relations between them" (8). As professors, we embrace the collective space in which we share our selves through emotion, and through developing this space in our writing classes, we hope to create a culture of belonging. Thompson aptly describes the development of such a culture:

> The place of connection and joy that we hope for in the classroom asks us to invite in a culture of belonging. Such an invitation requires understanding "belonging" in the big sense of the word—not only to the people who are physically present but also to all of their relations, both living and ancestors ... I have come to see that students bring into the classroom their own individual stories as well as those of many others (biological and chosen family, friends, spirits). Nurturing high-quality and original writing and discussion asks us to see students as capable of tapping into knowledge and wisdom that predated their current physical presence on earth. And tapping into emotions related to this historical memory as well (85).

Through this work helping students develop their emotional literacy while growing as writers, we can nurture the development of whole learners. After establishing our shared values and goals, we agreed upon a connecting-composing-cultivating approach toward integrating emotional literacy into first-year writing pedagogy. Later in this chapter, we discuss how our classroom environments fostered improved opportunities for emotional literacy through an interplay of *connecting* to each other as humans, *composing* with and about emotion, and *cultivating* individual and collective well-being.

Emotional Literacy in Action

Jessica's Story: Defining and Describing Emotions through Writing with Photographs

Meaningful learning experiences often start from a point of connection. I wanted to help students develop pathways to connect to me, each other, and their writing in ways that might improve their educational experience.

I hoped to encourage students to develop more caring relationships in the classroom and for this to assist in meeting learning outcomes. After contemplation, I revamped our daily writing exercises and longer writing prompts to integrate discussion of emotional literacy.

First, I considered my goals for our daily writing exercises and what outcomes I had previously achieved. My overarching goal for the exercises is for students to learn that they can write every day, develop their creativity, and be descriptive. Students have reported that these quick exercises improved their confidence as writers, provided opportunities to get to know their classmates, and helped them become more descriptive. As I further reflected on the outcomes, I noticed that while students had been eager to express a broad range of feelings, they often wanted to keep this writing private. Therefore, I began exploring intentional ways to use this writing to develop their connection with others, and to better understand their own experiences and feelings. To do this, I piloted efforts incorporating emotional literacy into the curriculum while simultaneously developing reading, writing, and thinking skills. I felt it was important to do this early in the semester, so started with very low-stakes writing.

On the first day of class, I projected a photograph from an online repository of a girl in a classroom, and asked the students to write a quick story about the character's first day of school. Later in the week, we read several short stories that included photographs and discussed the characters' experiences and how those were reflected by the photographs. At this point, rather than adding information about personal experiences, students wrote fictional accounts based on the photographs to make discussing emotions less personal and more about the writing itself. I chose photographs that included people who were engaging in diverse experiences and exhibiting different expressions. During the early stages of this exercise, most students tended to write simple descriptions with limited depth, such as that the person in the story was happy, sad, or mad. After engaging in this exercise for several classes, I introduced tools for naming emotions, including a chart featuring faces expressing different emotions and an image of an emotions model (Plutchik 349). We discussed how writers can use these tools to describe what the person in the photograph was doing and how they might react or feel within any given situation.

As noted, in the beginning of the semester, students wrote fictional narratives about characters in the photographs; however, as time went on, I would sometimes request that students imagine they were the person in the photograph or taking the photograph. I realized at this point that students in all of my sections were more openly sharing their writing than previous semesters and the writing was more descriptive. As the semester continued, students described more complex or varied emotions. Some chose to share personal experiences that mirrored things in the photographs. Overall, these exercises improved students' ability to write on demand; compared to previous semesters, students started writing more quickly and continued writing longer without prompting. The exercises also provided a way for students to get to know one another and to imagine another person's experience and perspective. One student, who began the class never speaking to her classmates unless assigned a group activity, told me that she had planned to keep to herself, but found herself curious about her classmates after hearing their stories from the writing exercises. She made several friendships by the end of the semester.

Importantly, incorporating these emotional literacy practices took no extra class time; I simply modified an existing practice to make it more valuable and engaging. I saw immediate improvement in the outcomes of the daily writing, and students were more attentive as they wrote and discussed their writing. It also elicited a different kind of response; for instance, students had to overcome a challenge when I gave them an intense image but asked them to cap their response at a certain number of words. Students used their learning from the exercises as they wrote their longer, higher-stakes pieces. For instance, as they crafted and revised their "Snapshot in Time" narrative writing assignments, they used more descriptive language in their writing and dialogue than they did in the daily writing exercises, and they chose very specific language to describe the characters' emotions. Many students commented in their final reflections about their narratives that the aspect of writing they spent the most time on was considering the best words to choose to describe the character's emotions to help make them more realistic.

Perhaps most importantly, students were talking and connecting to each other more before, during, and after class than I had seen in previous semesters. Instead of silent people playing on their phones before class, there was often lively conversation or laughter. More of them greeted me as I walked into the room. This leads me to believe that the connections made from these exercises allowed us to cultivate learning in a unique way: creating closer relationships, providing enhanced trust during our in-class and peer-review exercises, and allowing students to feel more fully engaged in the course. Over half of the student's course reflections noted appreciation for the relationships they had made with other students in the class and feeling like the class culture had made them work harder on their writing.

Laura's Story: Meditation, Mindfulness, and Happiness

As a professor with diagnosed generalized anxiety, I am keenly aware of the hidden anxieties of others. Human beings have a remarkable ability to hide mental illness, and often in students, it resurfaces in other ways—absenteeism, distraction, withdrawal, indifference, or even anger. Recent studies indicate that only 36.9% of those experiencing anxiety or depression while in college are seeking mental health services ("Understanding the Facts"). I can never assume that in a given semester that the students suffering from mental health issues are seeking appropriate treatment, but one of my biggest goals as a teacher is to make my classroom a safe, relaxing place of learning. I'm reluctant to even label this a feminist pedagogy; it's simply a practical teaching practice. I'm not trying to single out students who are depressed and anxious; I want my classroom to be a place where *all* students can flourish.

The first means of accomplishing this is by introducing meditation and mindfulness into my daily lessons. Beginning a class by creating a common emotional balance among my students has improved my students' attention and productivity significantly. College campuses are hubs of energy, but also incredibly arousing sources for those with anxiety. Beginning the class with a calming, contemplative mental exercise such as a guided meditation can allow students time to transition from the mayhem of the world to a place of greater serenity and peace.

Meditations can be chosen according to the class's agenda. There is a myriad of free meditation resources now that coincide with focus, motivation, and creativity, all of which are important in the writing classroom. A 2017 study investigated students' experiences in a course focused on meditation within a 15-week course: "Eighty nine percent of students (n=25) reported being more focused on the present moment . . . In addition, 86% of students (n=24) reported an increase in reflective thinking" (Crowley and Munk 94). The biggest takeaway for my students was that many of them began meditating outside of the classroom, as well as lamenting other classes in which they felt their performance would have been enhanced by pre-classwork meditations.

Facilitating a grounded start to each class opens the door for more willing conversations about emotions and well-being. My "happiness" classes, as they are now referred to by my students, bring the study of well-being to the forefront. We blend other disciplines into our writing to grapple with the question of what it means to be emotionally well; all of my composition classes research happiness. Along the way, we broaden our emotional vocabulary by not only learning new ways to describe our emotions in English, but by also tapping into other cultures and languages to find words to describe emotions that can only be captured in a foreign tongue. Students love sharing language from their cultures, and we have written about a time we experienced a hard-to-name emotion. Topics were aplenty, but these papers explored emotions such as the German feeling of *schadenfreude*, which means to take pleasure in another's misfortune, as well as a familiar feeling of college students: the Japanese declaration of *Koi No Yokan*, which is a phrase to describe the feeling upon a first encounter signaling the inevitability of falling in love with that person. Sharing emotional experiences and removing ourselves from the experience to look at the emotion as a cultural entity on its own is transformation; there is this realization that emotions are ubiquitous and, perhaps more importantly, worth sharing.

To cultivate our emotional journey, students ultimately present multimodal research projects sharing their top three keys to happiness. Their traditionally written literature reviews investigate how they define emotional well-being through rigorous inquiry into what the experts postulate, but the magic happens through the creation of their creative genres. By composing in different modes and genres, my students are able to enact their personal keys to achieving their own emotional well-being. Having students become more aware of what's important to their own emotional well-being has been enlightening to my students and to me as well.

Sabatino's Story: Memoired Commonplaces

My storied experiences with students who have composed and shared their memoirs in class have animated a core pedagogical belief: *memoir genres emotional commonplaces for selves, texts, and audiences to meet*. No matter the emotional tenor of our memoir topics, student stories resonated most with self and other when the authorship explored the emotional impact of the memoir's lived scenes. I became enamored with the idea of asking students to write a memoir that responded to this question: What specific scene in my life evokes powerful emotion?

In the time since, current student memoirs demonstrate more fully than past projects how genre conventions ask a memoirist to construct narrative scenes that show emotion and to interweave reflective insights that attend to the how, what, why, and when of the story's pathos. The memoir emerges as an emotional commonplace for the past-protagonist self and present author-self to meet—and when this text is presented to an outside audience, the other is invited into this space as well. In the pedagogical narrative I have coauthored with my students, emotion did not make explicit the need to explore memoir; memoir made explicit the need to explore emotion.

How do we travel to this memoired-commonplace of emotion? In addition to community building, conceptualizing emotion, interpreting emotion-expressive texts, and reading past student memoirs in our course digital archive, we foreground informal writing as an intertextual part of the memoir drafting process. Students author myriad genres and modes in social, low-stakes situations to navigate emotion before, during, and after they compose drafts of the memoir. In our first sustained in-class writing session, a Lee Martin prompt asks us to use a personal physical object so we can compose a scene that evokes "a moment of emotional resonance and complexity" (13). The next session involves composing "hiraeth" scenes to inhabit the Welsh concept of longing for a lost home. Other informal assignments, which ask students to interact with the emotional language and themes living in the memoir draft, include *remixes* (storyboards, six-word memoirs, found poetry), *reconsiderations* (counterfactual scenes to construct an alternate outcome as well as empathy letters from other characters or past protagonist-selves) and *reflections* (from vlogs to Wizard-of-Oz revelations about the heart, brain, and nerve of the story).

Students compose these informal assignments to generate content for the formal memoir, to remix the memoir in ways that make explicit the multiplicities of self, context, and emotion in and around the story, to revise the memoir's emotional language to mirror their broadening repertoire of emotional literacy, and to reflect on the affordances and constraints of the memoir-genre's relationship to emotion. In public blog reflections, writers' round-tables that follow in-class memoir presentations, and private conference conversations with me, students express recurring themes of how their memoir experience proved therapeutic, necessary, life-changing. Students share how they valued—often needed—a community to listen more than they voice a desire for editorial feedback. Our course-approach to memoir cultivates embodied social-inquiries into how the stories we tell ourselves shape our emotional-being, emotional-doing, and emotional-knowing in the world.

In this spirit, I share a continual class scene: we listen to a fellow author read the last word of her memoir. Instead of clapping, classmates leave their seats to hug the author. They offer each other tissues, share smiles and tears and eye-rolls as they commiserate and empathize over the story's emotional arc. I have not asked the students to enact such emotional bonding. I do not wish to disrupt the organic manifestation of shared emotions, so I participate by continuing to bear witness. The author waves me over to join the group. This gesture of kindness and trust allows me to join the author's convergence of past and current life scenes—disrupting the teacher-student binary so we can meet as authors and as storied human beings who belong to a community. The author says to us all, "It was hard at first, but I needed to tell that story. I feel better." I sense the vibrations of former students who have written and spoken their memoirs in this room. I hear emotion in the echoes of their authorial-ancestral voices. I wonder if my students in this moment feel their own memoirs extending beyond the page: past and present commonplaces of emotion interacting with selves, texts, and others. Our stories ongoing.

Experiential Data Themes

We used four lenses to view themes in our experiential data. First, we interpreted informal and formal student texts, with emphasis on the well-being research paper, memoir, daily writing exercises, and writing reflections. Second, we observed how our new curricular design impacted in-class student engagement and social interactivity. Third, we situated student-teacher conferences as sites to discuss emotion. Fourth, we dialogued our professor-experiences via personal pedagogy reflections and shared conversations among ourselves.

Together, we noted how the implemented pedagogy flourished within a fluid interplay of connecting, composing, and cultivating emotional literacy as a commonplace. We started the semester with a pedagogical intention: join students in making explicit emotional connections with each other as human beings. This intention proved prescient because students reflected on how our in-class commitment to ice-breaking exercises and informal conversations about emotion created a community of trust in the course and sense of belonging to each other. From there, our experiential data suggest when students composed informal and formal texts with and about emotion, as well as cultivated emotional well-being with self and others in the course community, they were better positioned to: (1) engage in composing processes that enabled us to interact with our own emotions and empathize with the emotions of other people; (2) investigate language's impact on our ability to express emotion; and (3) identify implicit and explicit manifestations of emotion within myriad literary and rhetorical genres.

By focusing on connecting, composing, and cultivating, we noted that we made more explicit our implied and long-held pedagogical aims of joining students to nurture individual and collective well-being within welcoming writing environments. The intentional shift to use emotion as space for unity—amid the diversity of human experiences—resulted in students demonstrating increased social bonding, reduced stress, and improvement in their confidence and ability as writers. As Micciche explains, emotion is central to the teaching and learning experience as we come together to make meaning, to share stories, and to think. She implores us "to stay with emotion" in the classroom and elsewhere, because "staying with emotion is staying with others, for, without others, emotion has no meaning or effect. In that sense, I see the power of emotion studies still in its ability to foreground how coalitions of people, of causes, of diverse others come together and/or break apart" (*Staying*). A pedagogical framework for emotional literacy allows students to incorporate their emotional growth alongside their academic and intellectual growth—as these phenomena are not only interconnected to each other but also to a students' sense of well-being. Given that emotional wellness complements students' academic and vocational success and helps students cultivate self-efficacy and social-belonging in varied writing situations, emotional literacy is a welcome addition to a student-focused composition pedagogy.

Jessica: Defining and Describing Emotions through Writing with Photographs

Readings and Resources

Photograph Repositories

I use a variety of online resources to find interesting photographs for exercises and writing prompts. Generally, I select and encourage students to choose photographs that are in the public domain or freely available for use, particularly since we sometimes do online multimodal writing. The following are a few sites that provide a good variety of images:

> "The Commons." *Flickr,* Yahoo!, https://www.flickr.com/commons/.
> "Free Photographs for Commercial Use." *Morguefile*, https://morguefile.com/.
> "The New York Public Library Digital Collections." The *New York Public Library*, https://digitalcollections.nypl.org/.
> "Stunning Free Images to Use Anywhere." *Pixabay*, https://pixabay.com/.

Readings about Emotions

Many of my students need more development of their reading skills and working on this often helps their writing. "Hard Feelings" is a reading that provides a challenge for them, as it is a lengthy piece with some high-level ideas and vocabulary. Because of those challenges, I ask them to work in groups to discern meaning and to then report back summaries of their group's paragraphs to the class. By dividing the article into parts, the reading is more manageable. From working with this article, students can get a better understanding of how scientists define emotions while practicing their reading, writing, and thinking skills.

Beck, Julie. "Hard Feelings: Science's Struggle to Define Emotions." *The Atlantic*, 24 Feb. 2015, https://www.theatlantic.com/health/archive/2015/02/hard-feelings-sciences-struggle-to-define-emotions/385711/

"The Nature of Emotions" provides several helpful paragraphs to help students recognize how scientists study emotions, the importance of understanding emotions, and it also provides several helpful visuals about naming and understanding emotions. While we do not utilize the entire article, using pieces of it has proven beneficial.

Plutchik, Robert. "The Nature of Emotions: Human Emotions Have Deep Evolutionary Roots, a Fact That May Explain Their Complexity and Provide Tools for Clinical Practice." *American Scientist*, vol. 89, no. 4, 2001, pp. 344–50. JSTOR.

Video about Emotions
To further explore the definitions and explanations of different words for emotions, this Ted Talk provides a historical and cultural perspective of how we think about and label emotions, and how our thoughts and language impact our understanding of emotion.

Smith, Tiffany Watt. *The History of Human Emotions.* www.ted.com, https://www.ted.com/talks/tiffany_watt_smith_the_history_of_human_emotions.

Exercises
Our in-class writing exercises are meant to build up and prepare for a longer, graded writing prompt. An important aspect of these exercises is building writing confidence while also gaining more knowledge about being descriptive and thoughtfully making writing choices. In this case, they are asked to be thoughtful about the definitions and descriptions for various types of emotions. This is an outline of one week's progression of daily writing activities:

Monday
Show students a photograph in which a person or people are displaying an exaggerated or obvious facial expression or body language. Ask students to write a detailed story about what is going on and how the person is feeling.

Wednesday

Show students two photographs where the people are displaying a similar emotion, such as sadness. Ask the students to write a story for each one. After the writing exercise, form small groups and ask them to compare and contrast the stories and how they imagined the people were feeling. As a class, have students create a list of as many specific emotion words as possible to describe a character's emotions. After creating the initial list, ask the small groups to use whatever tools they have, such as dictionaries, phones, or other books, to add to the list.

Friday

Ask the students to bring in four photographs in which people are engaging in similar activities, such as playing at the beach, walking a dog, or eating. Then, ask them to write about the people in their photographs and what makes them compelling characters. Using the word list created by the class during the previous session, have students apply the descriptive words to their photographs and write some dialogue that expresses these emotions for the characters. Then, form small groups to discuss how and why different activities or settings for those activities might elicit different types of emotions. Finally, ask the group to pick their favorite photograph and collaborate to write a detailed story using descriptive language and dialogue.

Prompts

After and along with working on various short writing exercises, students then compose longer pieces based on writing prompts. "A Snapshot in Time" is one of these prompts.

A Snapshot in Time

For this assignment, you will be expanding on our daily writing exercises in which we explored how to describe what a character is thinking and feeling. This narrative writing assignment asks you to write about a snapshot in time. You will write about a person or place in a very descriptive way from the perspective of the person in the photograph or the person taking the photograph. Your narrative should lead the reader to a revelation or broader understanding of the person or people you are describing. The subject of your writing is based on a photograph of your choice. You must choose the photograph from one of the online photograph repository links on our class website. This essay can be written in the first or third person, but is a work of fiction. Remember that you are striving for extensive description and interesting dialogue; you also want to clearly describe the emotions of the narrator or character. Remember to consider what about this snapshot in time is meaningful; why is this experience significant; and what larger idea or feeling about this person or place you want to emerge from the writing.

Laura: Meditation, Mindfulness, and Happiness

Readings and Resources

Some of the readings and resources pertaining to emotional literacy that I have used in conjunction with the aforementioned lessons and discussions are as follows:

> Robson, David. "Future—The 'Untranslatable' Emotions You Never Knew You Had." *BBC*, 26 Jan. 2017, www.bbc.com/future/story/20170126-the-untranslatable-emotions-you-never-knew-you-had.
> Smith, Tiffany Watt. "The Secret Joys of Schadenfreude." *The Guardian*, Guardian News and Media, 14 Oct. 2018, www.theguardian.com/global/2018/oct/14/the-secret-joys-of-schadenfreude-why-it-shouldnt-be-a-guilty-pleasure.

Specific meditations under five-minutes long that I have had success with in class:

> Insider Tech. "Deepak Chopra's Go-To 3-Minute Meditation To Stay Focused." *YouTube*, 20 Apr. 2017, www.youtube.com/watch?v=4Bs0qUB3BHQ.
> Pottenger, Chelsea. "3 Minute Guided Body Scan Meditation." *YouTube*, 18 Sept. 2017, www.youtube.com/watch?v=KcZ0aveOoJs.
> Stop, Breathe & Think. "3-Minute Mindful Breathing Meditation (Relieve Stress)." *YouTube*, 4 Mar. 2016, www.youtube.com/watch?v=SEfs5TJZ6Nk.

Suggested Meditation Apps:

> Mind Works: https://mindworks.org/
> Calm: https://www.calm.com/ (Calm College now available for free to select universities)

Exercises

Short Daily activities: Two fun, quick daily activities I have used to engage students in emotional literacy include "Tweet your feelings" and the "Emotion of the Day."

Emotion of the Day

Before class starts, I write a feeling on the board that I assume many of my students are unfamiliar with (for example, *empathy* or *bemused*). Then I ask students if anyone knows what it means; after it is defined, students complete a quick blog or journal entry in which they record this new emotion and their understanding of it, as well as a possible instance they have experienced this emotion.

Tweet Your Feelings

We don't always have time to learn a new emotion and write about them, but sometimes just sharing a feeling before or after our daily meditation can make students feel more connected.

Prompts

Untranslatable Emotion

After reading "Future—The 'Untranslatable' Emotions You Never Knew You Had," choose one of the following options: (1) In your own words, choose one of these "untranslatable" emotion mentioned in the reading that you have experienced. Then, write about your experience with this emotion, capturing the event behind the feeling; (2) Do you have an "untranslatable" emotion from your own language or culture that you would like to share? If so, please describe this word, its origin, and an explanation of a moment in which you have experienced this emotion.

#mymoments Multimodal Project

After tracking your sources of happiness this semester through the daily use of the hashtag #mymoments, formulate a thesis about your primary sources of happiness. We will then complete a multimodal project illustrating how you generate happiness. Sharing these projects is an excellent way to wrap up the semester.

Sabatino: Memoired Commonplaces
Readings and Resources

Our readings and resources are contextualized within the processes of the students own writing so they can interact with myriad genre conventions and authorial choices in ways that foreground "doing" the work within a framework of "knowing" the work of others. In the prompts section of this appendix, I provide examples of these contextualized in-process readings and resources. Here, I have selected five general texts that help to frame the memoir assignment:

> "The Fundamental Differences between Memoir and Autobiography." *Differences between Memoir and Autobiography—Author Resources*, www.liferichpublishing.com/AuthorResources/Nonfiction/Differences-Between-Memoir-AutoBiography.aspx.
> "Genre & Medium." *Purdue Online Writing Lab*, owl.purdue.edu/owl/subject_specific_writing/professional_technical_writing/business_writing_for_administrative_and_clerical_staff/genre_and_medium.html.
> Gutkind, Lee. "What Is Creative Nonfiction?" *Creative Nonfiction*, 2013, www.creativenonfiction.org/online-reading/what-creative-nonfiction.
> Martin, Lee. "Making Scenes in a Memoir." *Lee Martin*, 4 July 2016, leemartinauthor.com/2016/07/04/making-scenes-memoir/.
> "What Is a Memoir." *Creative Writing Courses and Ideas: An Online Resource for Writers*, www.creative-writing-now.com/what-is-a-memoir.html.

Exercises

Our in-class writing exercises can emerge as a two-minute written response to text or a 30-minute generative writing session framed by a productivity goal the students set individually (I will write nonstop for 15 minutes; I will compose 300 words in this session, etc.). At times, I ask students to coauthor texts and present the content on the whiteboard or via the projector screen (if they are live blogging, for example). After a writing session, I invite students to share their work in class on a volunteer basis. Our *HIIT (High-Intensity Interval Training) Writing Session* is one specific in-class exercise we enact during the revision process of the memoir. In the world of physical fitness, a HIIT writing session asks participants to perform one exercise at a high-effort level for a set time and then to rest for a set time (for example, 45 seconds of exercise and 15 seconds of rest) in cycles of alternating exercises that last for at least 20 minutes. In our class, I ask students to write within a specific genre for five minutes, rest for two minutes, and compose a new genre during the next five-minute writing exercise. I encourage students to develop these texts in future blog posts and/or reshape the content within the draft of their memoir. Here is a sample five-minute/two-minute HIIT writing session:

- **Empathy Letter:** Inhabit the self of a memoir character (another person or your past-protagonist self) and write a letter addressed to you that seeks your empathy about a decision or action/behavior that occurred in the scene of your story;
- **Sympathy Dialogue:** Create a dialogue shared between you and a memoir character (another person or your past-protagonist self) where you each express sympathy for each other's situation (experiences in the memoir scene as characters who lived the moment and/or in your current writing scenes as an author who is composing the story);
- **Counterfactual Scene:** Rewrite the memoir's pivotal scene of action to create a counterfactual alternative to the moment (this content might play out as a "what if" reflective moment in the memoir);
- **Reconsider POV and Tense:** Edit the language in the memoir to shift point-of-view from first-person to third person and tense from past to present (or vice versa).

Prompts

The following informal assignments connect to both the informal in-class writing assignments and to the drafting of the formal memoir assignment. To illustrate the potential scope of these assignments, I have included prompts that have appeared in my Developmental English course as well as my English Composition I and English Composition II courses. In each of these three first-year writing courses, I tailor the prompts to meet the course learning goals and attend to student needs. Below, I provide four prompts: one sample assignment format for each course (three total) and one universal reflection that is relevant for each writing context.

Developmental English: Writing Prompt to Explore Theme and Genre

Assignment Topic: Hiraeth
Assignment Focus: Longing for a Home

Assignment Process: Please complete the following:

- Interpret *Chef Table's Francis Mallman* episode for the hiraeth theme.
- Compose a 50-word introduction that connects Chef's Table Francis Mallman episode to your hiraeth composition about your longing for a "home to which you cannot return, a home which maybe never was . . ."
- Compose either a narrative scene, poem, song, sketch, painting, or photograph in your chosen design medium and mode (paper, video, an audio file, canvas, live performance, etc.).
- Share your composition with classmates during our in-class gallery walk.
- You can include this composition in your midterm portfolio to illustrate the breadth of your author-identity repertoire.

English Composition I: Writing Prompt to Generate Memoir Material

Blog Title: Composing an Emotional Scene with Dialogue and Symbolism
Blog Category: Memoir
Blog Text: Please complete the following in a Word or Google document so you can copy and paste the content into your blog post at the end of week __:

- Print out, read, and annotate: "Hills Like White Elephants" by Ernest Hemingway
- Write a 50-word introduction that connects a theme of emotion from Hills Like White Elephants to a theme of emotion in your memoir scene.
- Compose a 450-word scene that shows the reader an emotional moment you shared with someone in your life.
    - Please include dialogue. Use this article as a resource: "How to Format Dialogue" (https://firstmanuscript.com/format-dialogue/)
    - Please include at least one symbolic detail. Use this article as a resource: "Symbolism" (https://literarydevices.net/symbolism/)
    - Appeal to the five senses to animate the moment.
    - Remember: Description + Action + Theme = Scene.
- Please include at least one photo that shows a concrete or symbolic aspect of your written scene.

English Composition II: Writing Prompt to Remix Memoir

Blog Title: Found Poem of my Memoir
Blog Categories: Memoir, Remix
Blog Text: Please complete the following in a Word or Google document so you can copy and paste the content into your blog post at the end of week __:

- Print out, read and annotate:
    - What is a Found Poem? (https://poets.org/text/found-poem-poetic-form), "Sample Found Poem" (http://www.readwritethink.org/files/resources/lesson_images/lesson1034/sample.pdf)
- Write a 50-word introduction that provides (1) the focus of the blog post (summary of your memoir scene and transition to the prompt) and (2) a link to your memoir project web page.
- **This blog post should be arranged into two sections:**
    - **Section I: Found Poem**
        - Use the genre of found poetry to remix the first draft of your memoir.
        - Please use at least 100 words of material you "find" in the memoir.
        - Excerpt language from the memoir to create a title for the found poem.
        - Identify the type (sub-genre) of found poem you are composing: cut-up | cento | free-form excerpting and remixing | erasure
    - **Section II: Reflection (I encourage you to vlog this part of the post.)**
        - Please respond to these questions (you can copy and paste these questions into your blog post):
        - Do you think the memoir provides enough descriptive language to create a compelling found poem?
        - If not, how do you plan to revise the descriptive language in the narrative?
        - Do you think the descriptive language more so creates a setting or delivers subtext (consider your theme of emotion)?
        - In revision, will you focus on using description to develop more setting or more subtext?
        - Do you think the found poem explores the same emotions located in the story or does the remixed text foreground new or different emotions?

Reflection: Writing Prompt to Self-Assess Memoir

> **Blog Title:** My Memoir: A Wizard-of-Oz Journey
> **Blog Category:** Memoir, Reflection
> **Blog Text:** Please complete the following in a Word or Google document so you can copy and paste the content into your blog post at the end of week __:
>
> - Interpret the scenes in these video-text performances (videos available on YouTube):
>   o Wizard of Oz: If I Only Had the Brain, Heart, Nerve
>   o Wizard of Oz: Meeting the Wizard
>   o Wizard of Oz: You've Always Had the Power
> - Compose a 50-word introduction that provides the (1) focus of the blog post and (2) links to the three videos.
> - Compose a 450-word response to the following questions:
>   o How does your memoir allow you to travel into your <u>brain</u> (mind) then and now?
>   o How does your memoir allow you to explore your <u>heart</u> (emotions) about the event then and now?
>   o How does your memoir meet the <u>nerve</u> (high-stakes) element of meaningful storytelling?
>   o How does your memoir enable you to reexamine the power (agency) you have in authoring your life-story?
>   o What shapes our sense of identity: Life events or the stories we tell ourselves about life events?

Works Cited

American College Health Association. *American College Health Association-National College Health Assessment II: Undergraduate Student Executive Summary Fall 2018.* Silver Spring, MD, American College Health Association, 2018.

Brackett, Marc A., et al. "Emotional Intelligence: Implications for Personal, Social, Academic, and Workplace Success." *Social and Personality Psychology Compass*, vol. 5, no. 1, 2011, pp. 88–103.

Crowley, Claire, and Dana Munk. "An Examination of the Impact of a College Level Meditation Course on College Student Well Being." *College Student Journal*, vol. 51, no. 1, Spring 2017, pp. 91–98. EBSCO*host*, search.ebscohost.com/login.aspx?direct=true&db=pbh &AN=121530618&site=ehost-live.

Hughes, Morgan. "Mental Health Stigma on College Campuses Needs Revision." *Marquette Wire*, 6 Sept. 2016, marquettewire.org/3952764/featured/hughes-mental-health- stigma-on-college-campuses-needs-revision-mc1/.

Magnet, Shoshana, et al. "Feminism, Pedagogy, and the Politics of Kindness." *Feminist Teacher*, vol. 25, no. 1, 2014, pp. 1–22.

Martin, Lee. *Telling Stories: The Craft of Narrative and the Writing Life*. U of Nebraska P, 2017.

Micciche, Laura R. *Doing Emotion: Rhetoric, Writing, Teaching*. Portsmouth: Boynton/Cook, 2007.

———. "Staying with Emotion." *Composition Forum*, vol. 34, Summer 2018, compositionforum.com/issue/34/micciche-retrospective.php.

Plutchik, Robert. "The Nature of Emotions: Human Emotions Have Deep Evolutionary Roots, a Fact That May Explain Their Complexity and Provide Tools for Clinical Practice." American Scientist, vol. 89, no. 4, 2001, pp. 344–50. JSTOR.

Reilly, Katie. "Anxiety and Depression: More College Students Seeking Help." *Time*, 19 Mar. 2018, time.com/5190291/anxiety-depression-college-university-students/.

Spendlove, David. *Emotional Literacy*. Bloomsbury Publishing PLC, 2009. ProQuest Ebook Central, https://ebookcentral.proquest.com/lib/ccphiladelphia/detail.action?docID=601958.

Thompson, Becky. *Teaching with Tenderness: Toward an Embodied Practice*. U of Illinois P, 2017.

"Understanding the Facts: Facts and Statistics." *Anxiety and Depression Association of America*, adaa.org/.

Winans, Amy E. "Cultivating Critical Emotional Literacy: Cognitive and Contemplative Approaches to Engaging Difference." *College English*, vol. 75, no. 2, 2012, pp. 150–70.

Winerman, Lea. "By the Numbers: Stress on Campus." *Monitor on Psychology*, vol. 48, no. 8, Sept. 2017, p. 88.

Wolf, Jessica. "Study Shows Stigma around Mental Health on Campus Correlates with Students Not Seeking Treatment." *UCLA Newsroom*, 23 Jan. 2018, newsroom.ucla.edu/releases/study-shows-stigma-around-mental-health-on-campus-correlates-with-students-not-seeking-treatment.

10. Inverting Aristotle's Relationship between Invention and Pathos: 17 Students Write to the Freedom Writers

JESSICA ROSE COREY

I stressed to my high school "Introduction to College-Level Writing" students the importance of giving people emotional space to own and live their narratives. In that class, most students were from the Bronx, and all of them had received a scholarship to attend university the summer before their senior year of high school. Upon being assigned to teach the course, I struggled with the choice of materials, eager to reframe writing for my students not as a series of rules but as a social practice driven by rhetorical conventions. I chose to assign *The Freedom Writers Diary*, and the emotional connection students had to the book led them to ask if we could write our own letters to the Freedom Writers. I said "yes," and the project allowed students to experience writing as emotional and cognitive engagement with society's ideologies, conventions, and activities.

My desire for students to understand writing as a social practice was, in part, informed by scholarship that argues for emotion as "socially experienced and constructed" (Chandler 53) and meaningful to writing (Jacobs and Micciche; McLeod). McLeod, for instance, states that teachers can help students "control" their emotional responses to writing so that emotions prove beneficial rather than detrimental to students (433). But "controlling" emotion can come only after students have the emotional literacy to recognize their feelings and to consider how feelings influence identity construction and identity representation in a variety of forms, including writing. One student demonstrates this endeavor into emotional literacy in her letter to the Freedom Writers:

> I have never really been too good with words or expressing how I feel, which has been very problematic ... I wonder what made me this way, and the only things I could think of are how I was brought up, because my parents were never affectionate with me and I faced unfortunate bullying and discrimination ... I can recall my father saying he loved me only one time in my entire 17-year life, and my mother would probably say it a few times a year ... I always acted like things don't affect me but they really do and my feelings do get hurt. My one wish is to be able to express myself freely and comfortably, but it is going to take a while till I get there. Reading the *Freedom Writers Diary* allowed me to be able to write about my experience. I know that I always have a guard up and never want to open up with others, but writing has become my new outlet.

In this example, we see the student acknowledge her relationship with emotion and emotional expression, and question what this relationship means to her identity and the social relationships she forms. She also points out that writing provides a way to sort through these issues and express herself in a medium that feels safer than verbal expression, a place where her "guard" can be let down, if only temporarily. As the student identifies her understandings of emotion through her experiences and the contexts in which those experiences have taken place, she begins to practice a skill she would later practice in class: exploring the social influences on any production, and potential implication, of a text, thereby recognizing communicative acts as agents in shaping ideas and creating social change.

Drawing on additional excerpts from student letters to the Freedom Writers, I argue that Aristotle's conceptualization of *pathos* as an element of *invention* can be re-conceptualized so that *invention* serves as an element of *pathos*. Whereas Aristotle envisioned invention as containing *ethos, logos, and pathos*, with *pathos*[1] appealing to the emotions of the audience, in expressive writing[2] pathos contains invention and focuses on the emotions of the writer, not on those of the audience. In other words, the focus of *invention* and *pathos* moves from Aristotle's focus on audience to the writer, who uses emotion to invent ideas, invent oneself, and contribute to the invention of others. The implications of inverting this relationship include helping students explore and understand their emotions in relation to their subject positions and larger social and cultural narratives; helping students apply the analytical skill of exploring felt difficulty, subject positions, and context to analysis of texts and other cultural artifacts; and motivating students to consider the implications of the texts they produce. As a model of these implications, the Freedom Writers showed my students how awareness and understanding of pathos can enhance writing as a rhetorical practice and influence social change.

In Book 2 of *Rhetoric*, though defiantly, Aristotle recognized engaging the audience's emotions as useful in persuading its members to act in accordance with the speaker's desires (Corbett 23). Aristotle conceptualized *pathos* as "a will-to-act in a specific way—a mode of intentionality—which is prompted, quasi-syllogistically, by sensations and perceptions that are mediated by cognition or (in humans) by *logos*" (Walker 79). Put more simply, the glossary in Kennedy's translation of *Rhetoric* defines *pathos* as "a temporary state of feeling awakened by circumstances" (317).[3] So, a writer might certainly experience pathos as a "temporary state of feeling awakened by circumstances" (Kennedy 317) and compose expressive writing that motivates others to experience "a will-to-act in a specific way" (Walker 79).

Aside from the fact that Aristotle used the terms of pathos and invention in regard to speech and we use them in regard to writing, Aristotle seemed to understand the application of these terms differently than some writing teachers today. Anis Bawarshi begins the process of addressing this difference:

> In writing instruction, the shift in focus from production to product, from invention to arrangement, mirrored the displacement of rhetoric by philology within English studies. The English department built its research program around textual interpretation, not production, thereby marginalizing the teaching of how and why texts came to be (151).

Though writing sixteen years ago, Bawarshi describes a dynamic I see in every freshman writing course I teach: students easily analyze texts like literature, but when my assignments (and many others across college campuses) fail to tell them *what* to write, they are bewildered. They are unsure of how to construct an argument based on their *own* critical consideration of a text or concept. What are their emotional responses to the text, and what subject positions contribute to those responses? What are the contexts and cultural narratives at work in the production and potential implications of the text? Who might have a different emotional response or opinion, and why? Where do opportunities exist to enter the disciplinary conversation and how might students do that effectively based on the rhetorical situation? One student uses the Freedom Writers letter project, in part, to address the expectation for textual interpretation but not for invention:

> ... I had a feeling that my professor would tell the class to read *A Death in the Family* or *The Odyssey* or anything that is considered "college worthy." But a book that talks about personal life stories from urban students such as this was very surprising ... It was brain candy to me ... Most likely, the majority of people see me as just a Hispanic teenager who would constantly get arrested by the police or would drop out of high school in order to follow up with some local gangs. But what if I proved these assumers wrong?... This confidence that I have is what I gained after reading your book. I feel powerful even if I'm powerless in society. I feel great. I feel recognized.

This student's message shows a familiarity with "college worthy" texts (such as literary classics) but suggests a lack of familiarity with the notion of texts as socially constructed in varying contexts. This new awareness invokes a sense of power and recognition. Here, the text did not serve the purpose of standardized test prep, or as a premise for a generic academic essay; rather, the text served the purpose of allowing students to be "recognized." In this way, pathos that serves invention may yield self-awareness, intellectual stimulation, and a sense of empowerment.

Ken Kantor argues that in student writing assignments "we need to allow students some breathing room, some space in which to test out ideas, no matter how fanciful or far-out . . . we may want to accept, at least for a while, genuine expression of feeling" ("Evaluating Creative Writing . . ." 74). Rohman further argues many students, through the act of writing, gain a feeling of autonomy, satisfaction, and of being "capable of creating something new" (49). Kantor and Rohman, then, present emotion as a means of creating and working through ideas. Scholars attending the Dartmouth Seminar (1966), the first Anglo-American seminar on the teaching of English (Dixon), similarly advocated emotional response as a viable means of participating in "productive activities" (Kantor, "Creative Expression" 25), which we might interpret as invention.

James Britton also implies that pathos embodies invention by questioning whether "we may be under-estimating the value of 'shaping at the point of utterance' and hence cutting off what might prove the most effective approach to an understanding of rhetorical invention" (152). Moreover, Donald Murray describes expressive writing (which might also be conceptualized as "shaping at the point of utterance"), as "an emptying out of all we have said, read, thought, seen, felt" (Richards and Miller 68). I argue that through acts of expressive writing that employ pathos, writers in training learn not just about the rhetorical concept of invention, but also about how they themselves have been "invented" and "revised" by cultures and social systems; by extension, they also learn about relationships between author, audience, and context; the role of rhetorical appeals in shaping human responses, and the use of discourse (language of a particular community) and "Big 'D' Discourse" (ways of embodying an identity, the larger context of discourse) in effective communication (Gee 1–5). (For pedagogical practices that engage these skills, see the Appendix.)

Similarly, in consideration of backlash against expressive writing, Elbow argues for its potential to provide a "larger view of human discourse," stating that "rendering is not just an 'affective' matter—what something 'feels' like. Discourse that renders often yields important new 'cognitive' insights such as helping see an exception or contradiction to some principle we thought we believed" (137). In the following letter, for example, we see a student communicating a personal experience while also contemplating the meaning, and societal representation, of the abstract concept "happiness." The student engages in reflection and realizes the importance of distancing oneself from emotions and making a cognizant decision to help oneself:

> I personally think I deserve an academy award because from the time I wake up to the time I go to bed, I put on the performance of a lifetime ... Society depicts "true happiness" through media outlets such as television, computers, magazines, and movies, but I have never felt society's definition of joy. I dream of living a Disney fairytale where everything works out in the end, but when reality sets in I am reminded that Walt Disney is full of fiction and that all dreams do not come true. As time passed I held onto this notion and started to distance myself from my emotions. Upon reflecting, I realized that I feared feeling happiness because I knew sadness was inevitable. Rather than going on a roller coaster of emotions, I decided to remain emotionally numb ... The Freedom Writers taught me the importance of challenging my fears and mindset. Change begins with me and I have finally decided to liberate myself. No longer will I allow paranoia to dictate my actions and emotions. From here on out, I will seek help when needed; and I no longer feel alone because of the Freedom Writers.

The student uses emotion to invent, and that invention leads to cognitive realizations. Thus, pathos and invention have, from Aristotle's use of the terms as discovery of ideas and emotional appeals to an audience, developed into a practice of beginning with the author's emotions as a way of inventing oneself and one's relationship with texts.

Herrington and Moran further note "exploratory thinking and writing (that is, invention), and genres as potentially flexible guides for that invention and social action within a given discourse community" (10). Therefore, emotional, expressive writing and cognitive development continually inform each other, and contribute to one's personal growth. Expressive writing allows students to overtly examine their academic experiences as personal ones, helping them to locate themselves within disciplines. For instance, the letters to the Freedom Writers were expressive in nature but also revised to be rhetorically suited for their audience; the intersection of writing about personal experiences (and subsequent emotions) with writing rhetorically provided a different, more meaningful engagement with writing than students' prior experiences had provided. One student communicates a desire for more such writing:

> Writing for a grade does not allow us to liberate our thoughts on paper; instead it is a painful and dreadful activity to do. Therefore, I really liked the idea

Ms. Gruwell had of writing the diary entries. I believe that schools should do something similar to this because all of the students would be able to understand one another and provide support for one another. In high school, students try to conceal their feelings because they are afraid of what others may think. Through the diaries, students would feel a sense of community just as your class did, and it would provide motivation.

Though much evidence has demonstrated the re-contextualization of Aristotle's concepts of *invention* and *pathos*, some scholars remain hesitant to accept it. Herrington and Moran note how associations between genre and suppressed creativity led to unfair emphasis on expressive writing as compensatory (8). Expressive writing became associated with creative endeavors, and not with scholastic endeavors. Expressive writing, however, particularly in an environment supportive of taking risks with writing, may increase the opportunity for students to connect with disciplines, perhaps later using that connection to contribute to the progress of the field.

Many Writing Across Curriculum programs began with the incorporation of both expressive writing and transactional writing (writing for the purpose of communicating), which often showed expressive assignments *leading to* transactional formal assignments (Thaiss 4). Furthermore, Fred Carlisle, in *Essays on the Essay: Redefining the Genre*, points out the over-simplification of categorizing expressive writing and invention as separate entities. Again, pathos embodies invention, and all invention engages social experiences and responses. Specifically, Carlisle writes:

> [Loren] Eiseley has made explicit and functional aspects of discourse and of experience that are ... often absent in the writing of most scientists or poets. This alone suggests that he is not simply a scientist who writes well about science or about human values; nor is he simply a popularizer (if he is one at all) who explains science to others; nor is he just a writer who makes "poetry" out of science, thereby changing it into something else ...[He discovered] science which *includes* the self. Words give the scientist a means to explain and interpret research and discoveries, and even here they are not altogether transparent. They are a medium which shapes the scientist's insights and therefore affects his meaning. But Eiseley means even more, for words function sometimes as the *primary* instrument of the scientist; they become the medium within which the scientist's knowledge and imagination operate in order to discover something of the nature of the universe (187 & 189).

In sum, Eiseley's personal experiences served a scientific function in developing his ideas. Likewise, Bawarshi argues that students' understanding that invention remains personal and social allows them to "locate and invent themselves rhetorically within various sites of action" (154). Though maybe not in the way Bawarshi had meant, the Freedom Writers letters written by my students do, in fact, show students wrestling with identity (locating and inventing themselves) in different contexts, recognizing problematic social structures in various "sites of action." For example, one student wrote:

> In today's society, everyone believes that there are many opportunities, and if a child doesn't go to school, it's because they are lazy; but that is untrue. We as teenagers have to handle so many things, including family problems that no one will ever expect. There are teenagers who have to hold a job in order to help their family stay afloat. There are teenagers who don't have the resources to make it into good schools that would offer great internships and other opportunities. In many cases, the problem is not the children, but rather the system that degrades kids and makes them feel as though with every step forward, they take three steps back.

This letter shows identity as created and understood in relation to narratives of childhood, economics, family, education, the workforce, and "the system."

The integration of Aristotle's terms into the writing classroom, then, actually allows for wider application and more complex understanding of the dynamic he proposed. Though now modified to show more plainly a complex relationship among speaker/writer and audience, and the way in which these roles overlap, Aristotle lacked the context to consider these terms in the way we use them today; and his original conceptualization of invention and pathos stands firm in its relevance to multiple disciplines. I am an audience to another before I am a writer to an audience. In both roles, I am invented by my emotions, invent with my emotions, and contribute to the invention of others though the texts I produce in response to or consideration of those emotions.

Inverting the relationship between pathos and invention (so that pathos leads to invention, rather than invention leading to pathos) further moves the conceptualization of expressive writing and emotion from that which is self-centered and unintellectual to that which is a meaningful entry point into critical thinking and rhetorical communication that will serve students in academic, professional, and personal spaces. Expressive discourse is not a "way out" of critical thinking, writing, and revising. It is not a "way out" of avoiding our ethical responsibilities to an audience. Rather, beyond the relationship between emotion and invention long discussed in rhetoric and composition, emotional and expressive discourse can shed light on the social infrastructures that impact us as people and writers, and begin teaching students to contemplate the social, historical influences upon the process of producing texts, the rhetorical elements of communication, and ways of being in the world.

Appendix: Pedagogical Methods That Create Opportunities for Expression in the Classroom

- Double-entry journal: Students write summaries and analyses on one side of the page, and personal experiences and emotional responses related to the text or issues within the text on the other side of the page.
- Role playing: This can be done in large or small groups, and can revolve around any prompt you choose. I do this in small groups and assign students roles based on a text. For example, for a text about higher education, I use groups of three or four students, and assign roles such as university administrator, parent of a college student, college professor, and someone responsible for creating marketing materials for the university. The small groups and alternate personas provide a safe space in which students can explore social influences on texts, and emotion and empathy.
- Blog writing: Students may or may not be required to share blogs with fellow students, depending on the purpose of the assignment. Students might benefit from using their preexisting blogs as a space to write about their own experiences with course material.
- Epistolary writing: In the digital age, this has perhaps lost favor, but my students writing to the Freedom Writers found it liberating, and were able to disclose experiences they would not have felt comfortable disclosing in digital spaces.
- Makerspaces: Set up stations around the room with different materials (Play-Doh, paint, Legos/blocks, pen and paper, a computer, etc.) and ask students to depict their emotional response to a text or course concept. They will destroy their compositions before moving to the next station. Teachers can follow-up on this activity by having students write brief reflections on their experiences communicating in different modes. Which modes were easiest and most difficult for them to represent their emotions? Why? How can they apply what they learned from the activity to writing?

Notes

1. Aristotle posed means of persuasion as available in either non-artistic or artistic forms, with non-artistic forms classified as those which already existed (i.e., law), and artistic forms as those which required invention of ethical (ethos), logical (logos), or emotional (pathos) appeals (Corbett 22–23).

2. Expressive discourse is hereby defined as discourse which conveys the "experience of the writer" (Bizzell and Herzberg 1185) and "expresses and partially achieves [a writer's] own individuality" (Kinneavy 376). The "experience of the writer" and expression of identity inherently involves accounts of emotion.
3. Although the word "emotion" fails to create a direct translation (Hill 45), the word often serves as a substitute for, and for the purposes of this chapter, will be used synonymously with, the Greek term, *pathos*.

Works Cited

Aristotle. *On Rhetoric: A Theory of Civic Discourse.* Translated by George A. Kennedy, Oxford UP, 2007.

Bawarshi, Anis S. "Re-Placing Invention in Composition: Reflections and Implications." *Genre and the Invention of the Writer: Reconsidering the Place of Invention in Composition*, by Anis Bawarshi, Utah State UP, 2003, pp. 145–70.

Bizzell, Patricia, and Bruce Herzberg. "Introduction." *The Rhetorical Tradition: Readings from Classical Times to the Present*, edited by Patricia Bizzell and Bruce Herzberg, Bedford/St. Martin's, 2001, pp. 1183–1205.

Britton, James. "Shaping at the Point of Utterance." *Landmark Essays on Rhetorical Invention in Writing*, edited by Richard E. Young and Yameng Liu, Hermagoras Press, 1994, pp. 147–52.

Carlisle, Fred E. "The Literary Achievements of Loren Eiseley." *Essays on the Essay: Redefining the Genre*, edited by Alexander J. Butrym, U of Georgia P, 1989, pp. 184–91.

Chandler, Sally. "Fear, Teaching Composition, and Students' Discursive Choices: Re-Thinking Connections Between Emotions and College Student Writing." *Composition Studies*, vol. 35, no. 2, 1997, pp. 53–70.

Corbett, Edward P.J. *Classical Rhetoric for the Modern Student.* Oxford U P, 1990.

Dixon, John. "Growth through English, A Report Based on the Dartmouth Seminar 1966." *Journal of Research in Education*, Eastern Educational Research Association.

Elbow, Peter. "Reflections on Academic Discourse: How It Relates to Freshmen and Colleagues." *College English*, vol. 53, no. 2, 1991, pp. 135–55. Web Site: http://www.eeraorganization.org.

Gee, James P. "Discourse, Small d, Big D." *The International Encyclopedia of Language and Social Interaction*, edited by Karen Tracy et al., Wiley-Blackwell, 2015, pp. 1–5.

Herrington, Anne, and Charles Moran. "The Idea of Genre in Theory and Practice: An Overview of the Work in Genre in the Fields of Composition and Rhetoric and New Genre Studies." *Genre Across the Curriculum*, edited by Anne Herrington and Charles Moran, Utah State UP, 2005, pp. 1–18.

Hill, Forbes I. "The Rhetoric of Aristotle." *A Synoptic History of Classical Rhetoric*, edited by James Jerome Murphy, Random House, 1972, pp. 19–76.

Jacobs, Dale, and Laura R. Micciche. *A Way to Move: Rhetorics of Emotion and Composition Studies*. Boynton/Cook, 2003.

Kantor, Ken. "Evaluating Creative Writing: A Different Ball Game." *The English Journal*, vol. 64, no. 4, 1975, pp. 72–74.

———. "Creative Expression in the English Curriculum: An Historical Perspective." *Research in the Teaching of* English, vol. 9, no. 1, 1975, pp. 5–29.

Kinneavy, James L. "Expressive Discourse: Introduction and Terminology." *The Norton Book of Composition Studies*, edited by Susan Miller, W.W. Norton, 2009, pp. 372–86.

McLeod, Susan H. *Notes on the Heart: Affective Issues in the Writing Classroom*. Southern Illinois UP, 1997.

Richards, Janet C., and Sharon K. Miller. *Doing Academic Writing in Education: Connecting the Personal and the Professional*. Routledge / Taylor & Francis Group, 2009.

Rohman, Gordon D. "Pre-Writing: The Stage of Discovery in the Writing Process." *Landmark Essays on Rhetorical Invention in Writing*, edited by Richard E. Young and Yameng Liu, Hermagoras Press, 1994, pp. 41–49.

Thaiss, Christopher. *The Harcourt Brace Guide to Writing across the Curriculum*. Harcourt Brace, 1998.

Walker, Jeffrey. "Pathos and Katharsis in 'Aristotelian' Rhetoric: Some Implications." *Reading Aristotle's Rhetoric*, edited by Alan G. Gross and Arthur E. Walzer, Southern Illinois UP, 2000, pp. 74–92.

11. *Stirring Things Up: Rhetorical Dissonance in Writers' Revisions and Emotional Responses*

MATTHEW FLEDDERJOHANN

One writer felt anxious when the peer reviewers in her English class took issue with the argument she was making in her critical analysis about the Affordable Care Act. Another writer became afraid that the reflection she'd written in response to a James Baldwin essay for her intermediate composition class made her sound like she was prejudiced against black people. A third writer became angry as she realized the stance she was developing about the environmental impact of mining practices for an eighth-grade position paper was not generally embraced. These writers responded emotionally when what they were writing clashed with their personal expectations and what they understood to be their readerships' values and priorities. Challenging emotions emerged as these writers experienced dissonance.

In this chapter, I explore the relationship between emotions, writing, and dissonance by considering how one writer's encounter with what I call rhetorical dissonance elicited uncomfortable emotions which then subsided through engagement with various sustained revision activities. I expand upon traditional revision scholarship's understanding of dissonance as a motivating force for change and identify rhetorical dissonance as a clash of expectations that is incurred, sustained, and sometimes resolved in connection to writers' writing processes and/or written products. I find that the anxiety, fear, and anger that rhetorical dissonance can generate can become enmeshed in writers' decisions to alter their texts, reconsider their contexts, and even interrogate their own beliefs and perceptions. This finding is particularly manifested in the encounter one writer—Trevor—had with rhetorical dissonance as he tried to compose an acceptable preliminary examination essay. By understanding rhetorical dissonance and how it can converge with difficult emotional responses, composition instructors will be better equipped to comprehend and respond to the emotional challenges some writers face.

My construction of rhetorical dissonance as a discrete phenomenon draws from the substantial social psychological work that has been devoted to cognitive dissonance as well as the conceptualization of revision that John Hayes has referred to as "the dissonance model." As originally understood by social psychologists, dissonance is the clash between two mutually exclusive cognitions (Festinger). More recently, scholars have broadened their attention beyond just the cognitive to acknowledge that dissonance can also occur in relation to irreconcilable emotions (e.g., Abraham; Jansz and Timmers; Pugh et al.). But whether dissonance occurs because of incompatible thoughts or feelings, it is experienced when individuals find themselves trying to adhere to conflicting realities. And just as is true for the musical phenomenon which the term "dissonance" describes, the resulting discord agitates for resolution. Leon Festinger, the social psychologist who developed the theory of cognitive dissonance asserted that, "dissonance is a motivating state of affairs" (93). Dissonance prompts change.

Dissonance's capacity to motivate change has made it a phenomenon of interest to revision scholars. In the late 1970s and early 1980s, as composition pushed to conceptualize the complexities of revision activity, several scholars suggested that dissonance is a primary motivator for revision. According to this perspective, dissonances—the "incongruities between goals and instantiated text"—generate tension which writers attempt to reduce through revision (Fitzgerald 484). Writers' vision for what a text should be does not align with what that text is, so they work to change their writing. The dissonance model has been shaped by Scardamalia and Bereiter's compare/diagnose/operate (CDO) model, Bridwell's conceptualization of revision processes, Sommers' interest in the important role difference plays into meaning making, and Beach's pedagogical approaches to writers' self-evaluations. According to this model, after writers realize that what they wanted to have written is not manifested in their actual text, they work to absolve the resultant dissonance by revising their writing.

Of course, revision can be motivated by any number of impulses and experiences beyond an encounter with dissonance. John Hayes has justifiably criticized the dissonance model for its limited understanding of why writers revise. Yet while dissonance is not at the root of all revision activity, it still motivates some writers to alter their writing. However, I argue that when writers encounter dissonance, the tension is the result of more than just what Scardamalia and Bereiter identify as the perceived mismatches "between the text as written so far, and a representation of the text as intended" (69).

Stirring Things Up: Rhetorical Dissonance

Additionally, its effects transcend textual revisions. I argue that, in addition to writers' writing, rhetorical dissonance is influenced by and influences writers' spatiotemporal contexts and themselves as writers. Figure 11.1 presents a more complete understanding of how rhetorical dissonance emerges and what its possible effects can be.

Rhetorical dissonance occurs when writers experience the tension of conflicting expectations generated by what they are writing, when and where they are doing this writing, who they are and what they believe, and (sometimes) what their readership values. Writers attempt to alleviate this tension by revising their writing, their understanding of their surrounding context, and/or their own values or beliefs. Figure 11.1 draws upon the classic rhetorical triangle to represent rhetorical dissonance's occurrence and consequences.[1] The various sources of expectation that always contribute to rhetorical dissonance (i.e., the text, the context, and the writer) are shown through dark arrows merging at a point of contestation (represented by an exclamation mark). The "audience" component is lighter since this is a possible but not necessary element of writers' experiences with rhetorical dissonance. The differently shaded arrows pointing back from the site of dissonance to differently shaded "text," "context," and "writer" represent the changes dissonance pushes writers to make to one or all of these elements. Rhetorical dissonance does not alter audience's expectations, so this aspect is left unchanged.

I developed this model of rhetorical dissonance through a qualitative research project that explored what happens when writers find themselves

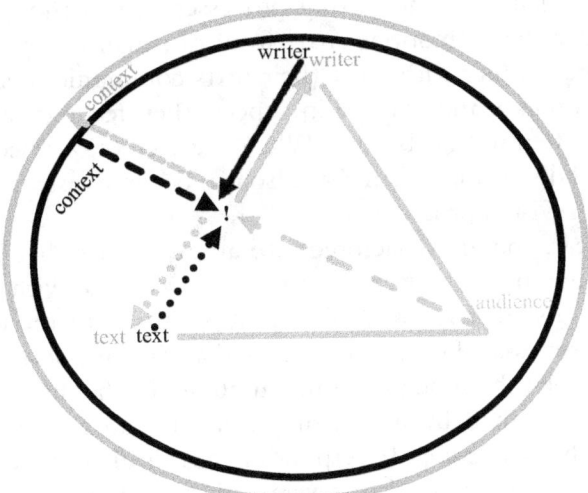

Figure 11.1. An updated model of rhetorical dissonance.

questioning their deeply held identities, values, and beliefs as a result of their writing. In order to understand more fully what occurs when writers encounter dissonance, I used archival and interview methodologies to track how fifteen writers arrived at and responded to these moments of difficult contestation. As I read some of their writing and talked to some of these writers, I was able to identify rhetorical dissonance as a particular kind of encounter with writing that motivates writers to make often substantial revisions to their texts, perceived contexts, and themselves. In addition to these noticeable trends in revision activity that point to and expand upon how the dissonance model scholars perceived the relationship between writing and dissonance, I found that rhetorical dissonance was also frequently experienced in association with the emotions of anxiety, fear, and anger.

Anxiety, fear, and anger can coincide with writing in many ways. Sometimes people write about these feelings in order to understand themselves better. Sometimes the topics they write about cause them to feel angry, anxious, or fearful. Both the practices of writing about emotions and writing about topics that generate strong feelings have been extensively considered in relationship to writing's potential therapeutic benefits (e.g., Anderson and MacCurdy; Bishop; Harris; Spear). Emotions also become entangled with writing as sometimes the process of composition itself evokes strong affective reactions.[2] Rhetorical dissonance can relate to all of these manifestations of writers experiencing emotions. As I discovered through my research, sometimes writers encounter dissonance as they are writing about their feelings or about topics about which they feel strongly. Sometimes dissonance emerges through emotionally fraught writing processes. And although writers certainly encounter these emotions apart from dissonance, when writers' personal assertions conflict with what their texts communicate and what their surrounding contexts and readership expect, then feelings of anxiety, fear, and anger are often not far behind. When these emotions become wrapped up in rhetorical dissonance, then they also can become instrumental in motivating writers' revision processes.

Anxiety, fear, and anger factored into an experience that Trevor, a PhD student at a large, public university in the Midwest, had with rhetorical dissonance when his advisor asked him multiple times to revise his preliminary examination essay. Dissonance emerged as Trevor's position as a writer, scholar, and student became incommensurate with what he was writing, the expectations established by his writing context, and the feedback he was receiving from his readership. In responding to this dissonance and the ensuing emotions, Trevor engaged in several substantial revision strategies. He revised his understanding of his writing context, his writing, and even certain values he associated with his scholarly identity. The anxiety, fear, and anger he experienced through this process made it one of the most challenging academic writing activities he's ever undergone, and these emotions were both a product of this dissonance and further impetus for Trevor to find his way to and through particular revision processes. His experience provides a rich example of how emotions, dissonance, and writing can converge to evoke both sustained discomfort and eventually productive revisions.

In Trevor's graduate program, preliminary exams consist of essays composed and defended after students have completed course work. These essays required him to position his ideas and academic interests in relationship to key conversations occurring within his field. One essay was based on a reading list prescribed by the program's faculty members. As Trevor described it, this essay, "asks you to sort of define your place in the field." Most obviously, the rhetorical dissonance Trevor encountered in conjunction with this essay was generated through his advisor's persistent request that he keep revising his writing. However, these requests—requests that Trevor felt were consistently identifying the inadequacies of his drafts—were primarily informed by a gap between how the advisor understood this writing assignment and what Trevor thought this essay was supposed to be.

According to Trevor, his essay drafts were sent back because he didn't initially understand the purpose or even the genre of this writing. Trevor said his first draft tackled the challenge of identifying himself within his wider field of scholarship by declaring, "I don't know, I think I'm this kind of guy. I think I like these sources and don't like those ones and that's why!" But when he started receiving feedback on this draft, he realized that he had been misunderstanding the prompt. Instead of picking the sources "that are kinda most like the work you're doing, and tell[ing] us why the other ones are not like the work you're doing," he was supposed to be making, "an argument for your dissertation interests that situates it in the field in relation to these other works." "[I]t sounds like a subtle shift," Trevor said, "but for me it was like a big shift. It was like, 'Oh ... this is an academic paper! ... Not like an off-the-cuff reflection paper.'" Getting to that realization involved a certain amount of angst. To continue through this emotionally fraught, dissonant experience, Trevor had to revise his perceptions of his writing context by developing a new understanding of what he was writing.

Trevor's evolving understanding of his writing context manifested in his sustained engagement in substantial revision processes—processes that were prompted by his advisor's consistent feedback. But as he struggled through this process, this feedback became a source of considerable emotional disturbance. Trevor remembers developing three or four full drafts of this essay over the course of several months before he started getting it right, before the feedback from his advisor was something other than a rejoinder to, "Start over."[3] And as these rejections of his drafts began stacking up, Trevor became more and more agitated. "I mean," he said of his response to this difficult feedback, "there's a whole, like sort of mental hoops you go through of like being angry at people, being angry at yourself, and like, bummed out and worried, sort of all that ... Usually it was like being angry for a day and confused for a day and putting it off." But the situational necessity of completing this essay in order to move forward in his pursuit of a PhD always drove him back to develop another revision. "[T]hen you fuckin' sit down and write," Trevor said of his eventual return to his essay. "Because you don't have another choice, right?" He understood that not writing this essay would mean not getting his PhD. "And that means you're making a different life choice," he admitted—a choice in line with an alternative life away from the academy that would come with its own stressors, difficulties, and unknowns which he wasn't interested in facing.

So, Trevor moved through the anger and the feelings raised by the dissonance he experienced in the contested space between how he had expected this writing process to proceed and what was actually happening. He revised—a process that involved:

> sitting down with the [advisor's] notes again a day or two later [after receiving feedback] and ... taking stock. Like, "This one I'll ignore. This one—okay that's not as bad as I thought when I first read it. This one—oh, that's really helpful, actually." Right? And then, so sorting through the feedback so it's not so this wash of, "Oh, I've done it all wrong, and I can't do anything right." Now ... after sort of riding that emotional wave, you go back to it, and you're like, "I have to do it. So, what pieces of this are manageable? What's actionable? What can I actually do?" And then you start building sort of an idea of what, what to move forward.

As he revised, Trevor reached out to his advisor with specific questions. His advisor " ... was great about sort of throwing that back to me and giving me some notes for some kind of clarity." Then Trevor would:

> take another run at it. Sometimes it meant like completely redrafting. Sometimes it meant, like moving sections around and mostly redrafting. And then I would turn it in, and the feedback would come back and it was like, "Augh! Again!" And the second or third time I got that feedback was when it sort of, the worst, it just sort of builds: the feeling of, "Oh, I don't know. If this one doesn't work, I'm out of here." [laughs] That sort of thing.

Trevor became frustrated over not being able to successfully complete this writing task. Sometimes that frustration boiled into anger. It occasionally simmered into anxious concern that he was not going to be able to become the scholar he wanted to be.

The sustained rhetorical dissonance made Trevor question whether or not he could complete his doctoral degree. "Maybe I don't know how to do this," he worried as he continued receiving feedback suggesting he still wasn't getting this right. "Maybe I don't know how to [be] a PhD program guy. Maybe, maybe this is not for me." This fear became amplified. Trevor said the experience:

> brings out a certain level of identity crisis and, ah, stress that is, I mean, it is the writing, but also is, it starts to spread to your whole life instead of just the stress of like, "Hmm. How do I solve this little problem of communication?" It becomes, like, "Uh-oh, my whole life might not work." Right? ... I don't like feeling that way.

But in addition to fearing that he would not be able to complete this writing task and therefore not finish his PhD, Trevor found the writing assignment was also challenging him through its requirement that he specify his scholarly identity.

In both his original, erroneous understanding of this prompt as an informal reflection piece and what he came to realize was actually being expected of him, Trevor's identity as a scholar was a key part of this essay. Through this essay, he was answering the question, "Who are you as a scholar in relationship to these other works?"—something which he understood to be "very much an identity question." Trevor admitted that positioning himself as a scholar in relationship to others' ideas was "tough ... 'cause you don't know yet because you're not really a scholar in relation to anything yet. [laughs] Right? You're just kind of a PhD student just hoping to be something." As Trevor understood it, "figuring out what the paper is supposed to be is also a process of figuring out who I am in relationship, or how do I express some version of myself that fits" into his wider field and eventual job market.

In the midst of his uncertainty as to the kind scholar he was becoming, Trevor was sure of one thing. He wasn't "going to be one of those blowhard academics." He wanted to be a researcher whose work was accessible, and as his advisor continued pushing him toward more conceptual complexity, he became afraid that he was being told he should abandon clarity. This fear came to a head when his advisor sent him an example of scholarship that "he thought was a good example of the [preliminary exam] genre." Trevor resisted. He sent his advisor an email declaring, "I don't like how this person writes, and I don't like how they think."⁴ He felt like he was being asked to become the very thing he wanted to avoid. Dissonance existed in "feeling like I wanna be this kind of a scholar and feeling, resisting any sort of pressure to be something different." Trevor realized later that this pressure to become what he didn't want to be was not actually coming from his advisor. Trevor had misunderstood. This advisor emailed him back, assuring him, as Trevor summarized, "I just thought it [the recommended article] was a good example of these points. You don't have to do all that." Trevor acknowledged, "A lot of the resistance to me being that kind of scholar was just perception on my part and not real." But it still felt real to Trevor, and the anxiety it generated informed the difficulty he continued to encounter as he worked through his prelims writing process.

After months of uncomfortably muddling through the frustration, fear, anxiety, and even anger associated with this rhetorically dissonant experience, Trevor eventually started to make productive headway. By revising his understanding of the preliminary examination prompt, continuously altering his essay itself, and learning that he could be a scholar who writes both clearly and deeply, Trevor's dissonance began to abate, and the associated difficult emotions subsided. He clung to his insistence that, "No, I really want to get this PhD. This feels like the right thing." By continuing to adhere to his desire to complete his degree, Trevor kept on returning to his work and making progress. He told me:

> Eventually, though, I hit a draft, and [my advisor] was like, the feedback was, "This is close." Right? And then, that really shifted the dynamic of it. Like the feeling, that sort of frustrated, I-can't-handle-this feeling sort of evaporated 'cause like, "Oh, I can do it." [laughs] I landed in the safe zone. And now it's sort of tweaking and refining the thing that we have.

The rhetorical dissonance and his fears and anxieties subsided when he reached a consonance between what he was writing, what his writing context had outlined, what his reader expected, and how he wanted to present himself.

According to Trevor, one of the most influential changes generated through this experience was his understanding of what it means for him to be an academic. Through his continuous engagement in this process, he realized that being a clear, direct writer and building complex, sophisticated arguments are not mutually exclusive. "You can do both of those things," he said. At the time of our interviews, Trevor was working on his dissertation, and he told me his current writing process was guided by his now-joint motivations to be both clear and complex. "The tension is still there, but it doesn't feel like such a problem anymore." The emotionally fraught rhetorical dissonance he underwent and eventually resolved through the various revisions that informed his prelims process taught him that he could adhere to several writerly identities simultaneously.

In addition to showcasing how rhetorical dissonance occurs; how it can become wrapped up in emotions such as anger, fear, and anxiety; and what role revision can play in its possible resolution, Trevor's experience speaks to the importance of emotional intelligence in responding to this kind of compositional difficulty. As a mature adult who intentionally strives toward increased self-awareness, Trevor was able to recognize what was going on internally and choose to continue revising. As psychologist Daniel Goleman claimed in his seminal work on emotional intelligence, a key aspect of this intelligence is being aware of the emotion as it is occurring (43). Even through the difficult, Trevor said he was able to locate "some healthy part of me that in the middle of the emotional turmoil is like, 'Bro, we're going to just write it. [laughs] Like, take a day to be all weird, and come back.'" And that is what he consistently did.

Identifying rhetorical dissonance as a distinct phenomenon that some writers struggle with and that has the capacity of raising or amplifying writers' fears, anxieties, and angers bears significance for composition instructors committed to helping writers through the difficulties of writing. Even though rhetorical dissonance is only one of the many challenges writers can face, composition instructors who are aware of it can be looking expectantly for the fear, anxiety, and anger writers may encounter upon experiencing a profound tension between what they have written, what their context and/or audience expects, and what they themselves value. Knowing about rhetorical dissonance can advance instructors' emotional intelligence in relation to their own writing practices and across their observations of others' writing difficulties. By understanding how dissonance emerges, identifying the emotions that may become associated with this phenomenon, and recognizing the role revision can play in the resolution of dissonance, instructors can help writers whose writing product or process has made them uncomfortably question core aspects of their identity, belief system, or worldview. And if writers can be encouraged to recognize their emotions in light of rhetorical dissonance and dissonance as an invitation to engage in widespread revision practices, then maybe, like Trevor, these writers will be able to use revision to move from anger and uncertainty to a more developed text, a clearer understanding of their context, and maybe even an advanced perception of themselves as writers and learners.

Notes

1. In building this model around the rhetorical triangle, I am not suggesting the triangle provides a totalizing representation of rhetoric. Instead, given the triangle's foundation in rhetorical theory (Aristotle 1.2.2–3), its prominent application across composition pedagogy (e.g., Lunsford), and its flexible nature (Gorrell 401; Tinelli), it provides a productive theoretical framework around which I develop an understanding of rhetorical dissonance.
2. The prominence of this experience is underlined through the frequently studied phenomenon of writing anxiety (e.g., Bloom; Martinez et al.; Stewart et al.).
3. Through our interviews, Trevor admitted that the feedback he received was never actually this harsh. His advisor "never said that, but that's the feeling that I got was like, 'No, this is not what we want at all. Just start over.'"
4. Trevor said that in this moment, "I was really, like, in my resistant fussy mode."

Works Cited

Abraham, Rebecca. "Emotional Dissonance in Organizations: Antecedents, Consequences, and Moderators." *Genetic, Social, and General Psychology Monographs*, vol. 124, no. 2, 1998, pp. 229–46.

Anderson, Charles M., and Marian M. MacCurdy. *Writing and Healing: Toward an Informed Practice. Refiguring English Studies*. National Council of Teachers of English, 2000.

Aristotle. *On Rhetoric: A Theory of Civic Discourse*. Edited and translated by George Kennedy, Oxford UP, 1991.

Beach, Richard. "Demonstrating Techniques for Assessing Writing in the Writing Conference." *College Composition and Communication*, vol. 37, no. 1, 1986, pp. 55–65.

Bishop, Wendy. "Writing is/and Therapy?: Raising Questions about Writing Classrooms and Writing Program Administration." *Journal of Advanced Composition*, 1993, vol. 13, no. 2, pp. 503–16.

Bloom, Lynn Z. "Why Graduate Students Can't Write: Implications of Research on Writing Anxiety for Graduate Education." *Journal of Advanced Composition*, 1981, pp. 103–17.

Bridwell, Lillian S. "Revising Strategies in Twelfth Grade Students' Transactional Writing." *Research in the Teaching of English*, vol. 14, no. 3, 1980, pp. 197–222.

Festinger, Leon. "Cognitive Dissonance." *Scientific American*, vol. 207, no. 4, 1962, pp. 93–106.

Fitzgerald, Jill. "Research on Revision in Writing." *Review of Educational Research*, vol. 57, no. 4, 1987, pp. 481–506.

Goleman, Daniel. *Emotional Intelligence*. Bantam, 1995.

Gorrell, Donna. "The Rhetorical Situation Again: Linked Components in a Venn Diagram." *Philosophy & Rhetoric*, vol. 30, no. 4, 1997, pp. 395–412.

Harris, Judith. "Re-Writing the Subject: Psychoanalytic Approaches to Creative Writing and Composition Pedagogy." *College English*, vol. 64, no. 2, 2001, pp. 175–204.

Hayes, John R. "What Triggers Revision?" *Revision Cognitive and Instructional Processes*, edited by Linda Allal et al., Kluwer Academic Publishers, 2004, pp. 9–20.

Jansz, Jeroen, and Monique Timmers. "Emotional Dissonance: When the Experience of an Emotion Jeopardizes an Individual's Identity." *Theory & Psychology*, vol. 12, no. 1, 2002, pp. 79–95.

Lunsford, Andrea A. *The St. Martin's Handbook*. 7th ed. Bedford/St. Martin's, 2011.

Martinez, Christy Teranishi, et al. "Pain and Pleasure in Short Essay Writing: Factors Predicting University Students' Writing Anxiety and Writing Self-Efficacy." *Journal of Adolescent & Adult Literacy*, vol. 54, no. 5, 2011, pp. 351–60.

Pugh, S. Douglas, et al. "Willing and Able to Fake Emotions: A Closer Examination of the Link between Emotional Dissonance and Employee Well-Being." *Journal of Applied Psychology*, vol. 96, no. 2, 2011, pp. 377–91.

Scardamalia, Marlene, and Carl Bereiter. "The Development of Evaluative Diagnostic and Remedial Capabilities in Children's Composing." *The Psychology of Written Language: A Developmental Approach*, edited by M. Martlew, Wiley, 1983, pp. 67–95.

Sommers, Nancy. "Revision Strategies of Student Writers and Experienced Adult Writers." *College Composition and Communication*, vol. 31, no. 4, 1980, pp. 378–88.

Spear, Rachel N. "'Let Me Tell You a Story' On Teaching Trauma Narratives, Writing, and Healing." *Pedagogy: Critical Approaches to Teaching Literature, Language, Composition, and Culture*, vol. 14, no. 1, 2014, pp. 53–79.

Stewart, Graeme, et al. "Anxiety and Self-Efficacy's Relationship with Undergraduate Students' Perceptions of the Use of Metacognitive Writing Strategies." *Canadian Journal for the Scholarship of Teaching and Learning*, vol. 6, no. 1, 2015, pp. 4–23.

Tinelli, Lisabeth. *Re-conceptualizing the Rhetorical Triangle: Informal Contexts in First-Year Composition*. Diss., University of Rochester, 2016.

12. First-Year Composition Students: Creating Their Own Stories

JEANNE HUGHES

"My history with writing isn't the greatest ... I believe that a main reason to why I struggle so much with writing is because growing up I have been told multiple times that I am not the level of writing that I should be for my age. As a result, I have become very insecure about my writing."—Abby, college freshman

Teaching composition to first-year students is not only about content. Students are exposing themselves emotionally when they share their writing. Some would rather stare at a blank page and fail a writing assignment by not doing it than be told, in some cases again, that their writing is not good enough. Insecurity about writing skill is not the only barrier. Students might lack the words or coping mechanisms to deal with the writing that spills out of them. They try to focus on writing something else, but the writing leads back to the same story pushing to be told. International students also struggle with words. Their new English vocabulary does not always provide the precise meaning they seek, which causes frustration, and, at times, plagiarism.

As a composition teacher of first-year undergraduates, I have seen students crippled in their writing process for all of the above reasons. I have sought ways to help them help themselves. Individual conferences, feedback, class conferences, writing practice, and frequent written reflections are all ways I have used to get students thinking about their own writing. I remember reading *Clearing the Way* by Tom Romano when I was an undergraduate student. I was struck by his genuine enthusiasm for student writing, and his words have inspired my teaching: "A teacher ... is in an excellent position to show students that someone is interested in what they have to say" (Romano 9). Emotions in a composition classroom do not always have to be negative. When faced with students' past failures or lack of confidence, a teacher can be a catalyst for change. Classroom communities can be built where students are working together. Romano's enthusiasm stuck with me because students want to be in a classroom where they are comfortable, engaged, and respected. There are multiple strategies I use to help students get past their own doubts, and each strategy has the same foundation: I am interested in what they have to say.

Individual Conferences

"I have never been a very good writer." This familiar greeting has been uttered by many students as they enter my office for a writing conference. We haven't even begun to discuss their ideas or what they have written, and they begin with a disclaimer.

My response used to be "yet." When I responded that way, it was meant to get students to reframe the way they think about their own skills. While positive and putting the responsibility on the student, I also gave them the idea that I had some cure to their problems—that students who came into my class were the lucky ones because they would learn to write. What I was not acknowledging with this response was the ability they already had. Clearly, this is where those conversations should have started.

My response varies now based on what writing I have seen and what else students have shared. I want them reflecting on their own abilities, thinking about what they can do and what they need to improve. Their writing should reflect their own intended purpose and direction, which was illustrated by a student named Max as he wrote about childhood memories.

Max entered my office with a draft of the first essay for our composition class. It was a narrative essay he was writing about his grandmother's art gallery. Before he even sat down, he uttered the disclaimer. Max explained that he had started college and then left after the first semester. He worked for two years before deciding to return to school, but he still had vivid memories of his unsuccessful semester. Max said he was not a good student or a good writer. I thought about how he had shown up every day and was very attentive in class. So far, I was not seeing a student who matched Max's description.

Then, we turned to his essay. He said that he was stuck. For many years, my first inclination was to help my students get un-stuck by telling them what they needed to do or asking leading questions. Fortunately, Newkirk's advice in *EdWeek* has helped me to "know when to stop talking." I asked Max to tell me the story. He discussed his grandmother, the art gallery, and his grandfather. He continued by telling how his grandfather set up the gallery and how he, his sister, and his grandfather would play games. He mentioned a painting he did in the story. I asked about it, and he answered quickly before telling more about his grandfather. Although I was curious about how the painting fit into the story, Max's thoughts were elsewhere. He shared another memory that included his sister and grandfather. As Moher explains, "The purpose of the conference is not to praise or to judge the quality of the writing, but rather to encourage students to pursue ideas, feelings, or merely a sense of things which they may not yet have thought out or been able to express" (32). Max continued to talk about his gallery adventures and then told of their abrupt ending when his grandfather died.

We sat silently in my office looking at each other. Then Max said he didn't realize how much his grandfather was in the story. He said it was really hard to think about how things changed after his grandfather died. It appeared that Max intended to write one story, but another story was coming out instead. He said he had to think some more and left to write. Max's final essay about how the death of his grandfather changed a childhood tradition was much different than what he started with, but something else also changed. In his reflection, Max sounded different when discussing his abilities: "This is an example of how even though it may take me multiple drafts, I can make something great happen ... I learned from this essay how amazing it is how writing can evolve." I listened as Max told his story and discovered his own direction.

Teacher silence does not always elicit a student revelation, as exemplified by Abby's story. She came to my office per my request. Her class attendance had been inconsistent, she did not submit drafts, and then she handed in a largely plagiarized essay. When she came to my office, I had the essay with the highlighted plagiarized paragraphs to show her, but she started to cry and say she is not good at English. And even worse, it appeared I was confirming her evaluation with the highlighted copy of her draft. I wanted Abby to move past those feelings of self-doubt. She had already decided to attempt this paper after not submitting the previous one. There had to be something motivating her. I asked her how she chose her topic, which was serial killers. She stopped crying and told me about the mysteries that caught her attention, the crime shows she loved, and her passion for studying human behavior. It was clear she was interested in her topic.

I asked her how she gathered her information. She told me about the articles she read. I noticed how many details she recounted without checking the articles. Her entire demeanor changed as she excitedly discussed her topic. We then discussed her draft. She said she was unsure how to summarize and paraphrase, and since she was not a good writer, she was afraid she would leave out important information. When I asked how she would start this essay, she looked immediately at the highlighted draft still on my desk. I turned it over and handed her a clean sheet of paper, saying, "You know so much about this topic already. Write what you just told me." Abby looked at me skeptically for a minute and then decided to start writing. It was not long before she had written a detailed page-and-a-half from memory. Before coming to my office, she had done everything she was supposed to do to create her research essay. She had read multiple articles, highlighted them, and taken notes. But when she went to write, she had let her emotions cripple her.

However, Abby had just shown that she could write. She needed to do it and realize she could do it. She then confessed she had not done her previous essay because she said it was easier to get a failing grade for not doing it than to be told her writing was not good enough. Abby's plagiarized draft led to the conversation that revealed her angst about writing, but more importantly, her ability to write. Having the opportunity to learn about the negative emotions she tied to writing gave us the chance to talk about what she could do. Her actions showed she wanted a change. She came to my office and talked, and I saw her work through her emotions, move past her preconceptions, and give her attention to her writing. Abby's missing essay and subsequent paraphrasing failure could have perpetuated Abby's negative feelings about her writing abilities, but she was able to look at what she could write and start a new story for her writing self.

Feedback

I have seen students flip to the last page of returned essays to see their grades without reading the narrative comments. Their focus is on outside evaluation instead of their writing potential. Grades can be perceived as an ending; feedback facilitates new beginnings. I think prompt feedback is essential (Chickering et al. 4). Students want feedback as they are creating. Whether the feedback is from me or classmates, it helps students focus on their writing.

Feedback should facilitate student goals. Sommers discusses how some feedback can lead to student writers focusing more on responding to teacher direction instead of discovering their own purpose (149–50). At the beginning of the semester, students will ask, "What should I fix?" They are giving me too much power over their writing. Instead, I ask them about their purpose and goals for their writing. What do you like about this essay? What are you struggling with? What do you plan to do next? Frequent conversations allow students to talk out ideas.

By including students in the feedback process, they get the chance to evaluate others' writing and think about their own. Nick discussed how he benefitted from giving feedback: "Helping others with their essays did give me insights into my own writing. I was able to look for mistakes ... that I maybe wouldn't have originally looked for, or added details in places I wouldn't have originally thought of myself." Nick's feedback to others caused him to think about his own revisions. Whether they are getting or giving feedback, students are thinking about writing.

Even after an essay is handed in for a grade, feedback is still important. Bobby considered feedback an important part of his process: "The teachers that I had for my previous English classes didn't give me good feedback on my essays. They would circle a grade at the top and pick out all of my grammatical errors ... Having those short quick talks ... helped me." Although grades at most institutions are necessary, they should not be the story of a writer. The focus should be on the writer and the writing. Talk about writing allows writers to create their own stories.

Class Conferences

While sharing and discussing writing is a way for students to think about their own writing, it can also be difficult to do. Sharing writing is a risk, and students need a supportive, constructive environment. At the beginning of the semester, I use class conferences to have students share their writing. Class conferences are when the entire class focuses on one student's essay. The student volunteers to share, and a clear protocol is discussed before the conferences begin (Hughes). In these conferences, students analyze writing together.

When Ryan entered my composition class in the fall, he said, "Coming into the first day of English I was very nervous. I was not confident in my reading and writing abilities." He continued, "If you asked me the first week of classes this semester what course I was most nervous for in college I would have definitely said English." Ryan did not volunteer to share his first essay, but he was very busy providing feedback to others. He said, "Reading and commenting on my classmates' essays gave me more ideas on where to go with my own essay." Ryan went from not feeling confident to saying, "I enjoyed reading and commenting on everyone's essay as it was very helpful on what to look for when writing and editing my own."

Alex's narrative essay was the first one we discussed as a class one semester. I sought volunteers, but there was reluctance. Ryan was not the only one who did not want to share first. Hannah also said she was too nervous. Alex joked aloud that he "volunteered" (using air quotes as he addressed the class) after I said he wrote a lively story with action that others might appreciate.

The class laughed at how he explained his volunteering. Alex may not have realized it, but his use of humor benefitted our community building. Sharing essays can be very stressful for students, and Alex's humor relaxed others.

Alex's willingness to share his essay gave the class a chance to work on responding to writing together. His joke about forced volunteerism gained him some immediate allies who appreciated that he was sharing first and understood how hard it was to share writing with an entire class. Tobin states, "Writing students succeed when teachers establish productive relationships with—and between—their students" (6). Although Alex was not unwilling to share, he did let others know that he had to be nudged into it, and in the process, he became a catalyst in creating a community where those relationships could be formed.

After helping Alex and others improve their writing, Ryan volunteered to share his second essay. Class conferences gave Ryan confidence. In a reflection, he wrote:

> After the first couple of weeks of class, I started to become more and more interested in the course content. By the middle of the semester, I had seen huge improvements on [sic] my reading and writing abilities. By the end of the course, I started to enjoy reading and writing more and more than any other English course in the past.

Class conferences are a way to build a community in a writing class. Even when students are nervous about sharing writing, they can still participate by offering feedback. These conferences give students the chance to talk through ideas and evaluate their thinking. Participating in class conferences helps students develop their writing confidence.

Writing Practice

To get better at writing, students need practice. Kittle and Gallagher recommend writing notebooks where students can practice writing and take chances (18). Ungraded writing notebooks give students personal space to create and develop ideas. In addition to writing notebooks, I have students keep reading response journals and write frequent reflections. Students write often.

When students enter my FYC class, some view reading and writing as chores. They may have used online summaries to answer questions about reading in the past, and they create writing to fulfill assignments. There is a disconnect, and writing practice is one way to help students break out of rote behaviors and encourage them to make new discoveries.

At the beginning of the semester, Theresa shared how she lost her passion for reading and writing:

> Since the day I was allowed to have crayons and could make up stories out of the pictures in a children's book, I didn't stop for a while ... I would be reading, drawing, or practicing my ABC's. When I started school and the reading and writing assignments kept coming in, I felt out of touch with my love for it. Being assigned a reading or writing assignment felt as if my creativity was being taken away. Ever since, I have struggled with creative writing and I never have any free time to read. Throughout this semester, some of my creativity has returned. The journals we do regularly in class has [sic] helped a great amount.

Reading how she explained her disengagement with her creativity shows how student emotion can affect learning. Theresa was starting the semester feeling resigned instead of excited. It is an emotion I have seen on many students' faces as they enter my classroom. Students need the chance to rediscover that excitement.

Writing practice also helps students developmentally. Roger, an international student, began the semester in the back row with his head down on his desk. After failing to submit multiple assignments, I wondered how he could improve his writing if he did not even try. After he explained his struggles with understanding and writing English, I could see why he was so withdrawn in class. I encouraged him to just try. His early writing was labored. He struggled with clearly communicating his ideas. But, in the third week of class, he was already making progress because he was writing. Roger began listening to other non-native English speakers in our class. He realized he wasn't alone, which offered him some comfort in his language struggles. His journal writing started changing. Instead of quick responses with incomplete sentences, he was creating more complete ideas.

Roger's early literacy narrative writings were revealing. He would answer questions by first reading responses on the Internet. I noticed that he would begin with sentences or parts of sentences that did not sound like him at all. When I asked him to explain analysis, he began with the following sentence: "Analysis is the process of breaking a complex topic or substance into smaller parts in order to gain a better understanding of it" (an explanation he found on Wikipedia). He then went on to create a thoughtful response about his ideas:

> My first analysis paragraph is focusing on entrust of the paragraphs. I read a lot of articles in this semester, and I learned persuasiveness is totally difference depending on the paragraph order. So, I usually write about the composition of the overall sentences in first analysis. In the second paragraph of the analysis, I will find out the author's appeal, which are ethical, logical, and emotional

appeal. An ethical appeal is an opinion from expert or professional person. It can give authenticity to readers. Logical appeal is correct evidence, which include pictures, specific number of people, and specific percentage etc. It is also can give credibility to readers. Emotional is the author's emotion, which I can get from the author's words choice. By writing analysis, we can get into the deep of the article. And the ability is very helpful for other classes and our future.

Roger was getting himself started with words from other people. While his starts were actually patchwriting, I had to consider my response in terms of his development. Crook explains the need for educators to "develop developmental responses to patchwriting that allow students to grow as writers" (2). Roger was attempting to navigate a new language in a college level writing course, and he needed more time and practice.

Writing practice continued, and Roger's reliance on others changed as he grew more confident. After reading several essays and writing out his thoughts, he began to evaluate his learning: "I need to read more newspaper[s] because I do not have any knowledge when I [sic] reading the article in this semester." Roger realized that he was lacking background knowledge, and that was affecting his understanding. He became more attentive during discussions, and he read more. Practice writing his ideas helped him discover how to aid his own development. Roger's engagement continued as he worked diligently on creating his own essays. He left the patchwriting behind as he found his own voice in his newly acquired language.

Through writing notebooks, reading responses, and reflections, students can analyze their own writing processes and make decisions about what helps and does not help them. They are often in my class for only one semester, but if they have acquired tools to help them think about their own learning, they can break out of those progress-hindering narratives they have created for themselves.

Written Reflections

Students need time to think about their writing. Frequent reflection facilitates that thinking. I include the following quote on the initial reflection activity I give to students: "Reflection … is the … process by which we develop and achieve, first, specific goals for learning; second, strategies for reaching those goals; and third, means of determining whether or not we have met those goals or other goals" (Yancey 6). Just like listening while students talk out ideas, reflection facilitates metacognition and empowers students to recognize their own strengths and challenges. Students can get caught in a cycle of going from assignment to assignment without seeing the reason for the assignments or looking for connections. I want them to understand the intended goal for each class activity and to think about those goals in relation to their own learning. I also want them to think about what helps them learn, and reflection gives them the opportunity to think through these important ideas.

Before students even start to write reflections, we have explicit conversations about the purpose of reflection (Ratto-Parks). Students begin by writing about their past experiences with reading and writing. We discuss pausing periodically to reflect on what they are doing in and out of class and how it affects their reading and writing. In writing, students discussed their abilities and challenges. Many tied their feelings to past grades they received in English classes. They were connecting their perceived abilities to the assessment received from others. I explained to them that I wanted them to base their reflections on what they were seeing. What worked for them? What didn't work? Where have they improved? What do they still need to work on? These periodical reflections led to a culminating activity that took the place of our final exam. In this final reflection, students reviewed the entire semester and discussed their own progress. I have found these final reflections honest, amusing, sometimes too critical, but at the same time, forward thinking. Students recognize their strengths and weaknesses and discuss ideas about future learning.

Hannah's reflections show her changing perceptions over the course of a semester. She did not speak with confidence about her writing when she entered our composition class. She was a student who had struggled with English in high school, and she even considered taking Developmental English instead of FYC:

> Coming into this class I didn't know if I was going to be able to handle it. My advisor said I could drop down to the lower one if I wasn't comfortable ... I always hated English, I dreaded it. I never thought I was good at writing."

Hannah's first essay was about trying out for the volleyball team in high school with few expectations, only to make the team as a freshman when her friends did not. It was a difficult subject she chose because there were many complex feelings associated with the memory. Making that team caused an eventual change in her friend group, an unexpected life disruption after what seemed like an exciting accomplishment. Hannah's first draft was full of mixed feelings of pride and abandonment. I asked if she wanted to share with the class. Hannah said no because it would make her uncomfortable. After we discussed other students' essays in class the following week, she told me she wished she hadn't been too nervous to share. The memoir essay was one she thought about all semester:

> Reading back on this essay now if I were to change something it would be the way I put everything together. I would want to outline my paragraphs in a certain way, and I would especially make sure that every paragraph was started with a complete, clear statement. But also making sure I stayed on the one paragraph's subject and not run off."

Her assessment of this essay is very different than the original reflection about not being good at writing. She was evaluating her writing and developing plans.

Hannah also wrote essays that she considered successful: "The argument essay was by far one of the best essays I have done in a while. I knew what I was talking about. I had plenty of information for my paragraphs … I started out each and every one with a clear, to the point statement." After a semester of writing and thinking about her own writing, Hannah was able to identify things she liked about her writing as well as what she still wanted to work on. Her final reflective paragraph for FYC began like this: "I changed my writing a lot through the semester, but I also have things to work on in the future." There is no writing about dread or fearing English class; instead, she discussed wanting to improve her paraphrasing skills and planning to be "a master at it." There is a huge shift in the tone of her writing from the beginning of the semester to the end. Spending time writing, discussing writing, and reflecting on her own writing let her rewrite her English story.

Conclusion

Students come into FYC classes with baggage. They have experiences in previous classes or in other parts of their lives that have caused them to define themselves and their abilities, sometimes very negatively. Even multiple successful essays cannot take away the shame of the one that made them feel lesser than other students. It is important to acknowledge this reality when students enter the classroom. Those previous experiences and preconceived notions can turn into roadblocks if students are not given the chance to reconsider their perceptions and start a new story. Letting students voice their reservations is a way to get conversations started. I have begun classes by handing out index cards and asking for anonymous input about reading, writing, and students' expectations for the course. I collect the cards and then pass them out randomly. Students take turns reading the comments about how other students feel about the class expectations and their own abilities. By reading other students' concerns, my students are already helping each other have a voice in our classroom. This opportunity to speak their minds anonymously is what I hope to be a gateway to open conversations throughout the semester. I do not begin class with my plans and expectations for students. I begin with their thoughts and expectations for our class. My hope is that this student-centered activity sets the tone for a community where we listen to each other.

Being attentive to students, letting them tell their stories and share their concerns, and giving them tools to work through their challenges can allow them to take control of their learning. There is not one specific way to build a confident writer, but there are many ways a composition teacher can give students the opportunity to create their own stories.

Works Cited

Chickering, Arthur W., et al. "Seven Principles for Good Practice in Undergraduate Education." *AAHE Bulletin*, Mar. 1987, pp. 3–7.

Crook, Stephanie. "Moving Beyond Transgression: Contextualizing Plagiarism and Patchwriting." *Online Submission*, Mar. 2016, pp. 1–20. EBSCOhost.

Gallagher, Kelly, and Penny Kittle. *180 Days: Two Teachers and the Quest to Engage and Empower Adolescents*. Portsmouth, NH, Heinemann, 2018.

Hughes, Jeanne. "Learning Skills That Transfer: Using Class Conferences to Teach Critical Thinking." *The Journal of Student Success in Writing*, vol. 1, no. 1, article 3, 2017, pp. 1–29. Available at: https://digitalcommons.georgiasouthern.edu/jssw/vol1/iss1/3.

Moher, Terry A. "The Writing Conference: Journeys into Not Knowing." *Teaching the Neglected "R."*, edited by Thomas Newkirk and Richard Kent. Portsmouth, NH, Heinemann, 2007, pp. 26–38.

Newkirk, Thomas. "Teachers: Know When to Stop Talking." *Education Week*, 2015. Retrieved from http://www.edweek.org/ew/articles/2015/07/28/teachers-know-when-to-stop-talking.html.

Ratto-Parks, A. "Negotiating Chaos: Metacognition in the First-Year Writing Classroom" [Web log post], 2014. Retrieved from http://www.improvewithmetacognition.com/negotiating-chaos-metacognition-in-the-first-year-writing-classroom/.

Romano, Tom. *Clearing the Way*. Portsmouth, NH, Heinemann, 1987.

Sommers, Nancy. "Responding to Student Writing." *College Composition and Communication*, vol. 33, no. 2, May 1982, pp. 148–56. EBSCOhost.

Tobin, Lad. *Writing Relationships*. Portsmouth, NH, Heinemann, 1991.

Wikipedia contributors. "Analysis." Wikipedia, the Free Encyclopedia, 30 Apr. 2019. Web. 23 May 2019.

Yancey, Kathleen. *Reflection in the Writing Classroom*. Utah State UP, 1998.

13. We Awaken To Ourselves: Emotion, Reflective Writing, and the Study Abroad Experience

Todd Harper & Michayla Grey

Writing has always been an integral part of the study abroad experience. It allows students who are studying abroad to reflect upon the intellectual and emotional transformations that they undergo as they encounter and then adapt to obstacles and challenges within their new environment. As the well-known travel writer Pico Iyer so astutely observes, "It doesn't matter where or how far you go—the farther commonly the worse—the important thing is how alive you are. Writing of every kind is a way to wake oneself up and keep as alive as when one has fallen in love" (255). Although Iyer does not speak directly to the study abroad experience, his observation could very easily apply to it. Placed within a setting that is foreign to them, students become keenly aware of their own subjectivity, of who they are as cultural and historical beings who respond in certain ways to their environment—ways that are often different from their host culture. In short, they become awake to themselves.

In general, we ascribe reflection and writing—the two often go hand in hand on a study abroad program as reflective writing—to cognition. Reflective writing, from journaling to autoethnography, allows students to record their experiences encountering an obstacle or challenge within a certain frame of mind, only to realize that that frame is inadequate to address that obstacle or challenge. Through reflective writing, they then create a new frame. Iyer also reminds us that writing is an embodied activity, that writing, along with the reflection that accompanies it when we travel, awakes us to ourselves and reminds us that we are alive. We awake intellectually and emotionally.

In this chapter, we describe a reflective paper that was at the center of Dr. Harper's world literature class. As part of the Great Books study abroad experience, which included a lower level World Literature and an Arts in

Society class, Dr. Harper and his Art History colleague, Dr. Jessica Stephenson, asked students to create a personalized Google Map that would be used in both classes. Before departure, students pinned various sites that they would visit in Rome, Florence, Orvieto, Siena, and Montepulciano as part of the program. These initial pins included at least three facts about the site. When students eventually visited these sites on their program, they uploaded photos and journal entry recordings of their experiences (see Appendix A for a description of the Project). The personalized Google Maps were then used as heuristics for longer reflective papers. These papers asked students to discuss their journeys along with obstacles encountered within that journey, using the *Odyssey, Aeneid,* or *Ramyana* as touchstones (see Appendix B for a description of the Journey Paper).

In visiting several of the sites, which included a number of famous Roman Catholic cathedrals, Ms. Grey recorded, in surprisingly emotional terms, the unique obstacles she faced encountering these sites as someone outside Christianity. Ms. Grey is devoutly Jewish, having visited Israel on a life-changing study abroad program the previous year. Her reflective paper described the difficulty of trying to relate and understand a tradition outside her experience, especially after she discovers anti-Semitic images in a well-known fresco in Orvieto depicting the last days, final judgment, and the apocalypse (see Appendix C for images of the *Deeds of the Antichrist,* which was particularly troubling to Ms. Grey). Her paper reflects an internal struggle to add meaning to this troubling experience in a program she feels should be life-changing. More importantly, when brought into relation with the Google Maps project, her paper becomes more than a reflection of her experience; it evolves into an essayistic map of her attempt to locate herself, emotionally and mentally, within the program as well as within the larger trajectory of her life.

The guiding principle of the Great Books Study Program and its assignments was reflection-in-action within the context of mapping space. As Jessica Stephenson, M. Todd Harper, and Emily Klump argue in a separate article on the same Great Books study program, study abroad inherently forces students to adjust and readapt themselves to form new frames of reference in order to confront new obstacle and challenges (Stephenson et al. 2019). However, by placing reflection within the greater context of a cartographic framework within the Google Maps project, they attempted to enact a type of reflection within the students' literal and figurative sense of space. In short, the project these authors describe (and, which is, in part, detailed below) not only asked students to create a literal map of each of their destinations and how they arrived there, but also a figurative map of how they found themselves as cultural and historical beings within that space. Through the facts, photos, and journal entries that they included within each pin along with their paper, students were able to see themselves as twenty-first century subjects moving through and, in turn, shaping the multiple layers of history and culture that they encountered in one place (see Appendix A for a description of the Google Maps Project).

As an example, Stephenson, Harper, and Klump note how students included pins for the Baths of Diocletian and Santa Maria di Martyri and dei Angeli, which were two of the first sites visited. In those pins, students noted certain facts, such as the fact that the Baths of Diocletian were built in the third century in honor of Diocletian and that Michelangelo used the design of the Bath's vaults to design the church's dome and to attach it to the vaults over 1,200 years later. However, students also included their own photos and stories, depicting how they absorbed that space, especially its mixture of the Roman Republic, the Renaissance, and twenty-first century Rome; how they inhabited that space on the day they visited; and, finally, how they too shaped that space. Stephenson, Harper, and Klump argue that this blending of geometric coordinates with the sensory description of photos and journal entries allow students to experience space as something that is alive and constantly changing. Although they do not address emotion directly, the "sensory description of photos and journal entries" reflected the students visceral as well as cerebral responses to the various sites. Indeed, it was often the emotional content of their pins and the resulting narratives that students wrote for class is what gave the feeling of space as something living and constantly changing.

Where this chapter differs from the previous work of Stephenson, Harper, and Klump is in its focus on emotions, particularly the relationship between emotion and place, mapping emotions, and reflective writing and emotions. In short, this chapter not only seeks to examine how one student experienced and shaped these multi-dimensional sites through her presence and then later through her writing, but more specifically how she felt within those spaces afterwards. In describing her paper, Ms. Grey moves beyond a cognitive account of her experience to one that includes a strong sense of emotion, one that is ultimately an embodied experience.

However, before moving into a discussion of emotions, it is important to further elucidate reflection as a means of literally and figuratively locating oneself as well as to give this type of mapping a name—wayfinding. Although she speaks to reflective writing and not to mapping, Kathleen Blake Yancey's statement on reflection as dialectical has cartographic implications. She notes,

> Reflection is dialectical, putting multiple perspectives into play with each other in order to produce insight. Procedurally, reflection entails a *looking forward*

to goals we might obtain as well as a *casting backward* to see where we have been. When we reflect, we thus *project* and *review*, often putting the project and reviews in dialogue with one another (Yancey 123).

As an historical methodology, modern dialectics asks us to think spatially about time. Very loosely put, it allows us to locate ourselves between where we have been and where we are going. Reflection enables this process at the individual level when we put "multiple perspectives into play with each other in order to produce insight." We find ourselves *looking forward* by *casting backwards* in order to determine our goals.

Notably, Yancey's statement has interesting implications for study abroad. Study abroad, as we have noted, is inherently a reflective practice with the *casting backwards* and *looking forward* occurring within a new environment where a student must constantly adjust or even abandon existing frames of reference. Moreover, these experiences take place on a physical as well as textual level, making them embodied experiences. Our encounter with another culture, especially a culture whose history is as rich and deep as Italy's, leads us to think about who we are and where we have been, while also thinking who the host culture is and where it has been. Moreover, that sort of locating oneself also involves *looking side to side* at cultural and societal differences. Who are they and who am I? Finally, as an embodied experience, it is as much visceral as it is cerebral. We often arrive at certain places (literally and figuratively) through our emotions first and then our intellect second.

Within the context of study abroad, this type of reflection (an embodied experience that is at once physical and textual) often takes the shape of *wayfinding*. Wayfinding is the "use and organization of sensory cues from the external environment" to locate oneself within space and then to identify the path to a desired location as quickly as possible (Farr et al.). These sensory cues can include signage as well as geographical and topological features that can be read and then physically or mentally mapped out. With the advent GPS technologies, especially within the context of study abroad, wayfinding becomes a form of reflection. As Adam Stantz notes,

> Our mobile technologies literalize these emplacements, thereby enabling students to see relationships they have developed. While these traces are developed through mapping their own work, the use of GPS-enable mobile devices allows for a more distinct sharing of space and location with other users. Accordingly, mapping, sharing maps, and telling stories of movement externalize stories we have shared but also allows students heuristic memory and access to visual representations of their movement to which we simply have not had access. (165–66; also quoted in Stevenson et al.)

Stantz identifies a number of principles that were formative in Drs. Harper and Stephenson's creation of the assignment. First, the Google Maps project allowed students to see relationships, not only those that they developed within the group, but also their relationship to their external environment. Moreover, in providing journal entries and photos, they were visually able to externalize their own stories. Finally, that externalization allow those outside, not just their teachers, but parents and friends, access to their movement.

In the end, the Google Maps project and its accompanying reflective paper created a sense of "lived space" (Stephenson et al.). Through the pinned points on their personalized maps, students were able to see where their own experiences and sensory perception of those spaces intersected with the maps geometric coordinates to reflect how those spaces not only changed them, but how they too changed those spaces (Stephenson et al.). As the theorist Edward Soja argues, space is always dynamic, always changing, always more than a set of geometric coordinates when filled with living, perceiving bodies (Soja; Reynolds). The actual map the students created laid bare the raw recorded material within various spaces, while their narrative, reflective papers gave greater shape and definition to how they moved, experienced, and even changed those spaces they experienced.

In the case of Ms. Grey's paper, that "greater shape" and "definition" came in the form of her emotional response to the Christian symbolism and anti-Semitic images of a well-known cathedral in Orvieto. As Alenka Poplin notes, our response to space is not just cerebral, but also visceral and emotional. Indeed, emotion places an important role in how we approach and then understand space. Poplin quotes Roger S. Ulrich, "Affect is central to conscious experience and behavior in any environment, whether natural or built, crowded or unpopulated. Because virtually no meaningful thoughts, actions, or environmental encounters occur without affect" (Ulrich quoted in Poplin 292). We come to understand our world as much through our emotions as we do our mind. Moreover, emotions and mind are ultimately inseparable.

The obstacle that Ms. Grey describes is twofold. On the one hand, as a Jewish woman, she initially felt a certain ambivalence because she was unable to read the signs (meaning, the Christian symbolism within the art and the architectural design) outside of their aesthetic value. This was compounded even more when she entered into the church and encountered an anti-Semitic image on a well-known fresco by Signorelli. On the other hand, she wanted to make her experience in Italy—one that had been discussed and anticipated throughout the year in her honors cohort—as meaningful as possible. In terms of the former, she lays out her most central challenge:

> Considering the fact that I am Jewish, and the majority of the sites that we visited throughout our trip in Italy were either churches or served as some significant site in the Christian or Catholic religions, it was very hard for me to connect with things on any level outside of them being extremely aesthetically pleasing. This definitely stood out to me as some sort of adversity that I had to overcome. I ended up being able to really get past this feeling of adversity when visiting the Duomo di Orvieto. Much of the reason I was able to get past it was due to the murals inside the cathedral and the architectural structure of the building itself.

A feeling of ambivalence is still a feeling, and Ms. Grey's inability to connect leaves her feeling spiritually empty, though somewhat awed by the aesthetic nature of the church.

This feeling of ambivalence is even more pronounced in the following lines from Ms. Grey's paper:

> The front of the Duomo is incredibly ornate and beautifully arranged. The façade is covered in murals and mosaics dedicated to the Assumption of the Virgin Mary, with a large rose stained-glass window at the top. The tympanum is occupied by a statue of Madonna and Child. There are also several bronze sculptures across the top of the piers of the façade representing different biblical aspects. Lastly, there are four columns along the base of the façade. Each column depicts a different story from the Bible via images carved into the stone. The first column (going from left to right) tells the story of Genesis, the second tells the story of the Tree of Jesse and prophesies of Redemption, the third shows episodes form the lives of Jesus and Mary, and the fourth is the Last Judgment: Book of Revelations. The exterior of the building, aside from the façade, and the interior of the building, aside from the mosaics and murals was covered in a latitudinally striped, dark gray and light gray stone pattern.

Although she is able to interpret many of the Biblical symbols, including New Testament imagery, her sentences are focused on artistic structure of the façade, as evidence by the subjects of her sentence: "the front of the Duomo," "the façade," "the tympanum," "several bronze sculptures," and the "four columns."

Nevertheless, as Ms. Grey makes evident in her paper and in her discussions with Dr. Harper, she desires to find some sort of spiritual connection, one that might be similar, though not exactly alike, to the way that she felt touring the synagogues and temples of Israel. This leads her to try to attach some sort of significance to various artifacts, even if that particular significance was not the intention of those artifacts. In short, she begins to freely associate meaning to the signs and symbols that she encounters on the façade of the church.

In terms of the latter, that is, being mistaken about one's own environment, Ms. Grey finds herself freely associating the dark and light gray stone pattern of this Renaissance cathedral—a pattern attributable to the availability of basalt and marble located within the region—to the stripped pajamas that Jewish prisoners were forced to wear in twentieth century concentration camps:

> The exterior of the building, aside from the façade, and the interior of the building, aside from the mosaics and murals was covered in a latitudinally striped, dark gray and light gray stone pattern. This instantly made me feel a large pit in my stomach. I realized that the pattern in the stones caused me to think of the Holocaust and the uniforms that the Nazi's made the Jewish people wear in the death camps, now known as "striped pajamas". The prisoners of the death camps would have their uniforms changed around every six weeks. People had to work, eat, sleep [spend their entire life] in the same clothes, so the dirt accumulated very quickly. I could see images in my head of prisoners, with disgusting, filthy striped uniforms surrounding the exterior of the cathedral. Furthermore, I was reminded of the movie, "The Boy in the Striped Pajamas". This is a very horrific, vivid, gruesome, and touching movie about a young boy who was captured and forced to work in one of the death camps, where he was later tragically murdered in a gas chamber. Although, I am sure that my interpretation of the architecture was nowhere near what the architects had intended, it still managed to have a huge impact on me, and I was made to feel this intense personal connection to the Duomo.

To be certain, Ms. Grey understands that there is no connection between the interchangeable pattern of the walls and the striped pajamas of Jewish prisoners. However, without knowledge of the reasoning for the church's patterning, she finds her mind freely associating until it can find meaning.

Anna Charisse Farr et al. observe that a variety of human elements allow individuals to locate themselves, including "spatial orientation, cognitive mapping abilities, route strategies, language, culture, gender, and biological factors" (716). These "human elements" aid individuals in reading signs, and when one or all of these elements break down, the individual either reaches for what she knows (in the above example, the artistic features of the architecture), becomes disorientated (unable to read anything and thus lost), or grasps onto something associative. In any case, the experience of being unable to read one's environment can lead someone from feeling indifferent to feeling lost to feeling mistaken about one's environment.

While Ms. Grey admits that the connection between white and grey striped design of the church exterior and those of the pajamas worn by Jewish prisoners is simply associative, she eventually encounters anti-Semitic images that were unfortunately common during the Renaissance. When she enters the cathedral's Chapel of the Madonna di San Brizio, she discovers Luca Signorelli's frescoes depicting the Apocalypse. Among these frescoes is *The Deeds of the Antichrist*, which portrays the devil speaking into the ears of the antichrist sowing discord through his preaching. The Antichrist, who stands on a pedestal, is surrounded by various scenes of chaos, including several citizens being thrown down and beaten by a mob, soldiers who have laid siege to a church, the sick and poor begin neglected, etc. Amidst the chaos—in fact, at the very front and near the center of the painting—is a money changer who is bargaining with a woman. The conniving and sneaky money changer has swarthy features, a beard, and a hooked nose, stereotypical attributes that Signorelli's fifteenth and sixteenth century audience would have recognized as a Jewish money lender (see Appendix C for images of *The Deeds of the Antichrist*). Over six hundred years later, these stereotypical attributes that characterize Signorelli's money lender are still recognizable, and it is they to which Ms. Grey responds:

> Typically, when we visited these grand cathedrals, I did not understand nor recognize much of the Christian or Catholic art that was displayed in the murals and mosaics on the walls. However, in one of the side chapels in the Duomo di Orvieto, there was one mural that really stood out to me. It was the first mural on your left side when you entered the chapel. Depicted in the painting was the image of the antichrist, alongside the antichrist was a very anti-Semitic image of a Jewish man, with a stereotypical large nose, handling money and trying to persuade the Christian figures to also handle the money. This was a concerning image for me to see. I had heard many stories, seen many artifacts, and learned in history class all about acts of anti-Semitism, however, never in a sacred space like this. I was shocked by the fact that painted into these breathtakingly gorgeous, ancient murals was such a judgmental image that added no significant meaning to the story of the painting itself. Although this was a negative connotation of Judaism, it still stood out to me as something important and that needed to be recognized.

For Ms. Grey, this depiction and others that she would see later on the program set up the challenge or obstacle that she must overcome.

Ms. Grey's desire to first find an emotional connection and then meaning within the symbols and images of the cathedral and its frescoes reveals something fundamental to reflection and writing. On the one hand, the dialectical process described by Yancey, the *looking forward* and the *casting backwards*, becomes almost impossible because she does not have all of the necessary language and art history terminology (at least, in the case of the striped pattern of the cathedral walls) to fully understand the cathedral's architectural history. Instead, she is forced to cast about in her own experience. On the other hand, once she has responded emotionally to the basalt and marble pattern, and then to Signorelli's anti-Semitic depiction of the anti-Christ, she has no choice but to try to assign both meaning. Her emotions have grasped a hold of these symbols, and now her mind finds it impossible to let go until they can be given significance.

Victor Savicki and Michele V. Price argue that this sort of attempt to seek meaning, even when that meaning is associative or has negative connotations, is a part of the reflective process. Citing Victor Frankl, who studies the way how the victims of Jewish concentration camps had sought to find meaning within their experience, even while imprisoned, and his "will to meaning," they note, "Reflection can be seen as a fundamental expression of humankinds' 'will to meaning' (Frankl, 1962), the desire to make sense of life's events. Reflective thinking has been proposed as an important feature of study-abroad learning: the challenge for students to construct a meaningful understand of events during their encounter with a different culture" (588). In their own study, Savicki and Price examined the ways in which study abroad students constructed meaning within a blogging assignment; however, we can apply their statement about study abroad, reflective thinking, and an "inherent will to meaning" to most any form of writing, especially narrative writing, which allows students to situate their experiences within a framework of *looking forward* and *casting backwards*, that is, to impose a significance on their own encounters with a foreign culture.

Ms. Grey, in the recording of her own impressions regarding the religious symbols that she encounters in the façade, the layered pattern that she sees in the walls, and in the encounter she eventually has with Signorelli's anti-Semitic image, reports her experience in a meaningful manner. However, Ms. Grey's writing, like all good writing, is more than a recording and reporting of her experiences. Rather, it is an inventive vehicle that allows her to shape those impressions into a positive and, for her, more meaningful story. In her own case, Ms. Grey weaves the story of Trojan prince Aeneas, who also encounters obstacles when he is forced from a burning Troy, into her own. Much like Odysseus before him, Aeneas encounters stiff resistance from the Gods when he sets out to discover Latium, including falling in love with Dido, whom he must ultimately reject in order to fulfill his destiny. (Aeneas must overcome his love for Dido and leave her in order to fulfill his destiny.) In identifying with Aeneas, Ms. Grey writes,

> Although the adversity that Aeneas and I encountered were different kinds of adversity, they still both taught important lessons. Both were very meaningful and sensitive topics that were held very dear to our hearts, Aeneas' being his romantic love for Dido, and mine being my passion for my Jewish beliefs and heritage.

> Aeneas learned that sometimes one's duty to their country and their future is the most important thing; following one's destiny is a crucial part to ensuring what needs to happen will happen. If one does not follow their destiny, eventually, they will encounter even more hardship and adversity. Staying on the path that guides you can be the key to one's success. However, sometimes veering from that path can bring something great and unexpected. I believe that Aeneas would strongly agree with the saying, "It's better to have loved and lost, then not to have loved at all."

In this particular passage, she identifies with Aeneas in two important ways. First, she recognizes the love of her own religious beliefs and heritage in Aeneas' passionate love for Dido. Second, she sees it as her destiny to maintain a path, one that includes and is shaped by her religious beliefs, while at the same time acknowledging that she will occasionally veer from that path to learn valuable lessons.

One thing that is interesting about Ms. Grey's attempt to relate her own encounter with adversity with that of Aeneas and Dido is that the analogy breaks down in some revealing ways. In the *Aeneid*, Aeneas must leave Dido in order to fulfill his destiny. (This eventually results in Dido's tragic suicide.) While the passion that Aeneas feels for Dido can be compared to that which Ms. Grey feels for Judaism, the outcome cannot be the same, or it would suggest that Ms. Grey would need to abandon her religious beliefs in order to fulfill an even greater destiny. Clearly, Ms. Grey does not intend to draw this final parallel, but the incongruity that does exist within her analogy suggests the difficulties encountered when students (really, all of us) try to make sense of the obstacles and challenges that are set in front of them. Nevertheless, reflective thinking, in general, and reflective writing, in particular, not only allows students to situate themselves and their experience by *looking forward* while *casting backward*, but also to give shape to their experiences and meaning to their lives through the narratives they tell.

In conclusion, we return to Pico Iyer's statement on travel writing: "It doesn't matter where or how far you go—the farther commonly the worse—the important thing is how alive you are. Writing of ever kind is a way to wake oneself up and keep as alive as when one has fallen in love" (255). In this chapter, we have noted two important items. First, reflective writing not only allows us to acknowledge and then record those challenges and obstacles that we encounter through travel and that bring us to life, but also to shape those experiences within the larger narrative of our lives. Second, as we witnessed with Ms. Grey's paper, the material that forms the basis for our reflective narratives is as much visceral and emotional as it is cerebral and intellectual. Finally, when the emotional and the intellectual are combined, the kind of writing that Iyer describes, the type of writing that awakens us and makes us feel alive, is an embodied experience.

Appendix A

Google Maps Project

For this assignment, you will create a Google Map, where you will pin several of the places that we visit in Rome, Montepulciano, Orvieto, Siena, and Florence.

Dr. Stephenson and I will provide you with the places that we would like for you to pin, often before we arrive. Here are the instructions that Dr. S. provided. (You will do the same map for both of us.)

How to Create and Manage your Google Maps Journal

Before May 14 and the official launch of your Great Books classes, plan to create your own Google Map for use throughout the three weeks we are traveling in Italy. The Map will enable you to create pins to mark key monuments visited, track your journey from location to location, make notes of your experience at each monument, and upload photographs of locations. This documentation will serve as a textual and visual journal documenting your journey. You will use this material as source material for two final course papers to be submitted for Dr. Harper's English Class and the other paper to Dr. Stephenson's Art History class. Dr. Harper and Dr. Stephenson will review your Google Map project once a week and it forms part of your course grade.

Step One: Create a Personal Google Map

1. You must have a Gmail or Google account. Create one for this class if needed.
2. Make sure that you are signed in to your Gmail account and thus to Google by clicking on the Login icon on the top right of the screen.
3. Click on the Google Apps menu on the top right of screen
4. Select the Maps icon which pulls up a new page with Maps
5. Click on Menu icon located at far left of maps page
6. Click on Your Places icon
7. Click on MAPS
8. Click on CREATE MAP at bottom of tab
9. In search tab type in Italy to pull up map of Italy
10. Click on "Untitled Map" to give your trip pap a unique name, something like "Great Bools Italy Summer 2018"
11. Save

You are now ready to start adding Pins to mark monuments that you encounter during the Great Books study abroad program. You should document the key monuments assigned by Dr. Harper and Dr. Stephenson, but can add pins for any place of interest to you whether it be roads, builds, landscapes, restaurants, and so on.

Before May 14, plan to create one pin that serves as a test pin. Using the instructions below, make a pin to mark the location of the Roma Termini Train Station. We will use this train station extensively during or stay in Rome.

Step Two: Create a Pin and add Text and Images

1. From Google Maps click on Menu in top left
2. Click on Your Places
3. Click on MAPS
4. Click on the title of the map you created for your trip (e.g., Great Books Italy 2018)
5. In the search box type in the name of the first monument you plan to pin, such as "Pantheon," making sure to select the ancient monument and not a hotel or restaurant with that name.
6. Click Add to Map
7. A blue pin will appear on your map
8. Click on the blue pin to pull up a box. There are icons at the bottom of the box where you can change the color of the pin, pull up a tab in which to add notes, and upload photos you take of the site, or that you find using the Google Image Search.
9. Repeat this process to add more pins
10. You can plot distance between monuments or add lines to plot your journey from monument to monument using the icons located below the search box at the top of the map.

You can zoom in and out of your Google Map to see the relationship between the monuments we are visiting and track your journey through Rome and other cities.

You will repeat this process for all the other Italian cities visited during this program!

(Note: The project itself was the result of Dr. Stephenson and Harper's brainstorming for the program. However, the actual language for the assignment is Dr. Stephenson's.)

Appendix B

Final Reflective Paper

For this assignment, I want you to use the texts that we have studied as well as one or two scholarly texts to help reflect upon an important experience that you have had.

To do this, I would like for you to identify one or two important experiences that you had on the trip. What occurred during that experience, and what lesson or lessons did you draw from that experience? If you were to state that lesson as part of an epic, what would be its theme? For example, you experienced something where you gained insight, where you overcame adversity through strength or wiliness or fidelity to a cause. Maybe, you found that you had to let go of something (ghosts), or maybe you found that some behavior that had worked in one context no longer worked in another (adaptability).

Once you have identified your experience and its lesson or theme, I would like for you to locate that same lesson or theme as it developed in one or more of our texts? What happens within those texts that is similar? How do the insights of those characters or the text itself help you provide you with insight into your own experience? Moreover, as you research within the primary text, do a little secondary research upon the theme to help elucidate the primary text as well as your own experience.

The paper should be somewhere around 1,500+ words (6–8 double-spaced pages) and should include internal and external citations in MLA style. As part of the paper, you will want to include a summary of your experience, summaries of similar experiences within your primary text(s), analysis that helps to draw out and elucidate the common theme in both, and at least one secondary source. (You may want to use yours or another group's study guide. You will also want to review the answers to your book and discussion questions. They should be a good guide as well. Finally, look over your Google map to help think back on the program.)

Appendix C

Images of Luca Signorelli's Deeds of the Antichrist in the Cathedral in Orvieto, Italy

Figure 13.1

Figure 13.2

Figure 13.3

Works Cited

Farr, Anna Charisse, et al. "Wayfinding: A Simple Concept, a Complex Process." *Transport Reviews*, vol. 32, no. 6, 2012, pp. 715–43.

Iyer, Pico. *The Open Road*. Vintage, 2008.

Poplin, Alenka. "Cartographies of Fuzziness: Mapping Places and Emotions." *The Cartographic Journal*, vol. 54, no. 4, 2017, pp. 291–300.

Reynolds, Nedra. *Geographies of Writing: Inhabiting Places and Encountering Difference*. Southern Illinois Press, 2007.

Savicki, Victor, and Michelle V. Price. "Student Reflective Writing: Cognition and Affect Before, During, and After Study Abroad." *Journal of College Student Development*, vol. 56, 2015, pp. 587–601.

Soja, Edward. *Thirdspace: Journeys to Other Real-and-Imagined Places*. Hoboken, 1996.

Stantz, Adam. "Wayfinding in Global Contexts: Mapping Localized Practices with Mobile Devices." *Computers and Composition*, vol. 38, 2015, pp. 164–76.

Stephenson, Jessica, et al. "Google Maps as Transformative Learning Tool in the Study Abroad Experience." *Journal of Global Initiatives*, vol. 13, no. 2, 2019 (to be published).

Ulrich, Robert S. "Aesthetic and Affective Response to Natural Environment, Behavior and the Natural Environment." *Human Behavior and the Environment*, vol. 6, 1983, pp. 85–125.

Yancey, Kathleen Blake. *A Rhetoric of Reflection*. Logan, Utah State UP, 2016.

14. Honoring Contemplative Practices in the Writing Classroom: A Personal and Pedagogical Exploration

RACHEL N. SPEAR

JoAnn Campbell's 1994 article "Writing to Heal: Using Meditation in the Writing Process" stresses the need for composition faculty to merge meditation and writing practices while *mindfully* recognizing the field's historic and complicated relationship with meditation. Mindfulness, like meditation, has traditionally been "on the fringes of our discipline" (Campbell 246). But we have seen an increase in contemplative pedagogies within pedagogical and writing fields—even making prominent appearances at the annual Conference on College Composition. While I welcome this influx of attention to "contemplative education" (Simmer-Brown and Grace; Barbezat and Bush; Kirsch; Wardle and Downs) and recognize its potential to enhance focus, decrease stress, and tap into creative energies (Schoeberlein; Rotne and Rotne; Olson; Kirsch; O'Reilley), I have mostly positioned my scholarship and teachings in the margins. I have researched mindfulness, incorporated smaller writing activities, and believe in its benefits while acknowledging its limitations. However, my own insecurities have often prohibited my connecting pedagogical practices too much with contemplative studies—perhaps because my individual practice falls short when scholars highlight the importance of one's personal practices before moving to the class (Srinivasan 18; Moffett 246). Yet I return to the idea, recently exploring how mindfulness in writing classrooms might be both explicit and implicit and how these practices might better teach the whole person, focusing on students' writing skills and emotional well-being. Knowing others' successful integration of contemplative practices—such as optional mediation activities (Campbell), mindful walking (Bryant), five-minute meditations (Veenstra), reflective writing (Garretson), meditative yoga with revision (Wetzel)—I challenged myself to move beyond implicit pedagogical connections and to create a writing course that explicitly focuses on mindfulness.

This essay offers a look into one English Honors FYC course, taught in the fall of 2018, where readings, writing assignments, and activities were themed around contemplative practices and where my teaching relied on contemplative writing pedagogies. While the focus relates to an Honors course, my approaches could be adapted to other composition courses. Ultimately, I assert that explicit exposure to a range of contemplative practices holds positive outcomes for students' writing, experiences, and emotional states.

Brief Background on Contemplative Pedagogies

Arthur Zajonc highlights the increasing turn to "contemplative pedagogy" the past twenty years, indicating that "[t]his movement is being advanced by thousands of professors, academic administrators, and student life professionals" (83). He further explains that these efforts are supported by the Center for Contemplative Mind in Society and the Association for Contemplative Mind in Higher Education, along with conferences, fellowships, retreats, and texts (83) like Barbezat and Bush's *Contemplative Practices in Higher Education: Powerful Methods to Transform Teaching and Learning*.

Scholarship focuses on presence, embodying links between body and mind. For example, in *Mindful Teaching and Teaching Mindfulness: A Guide for Anyone Who Teaches Anything*, Deborah Schoeberlein connects mindfulness to "a conscious, purposeful way of tuning in to what's happening in and around us" (1), and Jan Chozen Bays frames it as "deliberately paying attention, being fully aware of what is happening both inside yourself—in your body, heart, and mind—and outside yourself in your environment" (3). Nikolaj Flor Rotne and Didde Flor Rotne extend the practice to being "fully present for ourselves and for others" (13). This emphasis between body and mind becomes intrinsically intertwined with the heart—something best understood when looking at the word itself. Engaging with artist Kazuaki Tanahashi, Santorelli illuminates this interconnection: "[T]he Japanese character from *mindfulness* [is] composed of two interactive figures. One represents mind and the other, heart ... From this perspective, Tanahashi translates mindfulness as 'bringing the heart-mind to this moment'" (188). The simultaneous emphasis of heart, body, mind, and presence is key and should exist throughout what Zajonc labels as four primary practices: mindfulness; focused concentration; open awareness, which extends to the creative process; and sustaining contradictions, which includes experiential learning (84). I, however, claim that mindfulness encompasses the other three practices, simplifying matters while embracing different ways in which mindfulness can be enacted in classrooms. Definitions even extend to the other practices. It has been explained as *"the art of observing your physical, emotional, and mental experiences with deliberate, open, and curious attention"* (Smalley and Winston 11, emphasis theirs) and as "awareness without judgement or criticism" (Bays 3). Thus, mindful teaching should cultivate learning environments that work to instill "deliberate, open, and curious attention" while reminding participants to make purposeful decisions, follow their curiosities, take creative risks, and practice compassion for both self and others.

Such learning experiences yield many benefits. Rotne and Rotne stress that "children implanted with seeds of mindfulness gain the tools that will help them in many areas of their lives" (90). They engage with scholars such as Greenland and Siegel to highlight increased concentration, strengthened awareness, feelings of ease, enhanced recognition of self and feelings and body, and decreased nervousness (Rotne and Rotne 90). Srinivasan cites Meiklejohn et al. to stress that mindfulness in educational systems strengthens "memory, attention, and academic skills, social skills, emotional regulation, and self-esteem, as well as [to result in] self-reported improvements in mood and decreases in anxiety, stress, and fatigue" (qtd. in Srinivasan 25). In his 2014 text titled *The Invisible Classroom: Relationships, Neuroscience & Mindfulness in School*, Kirke Olson reiterates these benefits and turns to scholars Wisner, Jones, and Gwin to cite additional improvements, such as "... self-control, and emotional intelligence; increased feelings of well-being; reductions in behavioral problems; decreased anxiety; decreases in blood pressures and heart rate ..." (qtd. in Olson 167). In short, scholars have consistently argued that mindfulness "improves mental focus and academic performance" (Schoeberlein 1) and holds benefits related to brain and body (Kabat-Zinn 58).

With such benefits, it is no wonder that "contemplative education" surfaced in the 1990s (Simmer-Brown and Grace xiv) and has become what Zajonc calls a "[q]uiet [r]evolution" that promises to "support the development of student attention, emotional balance, empathetic connection, compassion, and altruistic behavior" (83). There is no denying that emphasis on mindfulness in education is trending more than ever, from Mary Rose O'Reilley's *Radical Presence: Teaching as Contemplative Practice* text to Gesa Kirsch's "Mindfulness and Composition" podcast to Elizabeth Wardle and Douglas Downs's "Writing-About-Writing and Mindfulness" blog post. The list goes on, and scholars are convincing. Perhaps one of the most striking arguments within composition studies arises from Kirsch, who indicates that "[c]ontemplative practices ... can enhance creativity, listening, and expression of meaning—key goals of most writing courses. They do so by inviting students and teachers to practice mindfulness, to become introspective, to listen to the voices of others—and our own—and to the sounds of silence" ("From Introspection to Action" 828). The links between contemplative and composition practices feel obvious, intrinsic even.

Personal and Pedagogical Explorations

While scholars note limitations of integrating mindfulness and meditative practices into writing classrooms, such as the inherent link to religion and spirituality (Schoeberlein; Campbell), my main resistance had been less ethereal and more practical. I thrive on packing in objectives, questioned the slower pace, and felt like an imposter because I cannot seem to squeeze my own practice into my schedule. So how could I merge contemplative and composition practices when I do not identify as a practitioner? Yet I continue to incorporate tidbits of mindfulness into my life—my work, writing, and classrooms. Over the past six years, this has manifested in courses differently—yet nothing too overt. To explain, I did not chime bells. I did not ask students to close their eyes and quiet their minds for the first minutes of class. I did not light candles, bring blankets, or expect students to warrior pose themselves into focused awareness. However, my flirtations with mindful learning resulted in small-scale experimental activities and implicit links. In 2014, I developed a writing workshop that invited students to sit wherever and however they would like and facilitated a guided meditation related to their essays aimed at enhancing revision efforts and investment. This one activity was structured differently than previous activities and by default was welcomed positively, yet the experience was quickly forgotten when we returned to conventional practices. In addition, I have relied on implicit mindful practices by encouraging students to be present, to be engaged and (self)aware, to reflect on their writing, to embrace silence, and to follow their hearts and inner curiosities. Furthermore, I work to build writing communities structured around compassion and invite students to invest as contributing members of our class and as growing writers capable of change. Such philosophies resonate with the teaching and learning of mindfulness and can be broken down into tangible teaching strategies, including emphasizing the importance of presence and value of class time, developing purposeful activities and discussing that purpose, remaining attuned to students' writing needs and challenges, acknowledging and empowering students and their authorial agency, and cultivating a class built on and around process and reflection.

Recently, I began to wonder whether these implicit links were enough, whether they were as effective as explicit ones, and my question of whether I was capable of merging mindfulness fully with my writing pedagogies were replaced with more pertinent questions: (How) Do explicit incorporations of contemplative activities detract from writing objectives? (How) Do explicit incorporations isolate or hinder students and their needs? (How) Do explicit connections to mindfulness benefit composition students in ways that implicit ones may not?

Grappling with these questions, I developed a composition course, one that moves beyond flirting with contemplative practices, embracing concepts with "a kind, curious, nonjudgmental awareness that we try to bring to each moment" (Srinivasan 18). This particular course, the students in it, and my own experiences opened my eyes to what is possible when contemplative writing pedagogies are at the forefront.

Explanation of a "Contemplative Practices" Composition Course

Themed "contemplative practices," this course was structured loosely around Christy I. Wenger's emphasis on the idea that "contemplative writing pedagogies are built on mindfulness in much the same way [her] yoga practice is," meaning that "they teach writers how to develop a practice ... and how to pay attention [which] are skills that all learning requires but few of us teach explicitly in our writing classes" (102).[1] Wenger's words struck something within me. This aspect had become second-nature to writing instruction, yet when it came to mindful practices, I had been relying on *encouraging* students to do so without *instructing* them how to do it. Thus, explicit links overlap instruction, and theming allowed course readings, discussions, writing assignments, and activities to align with contemplative writing pedagogies.

To elaborate, while this Honors section held the same student learning objectives as other English 101 courses, this course was grounded in contemplative practices (see Appendix A). Thus, from day one, students were introduced to the concept of joining both mind and body in their writing experiences—even if they did not yet know or understand what exactly contemplative practice or mindfulness entailed—and they were aware that they would be exposed to different practices throughout the course.

To help acclimate and educate students, I paired their rhetoric with a primary reader edited by Barry Boyce titled *The Mindfulness Revolution: Leading Psychologists, Scientists, Artists, and Meditation Teachers on the Power of Mindfulness in Daily Life,* included some supplemental articles, and pulled from Gina M. Biegel's *Be Mindful & Stress Less*. To focus on the daily practice that scholars stress (Goldstein 26; Brantley 40), I zeroed in on daily writing by including a mindfulness journal titled *I am Here Now: A Creative Mindfulness Guide and Journal*.[2] Throughout the journal, mindfulness activities invite self-expression, creative thinking, and awareness of one's surroundings. Students were required to complete seventy-five journal activities, a number that allowed them to miss thirty days, which would relieve some pressure while emphasizing that practice takes *practice* and involves nonjudgmental commitment.

To focus on writing process, I turned to Dinty W. Moore's *The Mindful Writer*. His short excerpts work nicely with homework assignments, brainstorming activities, invention stages, and revision efforts—while reminding students that they are writers and that their writing requires its own, dedicated mindful practice. These readings often occurred between drafts incorporated into what I called a "revision and reflection form," a five-question form integrated between peer-review sessions and revised drafts (see Appendix B). In addition, I would occasionally open a workshop or class by reading one of Moore's lessons. The shortness of his passages and openness in writing struggles invited discussions while debunking preconceived notions that experienced writers have all the answers and words.

A number of course readings explained contemplative practices in higher education, different mindfulness practices, and the science behind such. Students were exposed to mindfulness as it relates to yoga, martial arts, sitting meditations, body scans, and mindful eating, to name a few (Stahl and Goldstein 29–32; Smalley and Winston 18–20). While these readings were meant to expose students to the field and existing practices, they also demystified what we meant when we referred to focusing attention, living in the present, or practicing self-care and nonjudgment. Furthermore, they often offered step-by-step methods, for those who wished to explore beyond reading, as well as memorable metaphors to aid in students' learning.[3]

Readings also played a role in developing the contemplative practices that intertwined with writing pedagogies. For example, after reading "The Blue Pearl: The Efficacy of Teaching Mindfulness Practices to College Students" by Haynes et al. and being exposed to the practices mentioned (the bow, six points of posture, mindful breathing, walking meditation, eye practices, beholding, contour portraits, talisman, freewriting, day of mindfulness, creating a work of art, cultivating visual memory, and hearing and deep listening), students had a list of possible examples that went beyond what we had already mentioned. Going over ways of bringing contemplative practices into classrooms provides an image of what students might encounter and offers a framework to invite students to identify what contemplative practices they wish to experience. Doing so allows students a sense of agency in creating the class while enhancing their investment. Some of what my students selected included opening each class with a bow, creating works of art, and being exposed to mindful walking, yoga, martial arts, and deep listening—most of which we were able to incorporate into our lessons.

While some activities related to course discussions, others held specific objectives associated to one (or more) of the class's major writing assignments. By intertwining writing lessons with contemplative practices, students practice what Wenger deems as "develop[ing] a practice of noticing: thinking actively about an idea or concept and seeing it from multiple perspectives without automatically rushing to judgment" (103). Thus, I attempted to expose students to writing situations where they would consciously work on practicing their mindfulness skills while exploring topics of interest. For example, the narrative essay encourages activities that involve focused attention to the senses while the analysis assignment opens opportunities for music meditation, and the place profile incites deep listening through observations and interviewing (see Appendix C). Furthermore, in-class activities honed skills. For example, after their scheduled place observations, we spent part of class creating art activity based on the visual memory of their selected locations. The art supplies alone sparked excitement, but the art activity helped to capture their space and their embodied experience of that place, creating a material object that represented both the physical and emotional. As a byproduct, their writing moved beyond mere descriptions and towards encompassing the many perspectives and feelings of the place they were profiling.

Not every lesson held a contemplative practice component; rather, contemplative practices grounded each class. Opening the class with a bow became a gentle gesture that symbolized it was time to focus because class was officially beginning. In addition, reframing "objectives" into daily "intentions" shifted attitudes from what must be done to what we purposefully intended to do—a small rhetorical move that held a large impact. As Wenger affirms, "Setting an intention is a conscious way to bridge the mind and body's intelligence and can help students learn to connect feelings and thoughts, increasing awareness of both" (viii). These two alterations—the bow and day's intentions—set the tone while providing consistent activities on which students could rely. Furthermore, they maintained a contemplative nature on days when weaving in any other activity may feel forced or may distract from the lesson.

In addition, some lessons went beyond my expertise, and I turned to guest instructors. I was able to host two guests—a certified yoga instructor and a qualified Mindfulness-Based Stress Reduction (MBSR) teacher. Students, some for the first time ever, participated in beginner yoga poses while sitting in each pose and in the present moments. The MBSR introduction offered concrete breathing practices and demonstrated the meditative body scan. These trained professionals were able to lead students in two powerful sessions. Students expressed how doing these and various other activities throughout the semester strengthened their understanding and impacted their relationship with writing and with themselves.

To gain insight into how students' viewed links among contemplative, composition, and lifestyle practices, I conducted an anonymous end-of-the-course survey.[4] In addition, their final project consisted of a reflective prompt that asked students to discuss any connections between their composition and contemplative practices. Turning to student voices conveys how effective contemplative writing pedagogies can be for students not only as writers but also as individuals.

Survey and Reflective Results

Out of the eleven students, ten found the class, in general and in relation to the contemplative and composition studies, beneficial. In their finals, the majority expressed positive changes about their relationship with writing. One particular student shares, "[M]any of the practices such as the mindfulness journal, the yoga, and the mindfulness workshop allowed me to be a more open writer[;] the practices allowed me to get more in touch with the true writer that I really am. Now at the end of this curse, I feel that I ha[ve] more voice as a writer . . ." Another student notes growth in her "voice" and "creativity": "I learned how to be creative, find my writing style, have an open mind . . . and have a strong work ethic . . .[and] gain[ed] more confidence in myself." Her writing confidence propelled to an increase in motivation.

Other emotional changes were noted—primarily in regards to stronger connections to writing purposes, writing processes, and writing community. One particular student reveals, "I had a bad attitude about English, but I grew to enjoy and love the writing process again. What encouraged me most to do my best and give my all was my peers. I wanted to have something for them to enjoy to read . . ." Focusing on the desire to share captivating writing with her classmates and demonstrating an increased awareness to audience, this student implies how contemplative activities strengthened the writing community and commitment to peer reviews. Another overtly linked her writing practices to her contemplative practices throughout her composition stages. She expresses, "I finally sat down and meditated before beginning the revision process. I have always felt that revision is overwhelming and tedious, but with meditation I found patience and the possibility to revise [in] my best mind frame." By altering her writing habits, this student discovered that meditative time preceding her revision efforts assisted in self-regulating her emotions and in managing her tasks. Another compelling comment comes from a student who explains how contemplative practices can transcend writing habits:

> I began to get a feel for how mindfulness would help not only my writing but my life ... I felt that I was becoming a new and better writer that I had never been before. Plus in class activities like learning to understand our breathing and doing a body scan helped a ton. Whenever I get writing blocks I simply do one of those two and it calms me down and helps me get back on track.

This student went on to share that he "felt connected in a way [he has] never felt before ..." He continued, "Practices that we did throughout the year ... will stay with me forever. My favorite practice however was being forgiving to self. That was a new concept that I really took to heart and love now." Such words echo Garretson's point that meditation holds the purpose of "accept[ing] the self as fully adequate ...[while] striv[ing] to deepen and further its grasps on its own insights and truths" (55–56). Self-forgiveness and self-compassion come in handy, in life and in the writing classroom, and I was surprised to learn just how much this concept needed to be heard.

When completing that final reflective prompt, students often highlighted the significance of how contemplative practices reduced writing stresses or relieved daily anxieties. At least six students mentioned a reduction in stress or anxiety or how the course, activities, or readings helped to calm their worries. One particular student explains her appreciation for her daily practice: "The mindfulness journal gave me a quiet time. It was the time where I would reflect on my day and let go of my stress." Another student pinpointed exactly how our yoga day played a role in her emotional well-being: "With the practice of yoga, it helped relieve me of the stress brought on by my very busy college life." In addition to offering a time for students to re-set and re-energize, contemplative practices assist students in learning to take control of their reactions and emotions when they are feeling blocked or over-anxious. Two students highlight this best. One declares, "I had never heard of mindfulness before this course and was initially quite skeptical about it. After the readings and exercises ... I have come around to the idea of practicing mindfulness. I have found the exercises to be very relaxing and they are helpful in relieving stress." He continues, "When getting stressed out over an assignment or deadline, they can help clear my mind and calm down and relax ...[and] can help me focus on my assignment." Another shares, "[T]his course taught me quite a few things about myself, like the fact that ... I was almost never truly in the present, that paying attention to my breathing can help calm my anxiety ... and lastly, that being shy's totally normal and can be worked with ..." This student further expresses appreciation for composition and mindfulness: "[W]e had a bow we did to begin every class. It helped set the mood, and it helped me to focus. We dedicated an entire day just to mindfulness practices ... That day helped me to calm down and left me ready to tackle the remainder of my essay. I learned that contemplative practices helped me in my writing because I was really present and focused." This student became aware of her intensified emotions—in general and in regards to writing. Her amplified stressors related to writing are common. Many first-year students lack writing confidence. In addition, gifted students tend to hold themselves to high standards. However, when stress and anxiety overwhelm students, they may be overtaken by fear. Thus, implementing lessons and activities that teach contemplative practices provide valuable skills that assist students in building writing confidence while offering strategies to manage one's thoughts and emotions and practice self-care.

End-of-the-semester anonymous surveys further highlighted students' increased confidence in regards to contemplative and composition practices (see Appendix D). To elaborate, surveys revealed that everyone's knowledge about contemplative practices went up by at least one point (on a scale of 1–5); the majority's base went up three or four points. Specifically, five students noted that their knowledge went up three points, and four students noted that they moved from a 1 to a 5 throughout the course. Ten out of the eleven noted that their writing confidence increased, again, by at least one point, whereas, again, the majority noted a two- or three-point increase.

When asked if the course theme played a positive role in their (a) composition experience, (b) investment in composition, (c) composition learning, and (d) composition process, the results were overwhelmingly positive. Ten out of the eleven circled "yes" to all four components. More impressive were the responses to the question of whether or not they relied on contemplative practices throughout their composition processes, specifically (a) inventing, (b) drafting, (c) revising, (d) peer-reviewing, (e) reading, and (f) researching. The results conveyed that students actively intertwined contemplative practices throughout their composition stages. Specifically, nine indicated "yes" to inventing, revising, peer-reviewing, reading, and researching while ten indicated "yes" to drafting. Perhaps more shocking was that ten students shared that they intended to bring contemplative practices into their composition practices beyond this course and that nine intended to bring contemplative practices into their life(style).

It is relevant to note that one student out of the eleven did not find the course theme beneficial, circling "no" for everything. That same student has no intention of bringing contemplative practices into her composition practices or life(style) beyond this course, and if given another chance to enroll in the course was the one outlier who shared that she would not. I do not fault her or blame the class. In fact, I commend her honesty and acknowledge that she did take something away, even if that something was learning that integrating mindfulness into her already-created writing habits was not for her, at least, not at this time or not in the method presented. Furthermore, I focus on the fact that ten out of the eleven valued the experience and recognized their growth as writers and people. Students connected to their writing, writing purposes, and writing communities on deeper levels—all while learning more about themselves as writers and as individuals who are in process and who can actively elect to practice and work on improving themselves.

This course taught me that contemplative practices can be woven naturally and effectively into writing courses and invigorated my desire to do so. Moreover, it gave me the opportunity to explore, accept, and own my own practice. As Rotne and Rotne affirm, "The practice gives teachers the ability to anchor themselves in their profession with greater inner peace, openness, and insight; from this starting point they can create a more harmonious and fruitful learning environment" (13). By theming this first-year writing course, I was able to establish an authentic framework, one that opened up learning spaces for all and one that I hope instilled lessons that will continually be practiced.

Appendix A: Shortened Syllabus

ENG 101—Honors: Analysis and Argument
Francis Marion University—Fall 2018

Course Description

Similar to other English 101 sections, Honors English 101 is dedicated to strengthening analysis, argument, and composition skills. However, our section, unlike others, will be grounded in contemplative practices. Specifically, we will read, discuss, and write on topics related to mindfulness, from meditation to yoga, while simultaneously integrating these practices into methods of learning and teaching through what has been called "contemplative writing pedagogies." As Christy I. Wegner explains in *Yoga Minds, Writing Bodies: Contemplative Writing Pedagogy*, "What distinguishes contemplative pedagogies [from traditional teaching strategies] is their attention to the body as a primary site for mindful reflection, contemplative awareness and centeredness" (15). Thus, our writing practices will be intrinsically linked with our own contemplative practices, where we will work to enrich and deepen connections between our minds and bodies—all the while meeting the English 101 student learning objectives.

Required Materials

The following are required:

- Edited by Lunsford, Andrea, et al. *Everyone's an Author*. (ISBN: 9780393617450)
- Edited by Boyce, Barry. *The Mindfulness Revolution: Leading Psychologists, Scientists, Artists, and Meditation Teachers on the Power of Mindfulness in Daily Life*. (ISBN: 9781590308899)
- Moore, Dinty W. *The Mindful Writer*. (ISBN: 9781614293521)
- Biegel, Gina M. *Be Mindful & Stress Less*. (ISBN: 9781611804942)
- *I Am Here Now: A Creative Mindfulness Guide and Journal* (ISBN: 9780399184444)
- *Final Draft 2018–2019: A Guide to the Composition Program at Francis Marion University Featuring Student Writing* (ISBN: 9781680367560)
- Regular access to Blackboard to download and print supplemental readings and submit assignments
- A three-ring binder to keep class notes, materials, writings, and supplemental readings organized
- A mindful presence—with the material, with yourself, with all course participants
- A positive attitude, open mind, attentive ears, and respectful tongue
- A willingness to grow as a reader, writer, critical thinker, and more mindful individual

Course Objectives/Student Learning Outcomes

Upon completion of this course, students will be able to demonstrate success in the below course objectives:

- Understand rhetorical situations, analyzing audience and purpose in order to compose in multiple genres
- Develop ideas and content appropriate to specific rhetorical situations, establishing control of thesis, paragraphs, and larger organization of the essay
- Develop drafts and revise writing based on feedback from others, recognizing that writing involves collaboration with others
- Write about and reflect on the strengths and weakness of their own reading and writing processes
- Understand and employ research methods at an introductory level, documenting sources appropriately
- Read, analyze, and create arguments with an awareness of rhetorical situations, exploring persuasive strategies and possible consequences
- Enhance language skills, establishing control of surface features such as syntax, grammar, and punctuation

Contemplative Practices Goals

Due to the thematic and pedagogical focus, our course holds the following additional goals, which were adapted from *Contemplative Practices in Higher Education* (Barbezat and Bush):

- "To engage students in their own learning" (53) and offer opportunities for reflective thinking and self-awareness to emerge (11) and promote greater understanding of writing and writing practices;
- "To stimulate" (53) students' attention to self, others, and texts in ways that foster understanding and compassion (53, 11);
- To enhance students' ability to explore with focused attention (53) in efforts to strengthen engagement with writing, reading, and research processes; and
- To expose students to an array of different contemplative practices and activities, providing a range of strategies that they may, if desired, carry with them beyond this course (11).

Assignments and Method of Evaluation

Writing, reading, and thinking are complex processes that take time and that are intrinsically linked, and we will be doing a lot of each while focusing on process-based writing. We will invent, draft, review, and revise essays.

You should keep ALL versions of your essays (drafts, revisions, copies with feedback, etc.). Assignments include, but are not limited to, essays, smaller writings, class workshops, and a final.

While detailed explanations of the major essays will be provided in class, the below outlines assignments and grading method on a 1,000-point scale:

Essays—Worth 550 Points: You will be asked to submit four essays. Exact assignments will be provided in advance, and each will be assessed on the indicated point scale.

- *Narrative:* A focused, personal essay related to our course theme
- *Research-Based Analysis:* A thesis-based essay that analyzes and researches selected "text"
- *Research-Based Profile:* A thesis-based essay that profiles selected place or person while incorporating research related to topic/angle; both *field notes* and *annotated bibliography* are due before the essay
- *Research-Based Argument / Revise and Redesign Project:* A research-based argument that considers the semester's research and writing in order to revise and redesign information into something new

Contemplative Readings & Writings (CRW)—Worth 150 Points: Throughout the course, you will be asked to read selected contemplative readings, reflect, and write; these smaller writings often relate to larger essays while giving focus to your writing process. You should type these when you can, and you should aim for the equivalent of one-typed page in length, knowing that prompts may vary or invite different mediums/structures. These assignments are forms of informal writings, which are vital to the development of ideas, understanding and application of readings, preparation for class discussions, and development of our own contemplative practices; in short, they strengthen your writing skills while enhancing both critical thinking and awareness. Prompts for each will be provided. They are evaluated on a 10-point scale, either numerically or using a √+, √, √- system (which equates to 10, 08, 06). Hard copies are required the day they are due and at the start of class, as we may rely on them for in-class activities or group work. Missed assignments (due to being absent or to coming in late or unprepared) cannot be made up and will be recorded as a zero.

Peer Reviews, Writing Workshops, & Reflections—Worth 100 Points: It is important that you come to peer reviews and writing workshops not only prepared but also with your reflective component (as outlined with each workshop). During these, you should be fully engaged in that day's activities/tasks. Being prepared means, but is not limited to, having your draft, offering constructive feedback to others, working to improve your own writing, and submitting the reflective component. Each workshop + reflection set is worth 25 points. To receive full credit, you must be fully prepared and actively engaged. Failure to have required materials, to actively engage, to offer constructive feedback, or to complete the workshop reflections will negatively affect your grade. You do not receive points for missed workshops (due to being absent or unprepared); however, you may make up a missed workshop for half-credit with a documented visit to the Writing Center within 24 hours of the missed workshop.

Contemplative Practice and Class Participation—Worth 150 Points: Participation includes, but is not limited to, discussing the readings, listening to your peers' comments, engaging with in-class activities, and receiving quiz points. You are expected to come to class ready and willing to participate, being physically and mindfully present during class, activities, and workshops. Failure to do so or to have assigned documents will negatively affect your grade. Assessment is on a point scale and assessed daily. In addition to class participation, you are expected to work on developing your own contemplative practice by completing a mindfulness journal. Assessment of the journal will be based on number of activities completed, expected at minimum seventy-five activities.

Final—Worth 50 Points: We will meet the day of our final to complete an in-class writing assignment. The final will include, but may not be limited to, a reflective writing component and will be assessed on a point scale.

Appendix B: Example of a Revision and Reflection Form

Author of Essay: _____

After reviewing your feedback, what are your **revision plans**? First, highlight specific feedback that you will act on, and then write out your **intention** for your revision process. Next, elaborate on your revision plan as desired.	

Read Moore's #26 (on "working in clay, not marble"), and take his advice re. "giv[ing yourself permission to write that lousy first draft" (79). Draft a new section to your essay; write anything, and then, revise, and revise again. Reflect on your different drafts, and explain how you've taken your "soft clay" and have "formed, and reformed, and reformed again" (79). Elaborate on specifics.	
Remember Moore's #45 "Kill Your Darlings," and then consider that writers have to be selective in what stays in and what goes. This applies to the writing and the research. Explain what parts of both you selectively took out.	
Once you have completed your revisions for the final draft, **explain and reflect** on specific content-related revisions (beyond what you've already stated above) and on specific research-related revisions. Bring in some specific examples from your essay. What are you most proud about? What are still concerned about?	
Once you have a complete draft, **explain and reflect** on revisions related to style and voice. Bring in specifics examples to show how you focused on style and voice in your revisions.	

Appendix C: Example Assignment: Research-Based Place Profile

Essay Two worked with developing our research, analysis, and writing skills, and we will continue to enhance those skills with this next assignment. As you will see, this assignment, too, requires both research and analysis, albeit differently.

For this third essay, you should select a place to profile. That sounds easy enough, but you will want to dedicate a good bit of time to both your primary and secondary research. In addition, you will want to enter this assignment with that "open mind, open heart" approach that is mentioned in Santorelli's piece in *Mindfulness Revolution*, meaning that you should research your subject with an open mind and an open heart. This does not mean that you ignore your assumptions; rather, you should recognize them for what they are—assumptions—and move forward with the intention to research, learn, find a particular angle worth sharing with others.

This (place) profile should include both primary and secondary research, and you are required to bring in at least four secondary sources where at least two of those are scholarly sources from the library database. In addition, you are required to bring in primary research, which should include at least an observation and an interview. To help with your research, you will be submitting your Annotated Bibliography (worth 30 pts) and your Field Notes (worth 20 pts) on the specified deadlines. (Refer to your syllabus for those dates.)

As we know from *Everyone's an Author*, profiles can "cross the line to analyze or interpret the information" related to the subject being profiled (257). You will be crafting your firsthand account, with that detailed information about the subject while taking on an interesting angle—making the profile meaningful to read for a general audience (who knows nothing about the subject). Remember those analysis skills from your previous essay—and your growth in developing a thesis-driven essay that works to prove your point. You will be establishing your ethos in this essay, and your writing should reflect both your heart's and mind's connection to the subject being analyzed. In addition, remember to "cultivate ... an inquisitive mind ... [and practice] patience ...[and] humor" (Karr and Wood 104–05). Approach both your research and writing with that open mind and open heart while practicing compassion to self and others.

Your profile should be the equivalent of 5–6 pages in length. Your *audience* for this essay is the general public. Feel free to bring in images or other elements that may add to the profile, if desired, but note that this is not required. If you do, however, those do not count toward page length and should be cited correctly. Be sure to include in-text citations and a works cited, using MLA style. (Yes, interviews must be cited.) Also, remember to rely on any of the contemplative practices and link those to your analyzing, researching, and writing process, and feel free to brainstorm about possible places that may extend to the contemplative theme of the course.

Appendix D: Contemplative Practices and Composition Survey

1. On a scale of 1–5, how would you rate your knowledge related to contemplative practices before the course?

    (weak)

    __1   __2   __3   __4   __5

    (strong)

2. On a scale of 1–5, how would you rate your knowledge related to contemplative practices after this course?

    (weak)

    __1   __2   __3   __4   __5

    (strong)

3. On a scale of 1–5, how would you rate your confidence related to composition before this course?

    (weak)

    __1   __2   __3   __4   __5

    (strong)

4. On a scale of 1–5, how would you rate your confidence related to composition after this course?

   (weak)

   __1   __2   __3   __4   __5

   (strong)

5. (Circle) Did the course theme of contemplative practices play a positive role in your . . .

   a. composition experience: YES   or   NO
   b. investment in   YES   or   NO
       composition:
   c. composition learning: YES   or   NO
   d. composition process: YES   or   NO

6. (Circle) Did you rely on contemplative practices in your composition processes, such as . . .

   a. Inventing: YES   or   NO
   b. Drafting: YES   or   NO
   c. Revising: YES   or   NO
   d. Peer-Reviewing: YES   or   NO
   e. Reading: YES   or   NO
   f. Researching: YES   or   NO

7. (Circle) Do you intend to bring any contemplative practice into your life(style) beyond this course?

YES   or   NO

8. *(Circle) Do you intend to bring any contemplative practice into your composition practices beyond this course (at any stage of your composition, see question 6 for some specific stages)?*

YES   or   NO

9. *English 101 has the below student learning objectives. Mark "X" next to any/all of the objectives that you feel as if you met:*
   ___ Understand rhetorical situations, analyzing audience and purpose in order to compose in multiple genres
   ___ Develop ideas and content appropriate to specific rhetorical situations, establishing control of thesis, paragraphs, and larger organization of the essay
   ___ Develop drafts and revise writing based on feedback from others, recognizing that writing involves collaboration with others
   ___ Write about and reflect on the strengths and weakness of their own reading and writing processes
   ___ Understand and employ research methods at an introductory level, documenting sources appropriately
   ___ Read, analyze, and create arguments with an awareness of rhetorical situations, exploring persuasive strategies and possible consequences
   ___ Enhance language skills, establishing control of surface features such as syntax, grammar, and punctuation

10. *Our course held additional contemplative goals.* Mark "X" next to any/all of the below goals that you feel as if the course met: (*For citations, refer to Appendix A, Shortened Syllabus, "Contemplative Practice Goals.")*
    ___ To engage students in their own learning and offer opportunities for reflective thinking and self-awareness to emerge and promote greater understanding of writing and writing practices
    ___ To stimulate students' attention to self, others, and texts in ways that foster understanding and compassion
    ___ To enhance students' ability to explore with focused attention in efforts to strengthen engagement with writing, reading, and research processes
    ___ To expose students to an array of different contemplative practices and activities, providing a range of strategies that they may, if desired, carry with them beyond this course

11. *If you had the opportunity to enroll in this course with the same "contemplative practice" theme, would you? Why or why not?*
12. *Please share anything else that you would like to share about your course experience, composition studies, and/or course theme:*

Notes

1. To contextualize the course, I teach at a small, public university that holds the mission to serve its region and prides itself on having a liberal arts foundation. The majority of students are from the state of South Carolina, and a number are first-generation students. Housed as part of the Honors Program and only open to Honors students, this course did not mirror institutional demographics. The class was 90% white and 82% female with the majority identifying as South Carolinians. No data was collected on the group regarding first-generation status.
2. The journal opens with a mindfulness timeline as well as a quiz, educating students while immediately engaging with self-awareness. To guarantee privacy, I told students I would not read their entries as the goal was not to learn about my students, but rather to instill a daily practice that they felt committed to completing.
3. For example, Flowers breaks mindfulness down, encouraging one to turn to their "mindful compass" (171). Similar to how the four cardinal directions offer guidance and assist in finding one's path, Flowers identifies mindfulness as having "four primary readings ... your thoughts, emotions, sensations, and behaviors" (171). Thinking about checking one's own "compass" and examining these four points helps novice practitioners to work through different reactions and actions that emerge.
4. Data collected from the course has been approved by the Institutional Review Board. The IRB approval number is Spear-03-06-2019-006. End-of-the semester surveys were anonymous and submitted after everything in the course had been completed. Furthermore, surveys were not reviewed until after final grades had been assigned. Some reflective comments were connected to coursework; however, students' names have been removed when known.

Works Cited

Barbezat, Daniel P., and Mirabai Bush. *Contemplative Practices in Higher Education: Powerful Methods to Transform Teaching and Learning*. Jossey-Bass, 2014.
Bays, Jan Chozen. "What Is Mindfulness?" Boyce, pp. 3–6.
Biegel, Gina M. *Be Mindful and Stress Less: 50 Ways to Deal with Your (Crazy) Life*. Shambhala Publications, 2018.
Boyce, Barry, editor. *The Mindfulness Revolution: Leading Psychologists, Scientists, Artists, and Meditation Teachers on the Power of Mindfulness in Daily Life*. Shambhala Publications, 2011.
Brantley, Jeff. "Mindfulness FAQ." Boyce, pp. 38–45.

Bryant, Kendra Nicole. *"Free Your Mind ... And the Rest Will Follow": A Secularly Contemplative Approach to Teaching High School English*. 2012. PhD diss., University of South Florida.

Campbell, JoAnn. "Writing to Heal: Using Meditation in the Writing Process." *College Composition and Communication*, vol. 45, no. 2, May 1994, pp. 246–51.

Final Draft 2018–2019: A Guide to the Composition Program at Francis Marion University Featuring Student Writing. Fountainhead Press, 2018.

Flowers, Steve. "Mindfully Shy." Boyce, pp. 166–76.

Garretson, Kate. "Being Allowing and Yet Directive: Mindfulness Meditation in the Teaching of Developmental Reading and Writing." *New Directions for Community Colleges*, no. 151, Fall 2010, pp. 51–64.

Goldstein, Joseph. "Here, Now, Aware." Boyce, pp. 21–27.

Haynes, Deborah J., et al. "The Blue Pearl: The Efficacy of Teaching Mindfulness Practices to College Students." *Buddhist-Christian Studies*, 33, 2013, pp. 63–82.

I Am Here Now: A Creative Mindfulness Guide and Journal. TarcherPerigee, 2016.

Lunsford, Andrea, et al., editors. *Everyone's an Author*. 2nd ed. W.W. Norton, 2016.

Kabat-Zinn, Jon. "Why Mindfulness Matters." Boyce, pp. 57–62.

Karr, Andy, and Michael Wood. "Mindfulness, Photography, and Living an Artistic Life." Boyce, pp. 101–05.

Kirsch, Gesa K. "Episode 17: Mindfulness and Composition with Gisa Hirsch." *This Rhetorical Life*. Syracuse University. 17 Jan. 2014.

———. "From Introspection to Action: Connecting Spirituality and Civic Engagement." *College Composition and Communication*, vol. 60, no. 4, June 2009, pp. 827–28.

Moffett, James. "Reading and Writing as Meditation." *Language Arts*, vol. 60, no. 3, Mar. 1983, pp. 315–32.

———. "Writing, Inner Speech, and Meditation." *College English*, vol. 44, no. 3, Mar. 1982, pp. 231–46.

Moore, Dinty W. *The Mindful Writer*. 2012. Wisdom Publications, 2016.

O'Reilley, Mary Rose. *The Peaceable Classroom*. Boynton/Cook, 1993.

———. *Radical Presence: Teaching as Contemplative Practice*. Portsmouth, Boynton/Cook Publishers, 1998.

Olson, Kirke. *The Invisible Classroom: Relationships, Neuroscience & Mindfulness in School*. W.W. Norton, 2014.

Rotne, Nikolaj Flor, and Didde Flor Rotne. *Everybody Present: Mindfulness in Education*. Paralax Press, 2013.

Santorelli, Saki F. "Caring for the Wounded Places." Boyce, pp. 185–90.

Schoeberlein, Deborah. *Mindful Teaching and Teaching Mindfulness: A Guide for Anyone Who Teaches Anything*. Wisdom Publications, 2009.

Simmer-Brown, Judith, and Fran Grace, editors. *Meditation and the Classroom: Contemplative Pedagogy for Religious Studies*. State U of New York P, 2011.

Smalley, Susan, and Diana Winston. "Is Mindfulness for You?" Boyce, pp. 11–20.

Srinivasan, Meena. *Teach, Breathe, Learn: Mindfulness in and out of the Classroom.* Berkeley, CA, Parallax, 2014.

Stahl, Bob, and Elisha Goldstein. "Mindfulness Meditation Instructions." Boyce, pp. 29–37.

Veenstra, Michelle. "Mindful Learning in an Age of Distraction: How Students and Professors Can Become More Present in the Twenty-First Century Classroom." *Human and Social Sciences Symposium.* Francis Marion University. 21 Jan. 2014.

Wardle, Elizabeth, and Douglas Downs. "Writing-about-Writing and Mindfulness: Some End-of-Semester Ruminating." *Write On: Notes on Teaching Writing about Writing.* Blogs.BedfordStMartins.com/Bits. N.p. 23 Dec. 2010.

Wenger, Christy I. *Yoga Minds, Writing Bodies: Contemplative Writing Pedagogy.* Parlor Press, 2015.

Wetzel, Grace. "'The most peaceful I ever felt writing': A Contemplative Approach to Essay Revision." *JAEPL: The Journal of the Assembly for Expanded Perspectives on Learning,* vol. 22, Winter 2016–17, pp. 33–50.

Zajonc, Arthur. "Contemplative Pedagogy: A Quiet Revolution in Higher Education." *New Direction for Teaching and Learning,* no. 134, Summer 2013, pp. 83–94.

15. Dear Professor: Forging Student-Teacher Relationships through Course Letters

Ann Amicucci

In 2016, third grade teacher Kyle Schwartz asked her students to write in response to the prompt "I wish my teacher knew," and their responses generated nationwide discussion of the challenges students face that are invisible to teachers (De La Cruz). College students face just as many challenges as their younger counterparts, including when it comes to writing, and such challenges are often invisible until teachers can forge a rapport and relationship with their students, which may not happen until late in the semester. By inviting students into one-on-one dialogue, we can do them a great service by fostering student-teacher relationships that promote writing development. I employ a pedagogy of course letters in which students write three letters to me—at the beginning, middle, and end of the semester—to describe their writing goals and achievements, and I write letters back to each. These letters engage first-year writing students in dialogue that fosters our student-teacher relationships. I present here a study of letters written by twelve students in a first-year research writing course and demonstrate how students respond to my invitation to forge a student-teacher relationship through writing.

Reciprocal Student-Teacher Relationships

We know from experience that making connections with our writing students has positive results. Yet the nature of these connections is complicated: the need to maintain professional boundaries, the demands of teachers' workloads, and students' reluctance to connect can all impact our desire to facilitate valuable relationships. Nel Noddings suggests we can best support students through a stance of caring, which she describes as a relationship that requires "receptivity" on the part of both individuals. In this relationship, the individual who cares "feels the excitement, pain, terror, or embarrassment of the other and commits herself to act accordingly" (76). In turn, the cared-for individual "responds to the presence of the one-caring" and "feels the difference between being received and being held off or ignored" (78). In an educational setting, Noddings argues, a caring stance means being receptive to students as individuals, not just to the words or work they produce (186). This stance can remind us to see students as people first and consider their work as writers within the context of their wider lives.

Yet simply caring is not enough. In calling for an approach to writing courses that emphasizes "hospitality," Janis Haswell et al. argue that Noddings' approach does a disservice to students because it positions students as merely recipients who either accept or reject the "care" foisted upon them (710). What is better, the authors argue, is for students and teachers to both be responsible for students' learning: for teachers to create classrooms where learning is reciprocal and students are welcomed as equals to teachers (716). Kristy S. Cooper and Andrew Miness describe what such reciprocal caring can look like, in a study of high school students' perceptions of teachers' care. Cooper and Miness found that personal connections between students and teachers enhanced their relationships—but only when students had agency to shape whether and how their teachers got to know them (283). The authors call for teachers to "use their time with students to develop understanding of students personally—*when students express a desire for such understanding*" (285, emphasis in original). Collectively, the work of Noddings; Cooper and Miness; and Haswell et al. shows that teachers' efforts to foster relationships with students are most effective for students' learning when such relationships are built on tenets of mutual respect and mutual agency.

A Pedagogy of Course Letters

My use of course letters draws on a tradition of using letters to facilitate students' writing practice. In K-12 education, letters find their way into the writing classroom through dialogue journals and pen pal activities (see Anderson et al.; Rankin; Reyes). In college contexts, letters are often present when students practice writing in public genres, such as in letters to the editor, and when students use letters as an idea generation tool (see "Brainstorming"; Gogan; "Integrating"). In my first-year research writing course, I assign students to write three informal letters to me: once at the beginning of the semester, once in the middle, and again at the end (see Appendix for assignments). The first letter asks students to think about their writing practices, writing education, and plans as a writer and researcher, then they set goals and explain the steps they'll take to reach them. For the midterm letter, students read their first letter, discuss the progress they've made toward their goals with evidence from their work in the course, and explain their plans going forward. In the final letter, students read both prior letters and examine all their work from the course, evaluate their progress, and discuss how they will take their writing and research abilities into future contexts.

This letters sequence is a reflective writing practice grounded in Kathleen Blake Yancey's theory of reflection, which posits that when students reflect on their learning, and on their writing process habits in particular, they become more aware of those habits and, consequently, are more likely to shape and change them (26–28). Drawing on this theory, I have found that having students write explicit goal-setting and retroactive reflections on their writing choices leads them to take ownership of the successes and shortcomings in their writing processes (Amicucci 46–47). The letters also give me a window into students' experiences through which I can reflect on the course and student learning (Yancey 125–27). The letters facilitate students' development as writers through reflection, and our letter exchanges allow us to form relationships that benefit their development. Our exchanges enact the reciprocity that Haswell et al. and Cooper and Miness espouse in that rather than "commenting on" writing, I am engaging with students' ideas in a written response equal in effort to students' own.

Methods of Data Collection and Analysis

I collected 35 letters to study with Institutional Review Board approval and students' consent after the course had concluded and grades were submitted. In studying these letters, I analyzed 114 pages of text: three letters from each of eleven students and two from a student whose first letter was unavailable. I assigned pseudonyms to students who consented to have me study their letters. From there, I replaced all identifiable details with suitable alternatives in the letters. Next, I analyzed the letters from a grounded theory perspective in which I remained open to emergent themes (see Strauss and Corbin 160–63). During my initial read-through, I marked sentences in which students talked directly to me as their reader or discussed our relationship. After multiple readings, I focused the final coding scheme on two categories: describing relationship with teacher and describing relationship with other students in the class (see Table 15.1). The length of each instance of coded text was one sentence.

The semester-start letter assignment invites students into a writing relationship, and the letters that follow encourage students to continue

Table 15.1. Occurrences of Coding Categories in Student Letters.

Pseudonym	Pages of writing	Sentences coded as: describing relationship with teacher	describing relationship with other students in the class
Christiana	9	5	2
Doug	7	2	2
Enzo	9	2	1
Grace	9	15	6
Imani	13	4	5
Jim	10	2	3
Karrie	8	10	0
Lina	7	4	1
May	9	13	1
Rhea	12	13	6
Shane	9	11	13
Vince	12	11	0

conversation within this relationship. The numbers of instances coded as "describing relationship with teacher" show the varying degrees to which students respond to this invitation (see Table 15.1). Some students write quite formal letters about their goals and processes as writers and say little in regards to our relationship, while some say quite a lot in this category. Students also vary in what they say about their relationships with others in the course. In what follows, I discuss how the letters describe students' relationships with me as their teacher and with their course peers.

Student Descriptions of Our Relationship

Many student descriptions of our relationship position me as a course resource. In semester-start letters, several state plans to seek me out for help, such as:

- "I will make appointments with you and hearing your input in what I need improvement on and what steps I need to take in becoming a better writer." (May)[1]
- "I also hope to spend more time with you or people in the writing center when it comes to finalizing my paper as I often fly through papers and make simple errors that are unnecessary." (Christiana)

- "Many times I accidentally use blogs or other sources that are not credible and it takes away from my personal credibility as a writer. To fix this flaw in my writing routine I plan to reference you, my professor, or the UCCS excel center to understand and grasp what qualifies as a credible source." (Grace)
- "As for making a connection with you professor, I am sure that will be more of a forced relationship as I will be bothering you for help." (Shane)

In the first three examples, students indicate they are going to follow a prescribed student role by capitalizing on the help I will offer. The final example lets me know Shane plans to reach out for help but also suggests he may not recognize I am hoping he'll do just that. In this sentence, I hear Shane testing the waters of our relationship by couching his plans to seek help in humor because he is not yet sure of how I will respond.

Students say less in general about our relationship in their semester-start letters than in subsequent letters: the number of sentences I coded as describing students' relationships with me averaged 1.91 in semester-start letters, 3.08 in midterm letters, and 2.92 in end-of-semester letters. Shane's comment highlights the fact that students do not know me at the beginning of the semester, so despite my invitation to write informally, they may be reluctant or think it is inappropriate to make a connection with me in their first letter.

In later letters, several students again position me as a resource by referring to my feedback or our conversations. Karrie writes, "I have taken the advice you gave during our meeting, that I should write outlines of the papers I do," and May writes that "having you look over my thesis and give me feedback is one of the main reasons my paper came out well." Yet in these later letters, students move beyond only positioning me as a resource to talk about our interactions and our relationship, such as in these examples from midterm letters:

- "I feel more comfortable with my writing and you as my reader because I think it gives you a better sense of what my writing is and my abilities and strengths and weakness that I know I have and you see that I try to work to fix." (Christiana)
- "I want to push myself to be successful, Getting an A would not [only] prove to you that I [am] a good writer but it would prove to me that I belong here." (Shane)

- "I am excited to be writing you once again, I really enjoyed writing you the first time. I feel as if it gave me a chance to show you my background and what I was expecting for the course. And vice versa I got to know you and feel like I have a relationship with my you." (May)

By the semester's midpoint, students are embracing the relationship I invite them into. These examples position me as Christiana's "reader" with whom she is becoming "more comfortable" and as someone to whom Shane wants to "prove" his strengths as a student. May's statement has a curious mistype: she refers to the "relationship" she has with "my you," which may indicate that she began to write "my teacher" or some similar term but changed her mind and opted for the second person. Incidentally, the letter assignments do not use the term "relationship." May's statement here and Shane's that anticipates "a forced relationship" are the only two cases in the letters in which students use the term.

In end-of-semester letters, students' descriptions of our relationship are marked by enthusiasm and confession. Many end letters celebrate achievements of goals, such as:

- "I achieved all my goals by going to office hours, asking questions, studying on my own time and having Jamie [a friend] help me read through my rough draft papers. Using sources through friends, teachers and resources helped me improve much in this course." (Lina)
- "Now that it is over I am glad I decided to go with it, Not only have I made new friends but I found a professor who wants their students to learn. You are the first professor I have had that has brought 100% every day, and on top of that forced us to participate in discussion making us take control of our own learning. Also, you tried to get to know us both on our style of writing and us as a person." (Shane)

Lina positions me as a resource in a manner that echoes how other students set goals at the start of the semester, and Shane describes the effects that my enthusiasm has had on his learning. Others share evidence of similar achievements, such as Vince celebrating his reluctant but successful use of outlining and Rhea identifying the value of my having students evaluate their progress toward goals.

However, other comments in end letters are quite frank, indicating students are comfortable being honest within our relationship. Several students write what I read as confessions—thoughts they feel comfortable sharing because the semester is almost over:

- "I did not necessarily agree with your viewpoints on certain issues ..." (Doug)
- "One of my downfalls with [research paper] was in not submitting a complete first draft and in turn not receiving all the feedback from you that I possibly could." (Jim)
- "It seems to me that becoming a better writer for school really means becoming used to what your teacher expects and writing for your teacher." (Karrie)
- "The deadlines came pretty quickly, as you warned us they would, and I failed to stay ahead of them, leading to sub-par work." (Rhea)
- "I feel safe telling you, now that I've turned in my final paper, that when you said we could use ANY six sources for our paper, I never once looked at books." (Vince)

At the end of the semester, these students are comfortable critiquing their own work or expressing hesitation about my choices, such as "viewpoints" with which Doug disagrees or Vince's recognition that I expected students would consult books in their research. Karrie's realization that being a strong college writer "really means ... writing for your teacher" comes in a letter that describes many writing achievements but simultaneously laments the process. She writes, "I did become a better writer for class, even if I am not sure if that transfer to my personal writing (possibly)." Taken as a whole, the letters show evidence of students describing our relationship, and students' descriptions of such grow in frequency as the semester goes on.

Student Discussion of Classmate Relationships

Although I set out to study how students describe their relationships with me, I found that students also describe relationships with classmates in valuable ways. A few students name peers as resources that contribute to their writing success, such as Christiana's comment that she finds "partner work" to be valuable because "my writing becomes very 'tunnel viewed' and I only think of my topic in the way that I want to see it." Enzo says classmates' diverse range of perspectives "made for more interesting talks when discussing the different articles," and Imani notes that "reading others papers was a great strategy in gaining ideas on how my work should look like and be organized."

Several students comment on the comfort level they developed with peers during the semester, such as in these end-of-semester excerpts:

- "During these discussions, I really felt a sense of comfort when it came to give feedback or talk about any topic. This was due to the respect that the classmates had for each other, which made it easier for us to express how we feel about a topic." (Imani)
- "I also recognize that I have become more comfortable with sharing my thoughts with my peers without fear of judgment." (Grace)
- "Overall, I was impressed by the general level of respect demonstrated by everyone in our class, despite occasional incredulity and/or ignorance." (Rhea)

These students describe peer relationships characterized by respect, such as Imani's assertion that respect among peers "made it easier" to join class conversation. Grace's comment that she has "become more comfortable" indicates that achieving a comfort level is a process. Rhea's comment is marked by surprise: she is "impressed" by her classmates, "despite occasional incredulity and/or ignorance." In the same letter, Rhea refers to a divisive class discussion in which she perceived "a lot of confusion and distinct reluctance" from peers yet concludes that the discussion was worthwhile.

Shane stands out for his focus on peers, and I quote him at length here to show the value he places on these relationships. In his first letter, Shane sets "a connection with the students and faculty of this class" as a goal. He explains, "Coming from last year, I did not have too many friends in my English class ... Working on my own not only cost my grade but also made it where I was not able to compare my paper to others, or have a chance for a new set of eyes to read my paper and help catch a lot of standard errors." Shane decides he will "make conversation with classmates and reach out to others for help" in order to forge friendships.

Shane knew one classmate prior to the semester's start and reports in his midterm letter that he has made other connections:

> As you know, Nyla and I are pretty close, but recently we have been hanging out with Enzo. This past weekend we all drove up north of Denver to the haunted corn maze and well just picture Nyla running through corn and crying a little. We can just conclude that the night was amazing for Enzo and I, Nyla well she threatened to kill me for dragging her along ... Jason and I have bonded over hunting and adventure while Vince and I have connected through bashing Nyla (in a nice-ish way) ... I can see that many of these students will be a friend throughout my college career.

Shane's description of these connections shows his success in making friends, but his discussion is also indicative of the relationship he and I had formed by this point in the semester. Whereas at the semester's start he names peer connections as a support system for academic success, by the midterm letter, he feels comfortable sharing social details of these connections. Shane's end-of-semester letter also gives attention to peer connections, including a mention that he has "made new friends" and has learned from his peers.

The Value of Letters in College Writing Education

As the excerpts show, these letters offer great insight into students' experiences and their perceptions of our relationship. Each time a student writes me a letter, I write a letter in return that is more conversational than my feedback on their other projects and that responds to the ideas they raise. Students' goal-setting gives me the opportunity to weigh in with suggestions, and my responses in turn validate students' choices to pursue particular goals. By inviting students into dialogue through letters, and by asking them to write an informal letter prior to any formal texts, I take some pressure off of students who may struggle to perform at college writing tasks. As Sheldon George notes, students face a challenge in attempting to perfect an expected identity in the college classroom. He argues that "students may experience a frustrated sense of self that is caused by their struggles to decipher both the discourse of their professors and the identity roles their professors expect them to perform" (322). Starting the course with a letter gives students permission to just be themselves—at least temporarily, before they have to enact the performance of a student writing a research paper.

Cooper and Miness stress that "not all students seek a strong relationship with each teacher, but teachers must provide opportunities for students to share themselves if they so desire" (285). Many students' end-of-semester letters contain language expressing gratitude for my teaching. I recognize that some of this gratitude is performative, part of a role students are enacting as the course comes to a close. But these moments of gratitude also highlight the values students perceive in their learning. Students thank me for:

- "making me feel comfortable" (Imani)
- "your class, it really did teach me a lot about myself" (Karrie)
- "trying to keep your classroom a safe space" (Rhea)
- "challenging my thinking and helping me to grow in my education" (Doug)
- "making it interesting, and keeping a good vibe throughout the semester during what could easily have been an extremely dull and mentally taxing experience" (Vince)

In capping off our semester-long relationship by thanking me for learning, or a sense of comfort, or even "making it interesting," students identify these gains from the course. Not only does the relationship we build with students help support their progress as writers, the dialogue within that relationship makes students' progress visible to them when it occurs.

Appendix: Letter Assignments

Course Start Letter

What are your goals as a writer and researcher in this course? What steps will you take to achieve these goals? In this assignment, you will write a letter to me to identify your goals for the course and discuss the steps you will take this semester to achieve these goals.

As you consider what goals to identify in your letter, it may help you to think about:

- *Your current writing practices:* What types of writing do you do in everyday life? How can this course help you in your everyday writing, and how can your everyday writing help you in this course?
- *Your recent writing education:* What was the last writing course you took? What did you learn in it that was useful to you either in school or outside of school? How will you use or build on what you learned in this course?
- *Your plans as a writer at UCCS:* What types of writing do people in your major or your planned career do? (Hint: If you think people in your major or planned career don't write much, ask me or a professor in your major. Everybody has to be a good writer in every career.) Which of your writing abilities do you need to strengthen in this course to help you in courses in your major? What writing that we do in this course will help you become a stronger writer in your career someday?
- *Your plans as a researcher at UCCS:* What types of research do people in your major or planned career do? (If you don't know, ask.) Which of your research abilities do you need to strengthen in this course to help you in courses in your major? What research that we'll do will help you become a stronger researcher in your career someday?

Note: These questions are meant to get you thinking. You are not required to answer any (nor all) of them in your letter.

This assignment requires that you:

- Identify your goals as a writer and researcher for this course.

- Fully explain the steps you will take to reach those goals. Provide specific examples and details to support the steps you present, and explain how each step will work.
- Write about your goals and steps in the form of a letter addressed to Dr. Amicucci.

In completing these assignment requirements, you will write a 3-page (typed, double-spaced) letter. This letter is the start of a conversation between us, so it can be as formal or informal as you like. Make sure to proofread your work carefully from a printed copy to ensure that you submit your best, polished writing. This assignment is due on Canvas by the start of class on Thursday, Aug. 23.

I will grade your paper using the following rubric:

Identification of goals as writer and researcher		
5–4	3–2	1–0
Identifies goals for both writing and researching. Goals are presented clearly and explained fully.	Identifies goals for both writing and researching. Goals are partially explained or not explained at all.	Does not identify goals for both writing and researching.

Explanation of steps to achieve goals		
10–8	7–4	3–0
Identifies steps to achieve each goal. Steps are fully explained and make clear how writer will achieve goals. Provides specific examples and details for support.	Uneven or incomplete identification of steps or examples and details are not relevant to goals.	Does not identify steps to be taken or does not explain any steps. Provides no examples or details to support any explanations.

Professionalism		
5–4	3–2	1–0
Follows assignment guidelines. Is free from typographical errors. Is free from sentence-level errors according to the language variety the writer uses.	Follows some but not all assignment guidelines; writing is careless and contains some typographical or other sentence-level errors.	Does not follow assignment guidelines; contains numerous typographical or other sentence-level errors.

This assignment is worth 20 points, or 4% of your total semester grade.

Midterm Letter

In the Course Start Letter you wrote in Aug., you identified the goals you have as a writer and researcher in this course and the steps you planned to take to achieve these goals. In this assignment, you will go back and review these goals and write a letter to me discussing the progress you've made toward your goals and what you still need to do to achieve them.

As you consider what to write about in your letter, you will want to do the following:

- *Read your Course Start Letter:* Review the goals you set and the steps you outlined in this letter.
- *Evaluate the progress you've made so far:* Have you achieved any of your goals yet? If so, how? What evidence from your work in our class can you discuss to demonstrate that you've achieved them? Have you made progress toward some of your goals? If so, how, and what evidence from your work in our class can you discuss?
- *Identify what steps you need to take next:* If you have not yet achieved your goals, what will you do to achieve them now that you know how this class works? (Note: Don't just repeat what you said in your Course Start letter—you didn't know how our class worked when you wrote it.) If you've achieved all of your goals, what new goals can you set for the second half of the semester, and what steps will you take to reach them?

This assignment requires that you:

- Evaluate the progress you've made toward each goal you set in your Course Start letter.
- Provide evidence from your work in our class for why you have or haven't reached each goal, and fully discuss this evidence.
- Fully explain the steps you will take, now that you know how our class works, to keep working toward your goals. If you've already achieved your goals, you should identify new goals and fully discuss the steps you will take to achieve them.
- Write in the form of a letter addressed to Dr. Amicucci.

In completing these assignment requirements, you will write a 3-page (typed, double-spaced) letter. This letter is the continuation of a conversation between us; just as with the Course Start letter, it can be as formal or informal as you like. Make sure to proofread your work carefully from a printed copy to ensure that you submit your best, polished writing. This assignment is due on Canvas by the start of class on Tuesday, Oct. 16.

I will grade your paper using the following rubric:

Evaluate progress made toward Course Start Letter goals		
5–4	3–2	1–0
Evaluates progress toward each goal honestly and identifies why writer has or hasn't achieved each goal.	Evaluates progress toward some but not all goals and identifies why writer has or hasn't achieved these goals.	Does not evaluate progress toward each goal.
Provide evidence to support evaluation of progress toward goals		
5–4	3–2	1–0
Discusses specific evidence from writer's own work in the course to support each claim about achieving/not achieving a goal. Explains evidence fully.	Discusses specific evidence from writer's own work in the course to support some claims about achieving/not achieving goals. Does not explain all evidence fully.	Does not discuss specific evidence or does not explain evidence fully.
Explanation of next steps		
5–4	3–2	1–0
Identifies next steps writer will take to achieve goals or identifies new goals and planned steps toward them. All steps are fully explained and make clear how writer will work toward goals now that writer understand how the class works. All ideas are fully explained.	Uneven or incomplete identification of steps or new goals. Some ideas are not fully explained.	Does not identify steps or new goals or does not explain ideas fully.
Professionalism		
5–4	3–2	1–0
Follows assignment guidelines. Is free from typographical errors. Is free from sentence-level errors according to the language variety the writer uses.	Follows some but not all assignment guidelines; writing is careless and contains some typographical or other sentence-level errors.	Does not follow assignment guidelines; contains numerous typographical or other sentence-level errors.

This assignment is worth 20 points, or 4% of your total semester grade.

Course End Letter

In our final assignment in English 1410, you will examine all of your work to determine how well you've met your goals for the course and to identify what you've learned that you will take into future writing and research settings.

To prepare to write your Course End Letter, take the following steps:

- *Read your Course Start Letter:* Review the goals you set and the steps you outlined for yourself at the start of the course.
- *Read your Midterm Letter:* Review where you were at the halfway point of the course and the progress you had made toward your goals at that stage.
- *Review all of the writing and research you've done in this course:* Go back and look at all of it! Read your Rhetorical Analysis essay, your Facebook Posts and Responses, and all the materials you worked on as you drafted and wrote The Best Research Paper You've Ever Written. Ask yourself questions like:
  o What are you most proud of? Why?
  o Where could you have done better? Why?
  o Is your research paper really the best research paper you've ever written? Why or why not?
- *Evaluate your overall progress in this course:* What goals did you achieve? How did you achieve them? What evidence from your work can you discuss to show this?
- *Reflect on what you've learned about our course theme of Social Justice Issues in Language Diversity:* What did you learn about this theme that holds value for you? Feel free to be critical here—if you didn't learn something of value, explain why.
- *Identify what you'll take from this course into future writing and research situations:* What strategies or skills have you learned as a writer or researcher that you'll use in the future? How will you use these strategies or skills?

This assignment requires that you:

- Evaluate the progress you made toward the goals you set for yourself in this course, provide evidence from your work for why you have or haven't reached your goals, and fully discuss this evidence.
- Discuss what you've learned about our course theme and why this learning is (or isn't) important to you.

- Identify and discuss the strategies and skills you will take from this course into future writing and research situations and fully discuss how you will use these strategies or skills in the future.
- Write in the form of a letter addressed to Dr. Amicucci.

In completing these assignment requirements, you will write a 3-page (typed, double-spaced) letter. This letter marks the culmination of a semester-long conversation between us. Just as with your previous letters, it can be as formal or informal as you like. Make sure to proofread your work carefully from a printed copy to ensure that you submit your best, polished writing. This assignment is due on Canvas by midnight on Tuesday, Dec. 11.

I will grade your paper using the following rubric:

Evaluate progress made toward course goals		
4–3	2	1–0
Evaluates progress toward each goal honestly and identifies why writer has or hasn't achieved each goal.	Evaluates progress toward some but not all goals and identifies why writer has or hasn't achieved these goals.	Does not evaluate progress toward each goal.

Provide evidence to support evaluation of progress toward goals		
4–3	2	1–0
Discusses specific evidence from writer's own work in the course to support each claim about achieving/not achieving a goal. Explains evidence fully.	Discusses specific evidence from writer's own work in the course to support some claims about achieving/not achieving goals. Does not explain all evidence fully.	Does not discuss specific evidence or does not explain evidence fully.

Discussion of learning in course theme		
4–3	2	1–0
Fully discusses what writer has learned about course theme that is/isn't valuable and why.	Discusses what writer has learned about course theme that is/isn't valuable.	Does not discuss what writer has learned about course theme or does not discuss this learning's value.

Discussion of strategies writer will carry forward		
4–3	2	1–0
Identifies and fully discusses strategies or skills in writing or research that writer will carry beyond this course.	Identifies but does not fully discuss strategies or skills in writing or research that writer will carry beyond this course.	Does not identify or does not discuss strategies or skills that writer will carry beyond this course.

Professionalism		
4–3	2	1–0
Follows assignment guidelines. Is free from typographical errors. Is free from sentence-level errors according to the language variety the writer uses.	Follows some but not all assignment guidelines; writing is careless and contains some typographical or other sentence-level errors.	Does not follow assignment guidelines; contains numerous typographical or other sentence-level errors.

This assignment is worth 20 points, or 4% of your total semester grade.

Note

1. All student examples are presented as written except where bracketed material is inserted for clarification. Several sentence-level errors appear in examples, likely due to my encouragement for students to write informally. Though the assignments directed students to proofread their work and submit polished writing, the letters indicate that not all students did so.

Works Cited

Amicucci, Ann N. "Using Reflection to Promote Students' Writing Process Awareness." *The CEA Forum*, vol. 40, no. 1, 2011, pp. 34–56.

Anderson, Darlene H., et al. "Using Dialogue Journals to Strengthen the Student-Teacher Relationship: A Comparative Case Study." *College Student Journal*, vol. 45, no. 2, 2011, pp. 269–87.

"Brainstorming and Free Writing." *Naropa Writing Center*, https://www.naropa.edu/documents/programs/jks/naropa-writing-center/brainstorming-and-freewriting.pdf. Accessed 17 Feb. 2019.

Cooper, Kristy S., and Andrew Miness. "The Co-Creation of Caring Student-Teacher Relationships: Does Teacher Understanding Matter?" *The High School Journal*, vol. 97, no. 4, 2014, pp. 264–90.

De La Cruz, Donna. "What Kids Wish Their Teachers Knew." *The New York Times*, 31 Aug. 2016, https://www.nytimes.com/2016/08/31/well/family/what-kids-wish-their-teachers-knew.html. Accessed 16 Feb. 2019.

George, Sheldon. "The Performed Self in College Writing." *Pedagogy: Critical Approaches to Teaching Literature, Language, Composition, and Culture*, vol. 12, no. 2, 2012, pp. 319–41.

Gogan, Brian. "Expanding the Aims of Public Rhetoric and Writing Pedagogy: Writing Letters to Editors." *College Composition and Communication*, vol. 65, no. 4, 2014, pp. 534–59.

Haswell, Janis, et al. "Hospitality in College Composition Courses." *College Composition and Communication*, vol. 60, no. 4, 2009, pp. 707–27.
"Integrating Reading and Writing." *Institute for Writing and Rhetoric*, 14 Apr. 2016, https://writing-speech.dartmouth.edu/teaching/first-year-writing-pedagogies-methods-design/integrating-reading-and-writing. Accessed 17 Feb. 2019.
Noddings, Nel. *Caring: A Relational Approach to Ethics & Moral Education*. 2nd ed. U of California P, 2013.
Rankin, Joan L. "Connecting Literacy Learners: A Pen Pal Project." *The Reading Teacher*, vol. 46, no. 3, 1992, pp. 204–14.
Reyes, María de la Luz. "Process Approach to Literacy Using Dialogue Journals and Literature Logs with Second Language Learners." *Research in the Teaching of English*, vol. 25, no. 3, 1991, pp. 291–313.
Strauss, Anselm, and Juliet Corbin. *Basics of Qualitative Research: Techniques and Procedures for Developing Grounded Theory*. 3rd ed. SAGE, 2008.
Yancey, Kathleen Blake. *Reflection in the Writing Classroom*. Utah State UP, 1998.

16. Pet Pictures, Pop Culture, and GIF Game: (Re)Viewing Twitter as Multimodal Emotional Writing in First-Year Composition

AMANDA M. MAY

> "Pedagogies that embrace rather than excise emotion not only help students understand emotion as a part of reading and composing but also help them to consider what there is to learn from that which our culture would throw out."
> —Shari J. Stenberg, *Repurposing Composition: Feminism for a Neoliberal Age*, 66

In my first semester of PhD studies, I taught two sections of ENC 2135: Research, Genre, and Context, Florida State University's required composition course. It was my first time teaching a college course, so I relied heavily on a Wix website that houses different versions of the course for incoming graduate students. From these, I selected a syllabus that focused on digital writing developed by Molly Daniel during her PhD studies. Among other digital elements, Daniel's course implemented Twitter as a learning tool. Borrowing Daniel's syllabus language, I described Twitter in my own syllabus as a tool that "allows us to interact with the publicness of writing as you begin shaping your personal/professional identities. It also creates a space where we can interact with a variety of genre, contexts, and interact with users outside the classroom." Additionally, I utilized several aspects of Daniel's Twitter pedagogy: students created a new Twitter account, used course-specific hashtags to interact with me and with each other, and participated in live tweets at the opening of every class led by other students. To these three elements, I added in-class reflections when major projects were due, tweeting out a series of questions that students could respond to.

Before Fall 2017 started, I developed my own version of ENC 2135 focused on the visual, one shaped by both my experiences as a teacher and as a graduate student. During the past year, I had become more aware of my teaching preferences. I also developed an interest in visual rhetoric and, consequently, a strong belief that images could work well in FYC courses. Thus, I sought ways to incorporate images as objects of analysis, as part of other compositions, and as compositions in and of themselves.

I also continued to use Twitter, but I shifted my language away from identity and instead described the objective as "build[ing an] online community" in my syllabus. I further emphasized this importance by highlighting the need to like and reply during live tweets since such approaches were more in line with the objective. To better fit the focus of the course, I implemented small changes to my 2016 approaches. Students still created a new Twitter handle, which allowed them to create new online identities appropriate in classroom or professional settings. I continued to begin class with a student-led live tweet. The leader brought two questions—one about course readings or activities and one about an image that guided analysis and discussion—to which all participants of the class, including me, responded. I still sometimes integrated Twitter as a reflective space for projects and in-class activities, asking questions or soliciting GIF responses about students' feelings on their drafts. Finally, because I required students to tweet 150 times during the semester, I added syllabus language that explicitly invited them to tweet outside of class about genres they found around campus or any writing they were doing: "You can use Twitter to ask questions about the course (that are not in the syllabus), communicate about assignments and/or coursework, and about genres you happen to be seeing around campus and in your daily lives. I will also be tweeting out images on occasion." All of this activity took place under a course hashtag, one not in use by other composition instructors. While this didn't stop them from using other hashtags, it did simplify the process of finding one another's tweets for all of us—myself included.

My understanding of how students interpreted these guidelines, particularly "communicat[ing] about assignments and/or coursework," began to shift around Week 3 of the semester, when meteorologists predicted Hurricane Irma's potential impact on Tallahassee. As the storm approached, I used Twitter for more practical purposes, disseminating information about campus closures and hurricane safety. Student tweets, on the other hand, relied on emotions including concern and even humor; in some cases, they even used the images I valued through my course. In one such tweet, a student photographed their blank word document using her smartphone and wrote, "The only thing I'm more afraid of than Irma is this blank page."

Students responded with empathy; one even tweeted "Agreed!" with a GIF of a young woman hunched over a desk, suggesting engagement in coursework despite Irma's approach.

Hurricane Irma passed and the campus reopened, but the emotive tweets and their accompanying images continued. While beyond my initial vision, I felt positive about these tweets in reflection. The emotions they expressed did not read as complaints or criticisms but as everyday sentiments resulting from ordinary university student experiences. Further, such expressions both contributed to the sense of community on the hashtag and granted these students opportunities to support one another. Around Week 7, I opened class by acknowledging the work my students were doing on Twitter and encouraged them to continue tweeting about their experiences—both positive and negative—as writers at FSU, especially in terms of the images they continued to utilize in our online space. As the semester progressed, I continued to view this contribution as important, if not vital, to Twitter's success in my classroom. In the context of emotional writing, I read these tweets as successful because of their reliance on GIFs and on self-created images, both alone and as part of written posts. Before examining how this emotional writing unfolded through two notable examples from the last week of classes, I look to existing research on visual rhetoric and composition to contextualize both the links between emotions and images and existing social media pedagogies.

In visual rhetoric, scholars often discuss the links between images and emotions. Charles A. Hill relies on cognitive psychology to argue that images are more likely to produce an emotional response because the human mind can process them more quickly than written words, granting them a sort of immediacy (37). In Twitter's context, depending on the reader, a tweet that includes an image may create a more immediate and more potent emotional reaction than one that is purely textual. Hill refers to these emotional images as "[v]ivid images," which are "valued by rhetors ... because they tend to elicit strong emotions [that] will overcome and even inhibit analytical thinking" (33). Hill focuses on photographs that strongly reflect reality while noting that other images may also function in vivid ways (31), but what he fails to note is that such images, if used rhetorically, can also carry or suggest the emotions of those who utilize them.

To fully understand how students can use Twitter to express emotions, we first need to reconcile the divide between word and image. Anne Frances Wysocki conceives of this duality by acknowledging the separate communicative uses of picture and word: both have the potential to suggest identities that others can read and interpret (28). Thus, some situations call for a combination of word and text to express identity, and although they are different modes of communication, they can be used to communicate similar points. In *Non-Discursive Rhetorics,* Joddy Murray carries this further, arguing that all forms of communication are rooted in images because the human brain functions visually, including traditional language (3). Ultimately, both Wysocki and Murray show that while the ways that image and word communicate are fundamentally different, they do not function in opposition to one another. Instead, they often work together to create meaning, either through mental processing of a written or spoken word or through a combination of different forms of communication. Twitter bridges this gap in several ways: on profiles, users have the option of selecting a display picture and a profile banner, both of which can communicate different identities. Within individual posts, in both the browser and mobile app versions, Twitter includes buttons that enable users to post self-created photos. Twitter also provides a GIF keyboard in which users can search for premade images using key words like "scared" or "stressed." In October 2017, Twitter doubled its 140-character limit to 280 and implemented a thread option that allows users to more easily tweet multiple text-based posts with attached images.

While many social media pedagogies exist and a majority focus on the FYC classroom, few explicitly discuss the visual elements of such composing spaces. Lindsey Sabatino describes one approach to using the Xynga's Facebook game *Mafia Wars* to teach collaboration, critical thinking, analytical skills, and a greater literacy of visual cues (52). In addition to collaboration, often valued in the composition classroom, the visual cues within *Mafia Wars*—that is, the visual elements that help players learn how to use the game—help students recognize and interpret visuals in other spaces (42). Other scholars focus instead on teaching students how to use visuals rather than read them. Jennifer Swartz, another in-field scholar, discusses how profiles on MySpace and Facebook provide spaces for students to compose online identities. However, she also emphasizes the importance of being critical of such spaces, which enables students to better understand identity "as a set of rhetorical choices." Swartz is not alone in emphasizing the critical use of such platforms; Stephanie Vie also advocates for teaching technologies that "students are familiar with but don't think critically about" (10).

While such critical approaches help students view writing in new ways, they fail to account for how emotional writing can take place in public or semipublic online spaces like Twitter, and while Swartz privileges identity, neither Sabatino nor Swartz do not explicitly value emotional writing, as Shari J. Stenberg does in her book *Repurposing Composition: Feminist Interventions for a Neoliberal Age.* In her second chapter, she argues that to repurpose emotion and use it to make knowledge (44), instructors first need to "[study] it

Pet Pictures, Pop Culture, and GIF Game

as *a socially composed public text*, as rhetoric, *with our students*" (49, emphasis mine). This passage points out both the idea that emotion can take place in social texts, and that instructors participate in studying, a point that other researchers acknowledge directly in relation to social media. Bronwyn T. Williams notes in his chapter of *Social Media/Social Writing*, "Emotions have their social component, but explicitly enter the realm of rhetoric when they are performed and enacted" (137). Twitter provides an online space for such performance, and one option for which instructors can enact pedagogies that utilize emotional writing, suggesting that writing about emotion can take place in social media spaces. While not ideal for unfettered, unrestrained diatribes due to its semipublic nature, Twitter can provide opportunities for students to express their emotions using both words and images, and we can encourage students to use tools and technologies that they are familiar with to engage in emotional writing. Students in my Fall 2017 course utilized Twitter to express not only their experiences and consequently identities as students, writers, and human beings, but also the emotions that accompany moments situated within those identities. Two successful examples come from late in the semester, just before finals week: in the first, I invited responses, and in the second, another student invited responses.

During the last week of the semester, I tweeted to the class asking how they felt about the end of the semester and invited GIF responses, both because of the course's focus on images and the students' ongoing intentional and appropriate use of GIFs, what I colloquially call "GIF game." Student responses used GIFs depicting well-known television shows and only the class hashtag as additional text. One portrays a photo of Ryan from the American version of *The Office*, rubbing his head with both palms. In the GIF, his hair is unkempt, and after moving his hands in a half-circle, he slowly lowers them and closes his mouth before opening it again. As a class, we relied on *The Office* for several in-class activities, but here, the GIF serves as a marker for emotion: the student is very clearly expressing her stress as finals week approaches, and she is not alone. In another response, a different student relies on a GIF that other students had utilized earlier in the semester for numerous reasons. Leslie Knope from *Parks and Recreation* stands glancing to the left side of the image. In the background, viewers can see parts of her office: a computer, a door frame, and the walls. As the GIF progresses, she stops speaking, the camera zooms in, and she forces a smile, tipping her head slightly to the left. Her smile grows as the GIF ends. Throughout these motions, the caption "Everything hurts and I'm dying" remains visible in white text at the bottom of the image, the same well-known line that she utters during this scene. In class, as part of conversations and activities, students spoke about their familiarity with one or both franchises, showing a kind of audience awareness. Both GIFs draw on materials that most of the class was familiar with and responds to my invitation to express emotion. Furthermore, both images clearly and strongly suggest each of the students' respective emotions regarding approaching exams and deadlines, though arguably, the *Parks and Recreation* GIF does so with slightly more clarity due to the caption in the image, which reinforces the emotion and also highlights an attempt to remain outwardly positive. In my reading of these GIFs, both students are experiencing—and choosing to express—end-of-semester stress. Admittedly, one may read both GIFs as complaints about the work piling up and exam week stress. I, however, view them as invited but authentic expressions of emotion, and while these emotions are not positive, I chose not to invalidate my students' feelings by discouraging them in responses or verbally in class. Instead, as was the case with expressions of stress earlier in the semester, I empathized and encouraged.

A third response to my initial tweet, rather than focus on the current stress, looks ahead to the upcoming winter vacation. In this GIF response, the second in the thread, several women in full winter attire dance in the middle of a snowy landscape. Behind them, the viewer can see a fence and trees on a hill. At the top of the GIF, as the women dance, the words "Snow Party" remain visible, with the shadows of these words flickering light pink and light blue. While this student expressed her stress about the coming exam week in other tweets, her choice here is to focus on the positive. In an email early in the semester, this student disclosed that her hometown was not in a climate that often experiences snow, but the use of GIF in this instance still carries associations of winter via the snow and the attire of those in the GIF. Because the words are positioned at the top, my instinct is to begin with the words and then view the rest of the image. In combination, the text imposed on the image and the image itself emphasize the approach not of exam week but of the winter break that follows.

This GIF response was not the only attempt to generate positivity during what is arguably the most stressful point in the semester, and my invitation to post images was not the only one that occurred. Approximately 24 hours after my GIF invitation, a student in the class invited responses to a different prompt. She wrote, "I think we should start a dog thread to make everyone's morning a little brighter." While her invitation foregrounds her objective of "making a dog thread," she also emphasizes the emotional purpose that she has in doing so: "to make everyone's morning a little brighter." Her writing is emotional in its intent, and she expressed her hope to garner positivity with a thread of dog photos from classmates. This also connected to some of our in-class conversations about dogs, which, like pop culture references to *Parks and Recreation* and *The Office*, arose naturally out of our in-class dialogues. During such discussions, many members of the class asserted their identities as "dog people." The original tweeter posted the first response: her chocolate lab laying on a bed with an open mouth.

In all, the positive dog thread attracted ten responses, nine from students and one from me, almost all of which include both writing, image, and threads of responses to responses. One student who commented without a photo wrote, "this thread is making me miss my dogs even more" with a crying emoji. The student who started the thread commented, "same my parents keep sending me pics of my dog which doesn't help." While mostly textual, like the premade GIFs, the crying emoji provides another way that students can express emotion in an online space using premade images. In this instance, the emoji in question ties directly to the writer's homesickness, and the feeling of "miss[ing her] dogs."

The next poster returns to the self-made image and says simply, "This is Ruby." The photo he posts is of a black and white terrier sitting on a white surfboard with a blue wave pattern. In the ocean in the background, viewers can see two kayaks, one white and one red. It is unclear from the photo whether or not these two kayakers have any connection to the student who posted his dog, but responses focused on whether or not this was normal behavior for the dog. The original poster responds, clarifying that Ruby does "come out in the kayak with [him] to go fishing too." Thus, the photo of Ruby is not simply an expression of his emotions but of his connections to a place (the ocean) and to activities (fishing, surfing, and kayaking). Although the tweet itself contains no overt expression of emotions, the wording as well as the image itself suggest parts of his life beyond the classroom, connections that he feels passionate enough to post about and to respond and clarify those connections.

Because this thread also came just before the holidays, two students further contributed to the feeling of homesickness and connections to family by posting photos of their dogs in Christmas hats, through which they showed both connections to their families as well as family traditions. In one case, a student wrote, "my mom took some christmas [sic.] pics" and added the laughing/crying emoji. The photo depicts a small terrier wearing a Santa hat sitting on carpeted stairs. A different student wrote, "Doodles . . . don't mind the cocker" and posted a photo of a cocker spaniel wearing a Santa hat sitting in front of a Christmas tree. In the foreground, there is a blurry object that looks like a blanket or possibly an arm. These tweets serve as a reminder of the approaching vacation and suggest both optimism about the coming holiday (Christmas in both cases) and a connection to family traditions.

There are several possibilities as to why this invitation garnered more responses than my call for end-of-semester GIFs. It is possible that the students felt a greater connection with their pets than they did my invitation, or that they responded more because the invitation came from a classmate. In addition, this thread gave them the opportunity to post images that people in their lives had taken or that they had taken themselves. Also unclear is whether or not this thread had the intended effect of generating positivity. While participants expressed positive opinions about some of the dogs—for example, someone responded to the photo of Ruby with the comment, "that's so crazy!! she's such a good pup"—the overt mention of homesickness and of missing dogs highlights the unintended emotional response of being disconnected from familiar places and family. Regardless, the thread shows the strong sense of connections that students felt towards their pets and homes, and the degree to which they participated in this space in addition suggests that their sense of community in class carried over at least in some ways to online spaces.

Initially, I did not intend Twitter as a space for my students to do emotional writing. I envisioned it as a space where they could ask questions about the course, discuss images, and do learning in a digital space outside of Canvas, our course management system. However, my experiences suggest that in some instances, students should be encouraged to do emotional writing online. Twitter takes learning out of the classroom and moves it into a digital space with which students can engage in dorm rooms, coffee shops, libraries, and unscheduled trips home due to approaching hurricanes. As such, I find that many of the feelings of success I have about this particular semester stem from my decision to see dog pictures, GIFs, and other images as valid and welcome expressions of emotion, ones that went beyond my original vision but that changed Twitter for the better and strengthened the sense of community through their content, not mine. While we continued to use Twitter to open each class session to share information and learn about writing, I continued to show interest in their emotional expressions about the everyday experience of being university students and ultimately discovered that Twitter, like most forms of writing, can be used for multiple purposes. Further, the rhetorical ways in which students expressed emotion here, following generic conventions like using hashtags and emojis, writing concisely, and using informal but appropriate tone, demonstrates that they can still maintain a level of audience awareness.

Additionally, my focus on the image in this course and the ways students used these images in online spaces to express emotions reinforce Hill's idea that we can and should embrace rhetorical images (37), though these are a different type of image than Hill originally envisioned. The GIFs and emoticons that students used in their tweets and responses can express emotion on their own or connect to the other writing that they have been doing in these online spaces. Their pet pictures responded to a prompt in ways that helped communicate their connections to home, holidays, family, and animals. In some cases, these photos also suggest a sense of homesickness. Embracing the image in online spaces and encouraging students to use whatever images they feel comfortable using, be they images created by someone else or images they created themselves, presents an opportunity for them to express both emotions and identity using word and image together. Ultimately, Twitter provides us with new ways to see—and new ways for our students to see—how their emotional writing matters.

Acknowledgments

My thanks to the students in my Fall 2017 section of ENC 2135 for their continued willingness to let me use their tweets in my research and for all the opportunities I had to learn with them.

Works Cited

Hill, Charles A. "The Psychology of Rhetorical Images." *Defining Visual Rhetorics*, edited by Charles A. Hill and Marguerite Helmers, Lawrence Erlbaum Associates, 2004, pp. 25–40.

Murray, Joddy. *Non-Discursive Rhetoric: Image and Affect in Multimodal Composition.* State U of New York P, 2010.

Sabatino, Lindsay. "Improving Writing Literacies through Digital Gaming Literacies: Facebook Gaming in the Composition Classroom." *Computers and Composition*, vol. 32, June 2014, pp. 41–53.

Stenberg, Shari J. "Feminist Repurposing of Emotion: From Emotional Management to Emotion as Resource." *Repurposing Composition: Feminist Interventions for a Neolibreal Age*, U of Colorado P, 2015, pp. 41–69.

Swartz, Jennifer. "MySpace, Facebook, and Multimodal Literacy in the Writing Classroom." *Kairos: A Journal of Rhetoric, Technology, and Pedagogy*, vol. 14, no. 2, 2010.

Vie, Stephanie. "Digital Divide 2.0: 'Generation M' and Online Social Networking Sites in the Composition Classroom." *Computers and Composition*, vol. 25, no. 1, 2008, pp. 9–23.

Williams, Bronwyn T. "Having a Feeling for What Works: Polymedia, Emotion, and Literacy Practices with Mobile Technologies." *Social Media/Social Writing: Publics, Presentations, and Pedagogies*, edited by Douglas Walls and Stephanie Vie, UP of Colorado, 2017, pp. 127–43.

Wysocki, Anne Frances. "Drawn Together: Possibilities for Bodies in Words and Pictures." *Composing(media) = Composing(embodiment): Bodies, Technologies, Writing, and the Teaching of Writing*, edited by Kristin L. Arola and Anne Frances Wysocki, Utah State UP, 2012, pp. 25–42.

17. Performing Silence, Exhaustion, and Recovery: Articulating Faculty and Administrator Identity by Cultivating Mental Wellness

SHERRY RANKINS-ROBERTSON & NICHOLAS BEHM

This chapter shares narratives of shame, vulnerability, and fear, but these narratives also illustrate growth, strength, and ultimately healing, depicting the affective realities of the academy. This chapter opens with disciplinary discourse on mental wellness and self-care, so that those who experience challenges with mental health, whether singly, sporadically, or chronically, know that theirs is not a solitary experience. No matter how painful and desperate the lived experiences with mental illness may be, the journey of recovery and healing is possible as shown in this chapter. We begin with existing scholarship which we build upon by describing lived experiences with mental health issues. We move to a discussion of vulnerability, situating that discussion within the context of Judith Butler's theory of vulnerability and Gershen Kaufman's theory of shame. Lastly, we offer ways in which mobilizing vulnerability and resistance within writing programs could challenge stigmas of mental health in the discipline of teaching writing while strengthening interpersonal alliances not only between WPAs and with teachers but also between instructor and students.

Identifying Mental Disabilities in Writing Studies

According to the National Alliance on Mental Illness (NAMI), in any given year, approximately 43.8 million Americans experience an episode of mental illness. Annually, 16 million Americans experience a depressive disorder and 42 million live with anxiety disorders (NAMI). The NAMI statistics reveal more disconcerting realities: approximately 60% of Americans who experience a mental illness do not receive mental health services, and there exist significant inequalities with access to mental health services and the quality of those services among persons of different racial formations. Depression, according to NAMI, is the primary "cause of disability worldwide."

Though research in disability studies permeates rhetoric and composition scholarship, the same scholarship often discusses disability of students' learning experiences as the primary focus; the scholarship explores students' self-disclosure (Payne; Vidali, "Performing"); the accessibility of classrooms, curricula, and writing programs (Browning; McLeod and Garretson; Troia); and suggests how disparate abilities may influence students' literacy practices (Jurecic). Simi Linton's foundational work *Reclaiming Disability: Knowledge and Identify* (re)defines disability as "a group bound by common social and political experience" (12). This work makes way for rhetoric and composition scholar Margaret Price to argue for inclusion of mental disabilities within disability studies, particularly for faculty in higher education. Beyond her book *Mad at School: Rhetorics of Mental Disability and Academic Life*, which makes the argument for acknowledging faculty distress, she and colleagues coauthored the results of a study ("Disclosure of Mental Disability by College and University Faculty") examining 267 faculty on necessary accommodations and support for faculty mental health with particular attention improving work environments. This study acknowledges "individual revelations" by bringing attention to mental disabilities in higher education; however, the study shows very few faculty are aware of or request accommodations. Additionally, the work of Amy Vidali aims to "invite disability in new and diverse ways" particularly in the area of writing program administration (47). While the scholarship on self-care and emotional labor in the community of writing program administration is under development (Adams Wooten, Babb, Costello, and Navickas), a disparity exists in works on teaching writing, writing program administrative practices, and faculty who struggle with emotional management and mental wellness. While existing work has explored teacher and administrator burnout, directly addressing the promotion of mental wellness and acknowledgement of mental disability for writing faculty and administrators is insufficiently covered.

While the authors take journeys down different paths, the commonality of silent suffering and mental exhaustion exist; additionally, we agree that neither of us could move toward healing and recovery without intervention, space for sharing our stories with colleagues, and strategies for envisioning a different kind of performance in higher education. For Sherry, it was a slow unraveling that persisted over several years as the result of pushing toward what she perceived to be the expectations of the upward trajectory of the academy. For Nick, the first sign came as a debilitating, disruptive moment. For many of us, as it was for both Nick and Sherry, the healing begins with narration, allowing ourselves to become vulnerable not only with family members or mental health professionals, but also with our colleagues.

For too long, discussions of mental illness have been taboo; those who have experienced mental breakdowns have been stigmatized, alienated, and othered. The threat of how the revelation of a mental illness may negatively affect employment opportunities has prevented thousands from seeking and receiving help and treatment. However, taking issues of mental health seriously within disciplinary conversations subverts and ameliorates the stigmatization of those who experience mental health challenges, and just as importantly, works to change the culture of our discipline so that a positive and productive focus on mental health is normalized. Our aim is to normalize the individual narratives so the rhetoric and writing community, more specifically writing program administration, becomes a space of support for other WPAs and writing teachers, regardless of contingent status.

Sharing Lived Experiences of Silence

Successive panic attacks leave one desperately exhausted and unremittingly afraid of the next second, the next trigger, the next thought. In Aug. of 2017, Nick experienced a debilitating mental health crisis that dramatically impacted every facet of life. The signs and symptoms portending a crisis began a few months earlier. Shortly after submitting grades for the spring term, Nick experienced a traumatic physiological event during which his heart raced uncontrollably; he felt as if he had lost control of reality; tingling, numbness, and nausea pervaded his body. He thought he was dying. This was a severe, stress-induced panic attack that occurred after the most onerous year of his career during which he taught ten courses (four more than the contractual load); completed a book project and a book chapter; fulfilled roles with innumerable national and local disciplinary service positions; parented three children all under the age of six; and managed all of the diurnal, seemingly inane professional and personal challenges that manifest, in addition to other roles as a husband, brother, son, and friend.

Fissures and fractures in Nick's mental health materialized and proliferated. Over the course of two months, he reeled from one panic attack to another, feeling relentlessly edgy, suffocating from the powerful anxiety, and experiencing severe irritability and persistent insomnia. All of this continued, day after day, until it escalated into another disorder: a deep and debilitating depression that leveled him, drastically impeding his ability to think, work, or function. Unlike the majority of people who experience a mental disorder and who, because of the pervasive powerful stigma involved or lack of access or lack of time, don't receive support and help, he frantically sought out help. He was extraordinarily fortunate to possess a supportive family and a very understanding institution that allowed him to take medical leave with full salary. He benefited from accessible, effective mental health services. He could just be human for a time and focus on reassessing priorities and recalibrating investments of emotional and physical energy in attempt to reclaim some semblance of equanimity.

This process of reclaiming took time; for everyone, seemingly, it takes so much time. One of the most aggravating aspects of experiencing a mental health crisis is that there is no quick fix. Break an arm: doctors set the bone, restrict it with a splint or brace, and prescribe pain medication. Develop strep throat: you take antibiotics and the infection clears. With a mental disorder, depending on the severity, a person can languish for weeks, months, or even years with medical professionals, through endless trial and error, seeking the appropriate treatment regime of medication, therapy, and other interventions. Nick's journey to equanimity consumed several months, six weeks of an intensive partial hospitalization program, eight different combination of medications, and approximately a 100 hours of therapy. Not only is it aggravating that it takes so long to discern the right combination of medications and for them to actually work, but also the possible myriad side effects of those medications compound the distress and sense of failure one feels. The frustrating agony and disappointment, the vacillations between hope and despair that you have found the right treatment protocol, the acclimation to and coping with side effects are all part of the journey. There are setbacks; there can be incremental progress; there can be great leaps forward and backward, but no matter forward, backward, or sideways, one is always healing. Everyone's journey is distinctly traveled and felt, spanning a uniquely inscrutable timeline, because everyone's lived experience with a mental disorder is unique: although similarities exist, no two people experience depression, anxiety, obsessive compulsive disorder, or any other mental disorder exactly.

However, although a crisis in one's mental health can be frightening and excruciatingly painful, the lessons it teaches are invaluable. Part of healing is becoming more critically self-reflective, compassionate, and loving. Nick is passionately convinced that one can't help but become a better, more caring human while healing. At in-take of a partial hospitalization program, Nick felt ineffably scared. He quickly realized, though, that the patients in the program were exemplars of courage and strength. They were living the best way they could with what little emotional energy they had while enduring tremendous pain. What was he to them but a random person whose blindness to able-est privileges and entitlement had created a dangerous sense of invulnerability, which mutated into maudlin self-pity when a fabricated wall of invulnerability crumbled. Yet, they shared their experiences; they exposed themselves to the arbitrary judgment of each member of the group because of a collective responsibility to participate in the healing of others. They taught him how to be vulnerable—that, contrary to what we are conditioned to feel and believe in our individualistic, patriarchal culture, a deep and abiding strength constitutes vulnerability and circulates among expressions of vulnerability.

We see an opening for such transformative affective labor within writing programs and the academy with the application of how Judith Butler reconceptualizes vulnerability in "Rethinking Vulnerability and Resistance." For Butler, vulnerability is relational and sociopolitically constituted in highly dynamic social situations. This framing of vulnerability is rooted in Butler's earlier scholarship on gender and performativity in which people are interpellated into particular gender, racial, sexual sociopolitical norms: "We are treated, hailed, and formed by social norms that precede us and that form the constraining context for whatever forms of agency we ourselves take on in time" (18). Butler writes about the importance of "linguistic vulnerability," and how exposure to and experience with discursive categorization, epithets, processes of discursive definitions impose a generative and performative effect, acting on subjects, establishing constraints within and to which subjects perform sociopolitical identity formations. As she writes,

> There is a distinct performative effect of having been named as this gender or another gender, as part of one nationality or a minority, or to find out that how you are regarded in any of these respects is summed up by a name that you yourself did not know and never chose. (16)

Pertinent, here, is the linguistic vulnerability to which people who experience a mental health crisis are exposed—from diagnoses provided by medical professionals, to narratives one tells to oneself and others as part of therapy and processing a crisis, to epithets, like "crazy," "insane," "unbalanced," and other pejorative references to mental illness. The performativity of mental health is akin to, though not equivalent, and factors into identity formations of gender, race, sexual orientation, socio-economic status, or mental health; dominant discourses constitute, reinforce, and propagate norms and ideals that subjects embody and enact through language, "gestures and actions" and that deeply inform a sense of who we are and what we are about in terms of identity (17). Language acts on and the norms expressed interpellate subjects; however, this does not mean that language is entirely prescriptive, as the performativity of norms is inherently relational and relative to interpersonal interactions and performances of subjects within sociopolitical contexts. As Butler suggests, "performativity describes both the processes of being acted on and the conditions and possibilities for acting" (18). We are susceptible and vulnerable to norms constituted by and through language; however, for Butler, it is this very susceptibility and vulnerability that can enable the possibility for rejecting, revising, or reformulating norms (18). Spontaneously, inadvertently, or serendipitously, subjects can and do deviate from norms, "resignifying, and sometimes quite emphatically breaking [the] citational chains" imposed by those norms (18).

Months after his mental health crisis began, Nick reanimated. While hunched over the kitchen sink washing dishes, suddenly, he could feel each inch of his body enliven. It was a resurrection, and he could feel the full spectrum of emotions again. Cell by cell, ligament by ligament, muscle by muscle, mind to body, he felt whole and wept for the sheer, unmitigated ecstasy of the experience—the most astonishing, exhilarating moment of his life. Though not fully healed, he felt whole again.

Learning to Breathe through the Exhaustion

Sherry laid flat on her back. She had already received instruction to close her eyes but the exit sign captured her gaze. The red glow of the sign illuminating down onto her face in the dark room. She visually traced the capital letters E.X.I.T thinking about how she had not received the same kind of warning that Nick writes about above—or at least the inability to breathe and the urge to get herself out of the burning building of mind and body, which did not come to her with the ringing of a fire alarm or a clear sign out. The teacher's voice extended warmth through a second invitation: "Close the windows of your eyes." Perhaps now, the teacher had been speaking directly to Sherry—even though there were twenty other people laying on their mats positioned in neat rows against the hardwood floor. The instructor continued, "You are enough. You've given enough. You've made enough. You've taken enough." Her voice trailed off. Sherry felt the hot tears burn as they escaped her eyes and rolled over the temples of her head into her hair. The tightness in her chest and at the base of her throat resurfaced like it had thousands of times before—only now she was laying on the floor with the intent to learn how to breathe for the first time. It was as if she'd been watching the movie reel of her professional life for the past two decades, and now was the first time she was hearing someone say directly to her that it was time to exhale and let it go.

When Sherry moved into her first teaching position, as a non-tenure track faculty member at a two-year school, she took on extra courses and taught in the summer. Her daughter was five, and Sherry was newly married. Her 5–5 contractual teaching load quickly turned into a 7-7-3, and just as Nick described, Sherry was trying to offer thoughtful attention to novice writers while she could barely find the time to sleep. Naturally, when she accepted a seat in the doctoral program while being a full-time employee, wife, and mother, Sherry knew how to push through and use the rapid, short breaths (learned long ago during Lamaze class) to manage the anxiety of doing too many things and depriving herself of sleep.

When Sherry moved into an assistant professor position while simultaneously serving as the WPA, she already knew the trade-off of the physical and emotional demands needed from her body. With the new need to publish, Sherry moved her 60-hour work week to 80 hours. She somehow believed that with (more) dedicated time, she would not fall short of obtaining tenure and promotion. In her first year as a WPA, she read a cautionary tale of what could happen to any one of us as spouses and parents. In "The WPA a Father, Husband, Ex," Doug Hesse writes, "Especially for new assistant professors in competitive situations, there is already great pressure to define one's life narrowly as the pursuit of tenure" (47). The very ideas that he described about missing his children's events and his wife requesting separation created an immediate fear that prompted Sherry to wake up her husband in the middle of the night. With a tear-stained face, Sherry begged him to assure her that this narrative wouldn't be theirs. It was still her first year as WPA and assistant professor, so perhaps when you've been socially conditioned as the wife and mother to "take care of everything," you believe Hesse's narrative cannot, will not, happen to you. The verbal pact the two of them made that night didn't save them from what was to come.

After a few years of working as a WPA, Sherry was invited to apply for a position in the Provost's office. She felt confident that her on-the-job-training as WPA would serve as an ally to building programs, developing staff, and facilitating conflict in this new appointment. Even though she was still pre-tenure when she accepted this new appointment, Sherry saw this opportunity as an exciting role, and she believed with enough hard work, persistence, and quick breathing, she would be able to turn coal into diamonds, as she had in her previous academic positions.

Over the next 26 months, she wrote grants, developed a fully online campus for her university, took on new institutional initiatives, and hosted provost retreats—all tasks outside of the responsibilities listed in the job description of overseeing seven academic serving units that included a $5 million-dollar budget and team of 75 employees. At first, the signs were subtle; a dress that wouldn't zip or suit pants that became too tight. After six months, the persistent weight gain drove her to the doctor. She and her doctor talked through the limited options she had since she'd increased her work week to nearly 100 hours. Even though Sherry and her physician had laid out a plan, over the next year nothing changed except for escalated episodes of panicked breathing that turned to silent crying in stairwells and bathroom stalls. At the time, she hadn't reconciled that she was suffering in silence; she thought that all of this anxiety was part of learning this kind of job at this level and being able to produce the work. Looking back now, Sherry knows the exhaustion was suffocating her. Carefully twirling the plates and keeping them spinning had become a way of life, and she was fearful that she couldn't keep all of the plates in the air—that she wouldn't do enough or be enough because she'd allowed herself to be defined by her work.

Exposure to and performances of vulnerability are not new to academics, particularly those of us who frequently administer writing programs, writing centers, and other programmatic centers. We are inundated with stressors, responsibilities, our personal problems, as well as those foisted upon us by students, colleagues, and family members—all of which require our immediate and full attention. For many of us, the agonizing stress of these issues is exacerbated by precarious positions as adjuncts, graduate students, and non-tenured lines that may possess tenuous status within an institution and likely result in economic scarcity and exploitation. A few of us either possess or develop a seemingly superhuman capacity to manage all of these responsibilities and stressors; many of us struggle to calibrate our time and responsibilities in a way that is healthy and productive, shifting from one task to the next, completing projects excessively past deadline if at all, failing to process and make sense of mental and personal disarray; and after months or years of this, some of us cannot persist.

It's been two years since Sherry returned to her faculty position, and she's now teaching a course on the rhetoric of self-care, so she can offer graduate students a road map for healthy living in the academy.

Establishing Strategies for Recovery by Confronting Shame and Performing Vulnerability

In sharing these stories, we are performing vulnerability, and the worry, of course, is that we will be defined by the trauma of the experiences rather than the transformational experience of recovery. Too often, because of the pervasive and powerful stigmatization of mental illness in American culture, people who have experienced or who live with mental disorders feel deep shame because their mental disorders brand them as anomalous, as deficient, as unworthy relative to hegemonic portrayals of success, health, and well-being. Gershen Kaufman, an eminent psychologist, argues cogently in *The Psychology of Shame* that American culture is fundamentally "shame-based." So intensely integral is shame to the development of individual and cultural identity, Kaufman notes, that shame largely remains hidden and taboo because of the pervasiveness of feeling "shame about shame" (46). Instead of risking the exacerbation of the feelings of shame by exposing vulnerabilities and disclosing an event, behavior, or failure that causes one to experience shame, one internalizes it deeply, possibly to the detriment of one's own psychological and emotional well-being. Though the disclosure of shame maybe taboo and hidden as Kaufman claims, the act of shaming certainly is not.

It should come as no surprise that our departments, our writing programs, and our disciplines are fraught with shaming. Indeed, in "True Confessions: Uncovering the Hidden Culture of Shame in English Studies," J. Brooks Bouson delineates various scenes of shame the discipline is loathe to recognize as such but exist nevertheless, causing significant emotional and psychological suffering. For Bouson, scenes of shame are realized when academics participate in gratuitously agonistic scholarly discourse in which scholars viciously savage one another. For instance, many discussions on the WPA-Listserv have degenerated to what Jane Tompkins describes as "'ritual execution[s]'" (qtd. Bouson 627). Bouson identifies a second scene of shame as the shame/pride culture in which academics viscerally pay deference to and reinforce the alternating dynamic of fear of failure and pride in achievement that is inherent within the pervasive careerism of the academy. A third scene of shame exists among social relations established by academic ranking and the concomitant cultural, social, and economic capital of tenure, as those who possess prestige and tenure may or are perceived to shame non-tenured colleagues or who teach at institutions perceived as 2nd or 3rd tier.

As academic professionals and as teachers, most of us have been victims of shaming or maybe even witnessed students or colleagues shame others, and we might have even unintentionally participated in that shaming. Responding to Bouson's article in *JAC*, Jeffrey Di Leo notes that "shame is nothing less than a prominent, persistent, and dominant aspect of contemporary English studies culture" (227). For Kaufman, shame plays a critical role in the development and maintenance of identity. Feeling shame makes a person aware of transgressing a particular social or moral convention, motivating "self-correction" as a result (Kaufman 5). Shame's most important purpose, according to Kaufman, is its central role in identity formation throughout a person's lifecycle. Unlike other affects, shame is ontological, meaning that the onset of and experiences with shame can both develop and challenge deeply held notions about who one is and who one can ideally be and become. As Kaufman argues, identity is "forged in the crucible of shame" (5). When the affect of shame is activated, one feels acutely exposed or seen or revealed, which heightens one's self scrutiny, compounding shame and—as Kaufman notes—making one feel "fundamentally deficient ... diseased, defective" (17). "To feel shame," as Kaufman describes it, "is to feel inherently bad, fundamentally flawed as a person" (18).

Kaufman describes how shame is induced within a particular scene, which is an event or moment or experience as it is lived, constructed, and construed (59). He categorizes particular scenes during which shame permeates and may likely be elicited, including those that involve the expression and development of interpersonal needs; the exercise of primal drives, like hunger and sexuality; the communication of feelings; and the practice of expertise or competence. In sharing our stories of challenges to our mental health, we intentionally invoke the latter two of these scenes. Some readers may judge us harshly or attempt to shame us; however, we believe our experiences are more common than many are willing to disclose.

Indeed, we suggest that there are concrete strategies that departments and writing programs can implement to cultivate interpersonal bridges mitigating shame, destigmatizing mental illness, and affirming colleagues. The first is to foster awareness about the prevalence of mental illness among academics, as well as situations leading up to burnout and exhaustion in the academy. As Susan Guthrie and a team of researchers show in a recent study of mental illness among academics, burnout and episodes of mental illness among academics are comparable to those of high-risk populations, like healthcare workers (xv). There is high probability that several persons within any department, writing program, and institution have experienced or are currently experiencing an episodic or chronic mental illness. Spreading awareness can facilitate the realization that help and treatment are available and that living with mental illness does not have to be a solitary experience. To foster awareness, departments, programs, and/or institutions can easily distribute literature or facilitate reading groups, but more importantly these entities can ask mental health professionals to provide workshops at department meetings or faculty retreats: directly addressing the culture of busyness and its dangers along with how to effectively manage the expectations of higher education are critical. Departments can network and partner with local mental health providers to facilitate access to support and treatment for faculty. Spreading awareness also helps people understand that wellness, recovery, and equanimity are attainable after experiencing a mental health crisis.

Second, part of fostering awareness is also helping people understand the connotations of their words. In everyday conversations, "crazy," "insane," "psycho," and "losing it" are frequently and carelessly uttered to express busyness, stress, or having too little time. Even more disconcerting, people sometimes inappropriately express phrases idealizing suicide to express frustration or anger with a situation or colleague, as in "That meeting was so boring I thought I was going to shoot myself." Commonly uttering pejorative words frequently used to other and alienate those affected by mental illness only reinforces stigmatization.

Third, we have a powerful theoretical framework for not only delineating how norms constitute and inscribe the performativity of shame and shaming, but also making critical interventions that resist and subvert those norms by revising and reconfiguring them to generate performativity that is healthy and affirming. One way to intervene and to effect these positive affective revisions, Butler suggests, is to "foreground the ways in which we are vulnerable," emphasizing our human interdependency and privileging social networks and relations that can be mobilized for political purposes (21). Performing vulnerability, in sharing our experiences by deliberately exposing ourselves to the possibility of shame and stigmatization, enacts resistance to the very norms that shame and stigmatize because it strengthens interpersonal bridges among subjects and clarifies that "vulnerability is not a subjective disposition" but rather exists in relation to "a field of objects, forces, and passions that impinge on or affect us in some way" (Butler 25). If vulnerability to shame and stigma is collectively constituted and shared, that very sociality enables critical interventions that institute positive change.

Within writing programs, then, it is critical that we cultivate vulnerability and thereby resist dominant norms of shame, shaming, and stigmatization of mental illness. We can do this by making space for discussions of mental health in our individual programs and classes. Of course, we should not require students or colleagues divulge sensitive information; rather, fostering safe, affirming spaces for faculty to share narratives of lived experiences with mental illness and journeys to recovery. Doing so not only expresses and demonstrates solidarity with students and colleagues who may be experiencing mental health challenges, but also it exercises compassion and empathy for ourselves, colleagues, and students.

Works Cited

Bouson, J. Brooks. "True Confessions: Uncovering the Hidden Culture of Shame in English Studies." *JAC*, vol. 25, no. 4, 2005, pp. 625–50.

Browning, Ella R. "Disability Studies in the Composition Classroom." *Composition Studies*, vol. 42, no. 2, 2014, pp. 96–116.

Butler, Judith. "Rethinking Vulnerability and Resistance." *Vulnerability in Resistance*, edited by Judith Butler, et al., Duke UP, 2016, pp. 12–27.

Di Leo, Jeffrey R. "Shame in Academe: On the Politics of Emotion in Academic Culture." *JAC*, vol. 26, no. 1/2, 2006, pp. 221–34.

Guthrie, Susan, et al. *Understanding Mental Health in the Research Environment: A Rapid Evidence Assessment*. Cambridge, RAND Europe, 2017. royalsociety.org/~/media/policy/topics/diversity-in-science/understanding-mental-health-in-the-research-environment.pdf.

Hesse, Doug. "The WPA as Husband, Father, Ex." *Kitchen Cooks, Plate Twirlers & Troubadours: Writing Program Administrators Tell Their Stories*, edited by Diane George, Heinemann, 1999, pp. 44–55.

Jurecic, Ann. "Neurodiversity." *College English*, vol. 69, no. 5, 2007, pp. 421–42.

Kaufman, Gershen. *The Psychology of Shame: Theory and Treatment of Shame-Based Syndromes*. New York, Springer P, 1996.

Linton, Simi. *Reclaiming Disability: Knowledge and Identify*. New York, NYU P, 1998.

McLeod, Susan, and Kathy Jane Garretson. "The Disabled Student and the Writing Program: A Guide for Administrators." *Writing Program Administration*, vol. 13, no. 1–2, 1989, pp. 45–52.

National Alliance on Mental Illness (NAMI). "Mental Health by the Numbers." www.nami.org/Learn-More/Mental-Health-By-the-Numbers. Accessed 2 Mar. 2019.

Payne, Michelle. *Bodily Discourses: When Students Write About Abuse and Eating Disorders*. Portsmouth, NE, 2000.

Price, Margaret. *Mad at School: Rhetorics of Mental Disability and Academic Life*. Ann Arbor, U of Michigan P, 2011.

Troia, Gary. "Writing Instruction for Students with Learning Disabilities." *Handbook of Writing Research*, edited by Charles A. MacArthur et al., Gilford, 2006, pp. 324–36.

Vidali, Amy. "Disabling Writing Program Administration." *WPA*, vol. 38, no. 2, 2015, pp. 32–55.

———. "Performing the Rhetorical Freak Show: Disability, Student Writing, and College Admissions." *College English*, vol. 69, no. 6, 2007, pp. 615–41.

Wooten, Courtney Adams, et al. *The Things We Carry: Strategies for Recognizing and Negotiating Emotional Labor in Writing Program Administration*. Utah State UP, forthcoming 2019.

Contributors

Ann N. Amicucci teaches courses in first-year writing, research writing, writing pedagogy, and social media rhetorics at the University of Colorado, Colorado Springs, where she directs the First-Year Rhetoric and Writing Program. Her research focuses on college students' reflective writing and their digital and reading literacies. Her recent work has appeared in *Computers and Composition* and in Claire Lutkewitte's collection *Mobile Technology and the Writing Classroom: Resources for Teachers* (NCTE, 2016).

James P. Barber is the Senior Associate Dean for Academic Programs and Associate Professor at the William & Mary School of Education. His teaching and research focus on: college student development, liberal arts education, assessment, and integrative learning. Jim has published in the *American Educational Research Journal, Journal of College Student Development, Journal of Higher Education, and Change Magazine*. He currently serves as Editor of Oracle: *The Research Journal of the Association of Fraternity/Sorority Advisors*.

Nicholas Behm is the director of the Center for Scholarship and Teaching and a professor in the English department at Elmhurst University in Elmhurst, Illinois. He studies composition pedagogy and theory, writing assessment, and critical race theory. With Greg Glau, Deborah Holdstein, Duane Roen, and Ed White, he is coeditor of *The WPA Outcomes Statement—A Decade Later*, which won the 2013 "Best Book Award" from the Council of Writing Program Administrators. With Duane Roen and Sherry Rankins-Robertson, he is coeditor of *The Framework for Success in Postsecondary Writing: Scholarship and Applications*.

Julie Christen is a doctoral student in Rhetoric, Composition, and the Teaching of English at University of Arizona, where she researches user experience (UX) of education and online writing, technical and professional communication, and emotion in first-year writing. She is especially interested in UX research for creating inclusive and accessible technologies in education and beyond. When she's not teaching, researching, or writing, you can find her adventuring with her dog, Lily.

Jessica Rose Corey is Lecturer in Writing Studies; Assistant Director of First-Year Writing at Duke University. Jessica's primary research interests involve feminist rhetorics and feminist activist literacies, rhetorics of silence, multimodal composition, and composition pedagogy. She has taught a variety of lower- and upper-division courses in expository, research, business, argumentative, public, and creative writing, as well as digital and multimodal composing. She also trains, mentors, and supervises doctoral students in various disciplines as they teach freshman composition for the first time.

Diana Epelbaum, Ph.D., is Assistant Professor and Director of the Academic Writing Program at Marymount Manhattan College. Her scholarship is interdisciplinary, bridging, Writing and Rhetoric, Early American Literature, and History of Science. She is a reading specialist and educator trained in a balanced literacy approach, and has spent seventeen years in deep engagement—both in and out of the classroom—with best practices in writing, reading, and thinking pedagogies. In 2009, she was nominated by a student scholar and awarded *The New York Times* "Teachers Who Make a Difference Award," for teaching excellence.

Matthew Fledderjohann is the inaugural writing center director at Le Moyne College. His research interests include the enduring cultural significance of apocalyptic rhetoric, writers' experiences with dissonance, and the challenges and applications of writing center practice and pedagogy. Outside his academic work, Matthew spends a lot of time building LEGO with his young son, holding his infant twins, and playing word games with his spouse.

Dr. Rebecca Gerdes-McClain graduated from the University of Oklahoma in May 2017 with a PhD in Composition, Rhetoric, and Literacy. She is currently the Director of First-Year Composition at Columbus State University where she is also an Assistant Professor in the English Department.

As a teacher, her interests include responding to student writing, cultivating meaningful writing projects for students, and preparing students to effectively respond to a wide range of writing situations. As a scholar, she's particularly interested in the history of FYC, academic labor, feminist rhetorical practices, revisionist historiography, embodiment, and ethics. Finally, as an administrator, her goals include raising the profile of student writing across campus, building partnerships with faculty in all disciplines, and—most importantly—supporting the teachers and students involved in FYC. Her favorite professional moments occur when these roles and interests converge.

Of course, professors are more than their professional roles. Rebecca is also "mom" to four cats, four parrots, two bunnies, and a dog. She also enjoys traveling (most recently to Shanghai) and knitting.

Michayla Grey is in her third-year at Kennesaw State University, where she is pursuing a B.S. in Nursing. As a first-year student, she was part of a yearlong Great Books cohort, which culminated in a three week summer study abroad program in Italy.

M. Todd Harper, PhD, is an Associate Professor of English at Kennesaw State University, where he has taught for the last twenty years. In addition to his research and teaching in the field of Rhetoric and Composition, Harper has been involved in International Education since 2003. He has led over 17 study abroad programs to Greece, Turkey, and Italy, as well as taught on Fulbright and Rotary Grants in Greece and Turkey. He currently directs Kennesaw State University's largest and one of its oldest study abroad programs.

Dr. K. Shannon Howard is Associate Professor at Auburn University Montgomery where she specializes in material and popular culture. She has recently published the book *Unplugging Popular Culture: Reconsidering Analog Technology, Materiality, and the Digital Native* with Routledge. Her work has also appeared in the *Journal of American Culture, Present Tense, Pedagogy,* and *Studies in Popular Culture.*

Dr. Jeanne Hughes is an Associate Professor of English at Southern New Hampshire University where she teaches developmental, first, and second year composition. Part of her work includes teaching composition to International students as they transition from the bridge program into the undergraduate school. She also teaches foundational General Education critical thinking and literature. In all classes, her focus is on creating learning environments where students are both academically challenged and actively involved. Her current research is focused on creating readers, teaching writing through story, and using literacy narratives to increase student metacognition.

Laura Mangini completed her doctoral work in Composition and TESOL at Indiana University of Pennsylvania in 2015, earning the award of distinction for her dissertation defense on her research, which examines the dynamics of collaboration at the dissertation level while studying resistance to collaborative dissertations within the field of composition. She is an assistant professor of English at Community College of Philadelphia where she teaches composition and is working on revising the college's Accelerated Learning Program course. Her research interests include emotional literacy, writing in times of eco-trauma, collaboration, feminist theory, and multimodal composition. She resides in Chester Springs, Pennsylvania with her husband Sabatino, their children Elyse and Caius, and cat Gucci.

Sabatino Mangini is an associate professor of English in Communication, Arts, and Humanities at Delaware County Community College. He teaches composition, contributes to the curricular development and assessment of the English department's Accelerated Learning Program, and co-chairs a committee to create the college's first-ever First-Year Writing Program. Sabatino has published in *Teaching English in the Two-Year College*. His scholarly interests have explored composition pedagogy, narrative inquiry, multimodal writing, and collaboration. At present, his research focuses on the intersections of writing transfer and emotional literacy. When he is not teaching and writing, Sabatino enjoys spending time with his wife, Laura, and their two children, Elyse and Caius.

Amanda M. May is an assistant professor of English and director of the writing center at New Mexico Highlands University. She received her PhD from Florida State University, where she taught FYC, junior-level composition, and peer tutoring courses, often experimenting with social media in the classroom as a form of writing to study and to compose. She has also held numerous tutoring and administrative roles in several writing centers. Her recent research examines social media usage and non-usage among American postsecondary writing centers.

Contributors

Cathryn Molloy is associate professor in James Madison University's School of Writing, Rhetoric and Technical Communication where she also serves as director of undergraduate studies. She is the author of the book *Rhetorical Ethos in Health and Medicine: Patient Credibility, Stigma and Misdiagnosis*, co-editor of the volume *Women's Health Advocacy: Rhetorical Ingenuity for the 21st Century* and co-editor of the *Rhetoric of Health and Medicine* journal.

Sherry Rankins-Robertson is Professor of Writing and Rhetoric at the University of Central Florida where she serves as department chair. Her research has appeared in *Kairos, Computers and Composition*, and the *Journal of Writing Assessment* along with diverse edited collections. She has served as co-editor of the WPA journal. With Nicholas Behm and Duane Roen, she edited *The Framework for Success in Postsecondary Writing: Scholarship and Applications*. Her most recent co-edited collection is *Prison Pedagogies: Learning and Teaching with Imprisoned Writers*. Sherry is a co-author of *McGraw Hill Guide to Writing* 5th edition. She is an officer for CWPA and serves as a member of the executive committee for CCCC.

Crystal Sands holds a PhD in Rhetoric from Texas Woman's University and is a Senior Contributing Faculty at Walden University and an adjunct faculty at several online institutions. She is the former director of the award-winning Excelsior College Online Writing Lab and has directed national grants and research studies in her work for Excelsior College. She has been teaching writing for more than 23 years and designing curriculum for online universities for more than 12 years. During that time, she has worked as a Writing Program Director and Writing Across the Curriculum coordinator. With her husband, she helps run a small farm in Maine where they live with their two sons.

Jessica Schreyer is a Professor of English and Writing Program Administrator at University of Dubuque, specializing in Composition and Rhetoric. She teaches introductory composition, advanced writing courses, and environmental literature. Her most recent book chapter, *Composing and Researching on the Move* was published by NCTE. Previously, her book chapter *Adolescent Literacy Practices in Online Social Spaces* was published by Routledge. She has also published journal articles related to writing and program administration. She is on the editorial board for *JUMP: The Journal for Undergraduate Multimedia Projects*.

Rachel N. Spear is an Associate Professor of English and Coordinator of First-Year Composition at Francis Marion University, where she teaches Creative Nonfiction, First-Year Writing, and upper-level writing courses. Her primary research interests include writing pedagogy, trauma studies, life-writing, and the therapeutics of writing. Other scholarly and creative works have been published in *Pedagogy*, *NOLA Diaspora*, and *The Best Advice in Six Words*.

Sandra L. Stanko, PhD, is a teacher and educational writer who is committed to helping students become "deep learners," where students are given the freedom to adapt the course material to meet their specific personal and professional goals. Her personal teaching philosophy is to encourage each student to take an individualized approach to learning by choosing personally relevant projects and writing about personally meaningful topics. Sandra has won awards for her writing and has been published in numerous academic anthologies and other venues. She is currently an adjunct faculty member for Chatham University and a senior evaluation faculty member for Western Governors University. She earned her PhD in composition studies from Indiana University of Pennsylvania where her dissertation focused on the benefits of personal writing for working mothers.

Ethan Youngerman EdD, MFA, is a Senior Language Lecturer in NYU's Expository Writing Program where he's taught since 2001. His research interests include integrative learning, FYC, and writing in the disciplines. Ethan has published in *AERA Open*, *The Journal of Experimental Education*, *New Directions for Higher Education*, and *Learning Communities Research and Practice*. He's currently a Faculty Fellow in Residence in a first-year residence hall.

Jim Zimmerman started out as a reporter, moved into the cable TV industry, and eventually taught technical writing at The Ohio State University while earning his PhD. As a writing instructor, he worked at Case Western Reserve University, Stockton University, and West Virginia University before helping to create the School of Writing, Rhetoric and Technical Communication at James Madison University.

INTERDISCIPLINARY APPROACHES TO INSTRUCTION, PRACTICE, AND THEORY

Staci L. Shultz and CJ Kent, *General Editors*

This interdisciplinary series responds to the ever-changing educational landscape of the twenty-first century with practical writing support for students at the undergraduate and graduate level. This series offers material for a variety of courses: textbooks and resources for creative writing, composition, and literary studies classrooms; support guides for writing-intensive non-English courses; and resources aimed at supporting professional activities, such as grant writing and assessment reports. The broad scope of the series invites books on new approaches to established topics, such as teaching training, writing center pedagogy, and the use of technology as well as evolving and emerging topics, such as gamification, social media and writing, studies in language and power, writing across the disciplines at the graduate level, literacy councils, imagination and creative development, plagiarism studies, and writing competition.

For additional information about this series or for the submission of manuscripts, please contact:

> Patricia Mulrane Clayton
> Executive Editor & Publisher, Education
> p.mulrane@peterlang.com

To order other books in this series, please contact our Customer Service Department:

> peterlang@presswarehouse.com (within the U.S.)
> orders@peterlang.com (outside the U.S.)

Or browse online by series:

> www.peterlang.com

www.ingramcontent.com/pod-product-compliance
Lightning Source LLC
Chambersburg PA
CBHW071406300426
44114CB00016B/2199